RICARDO GÜIRALDES AND
DON SEGUNDO SOMBRA

RICARDO GÜIRALDES AND
DON SEGUNDO SOMBRA
LIFE AND WORKS

by

GIOVANNI PREVITALI

Forword by
ADELINA DEL CARRIL DE GÜIRALDES

Preface by
JORGE LUIS BORGES

HISPANIC INSTITUTE
IN THE UNITED STATES
NEW YORK
1963

245911

Cat. Spanish.

Printed in the U.S.A. by
Foreign Language Typographers, Inc.
New York 11, N. Y.

This Book is Dedicated

to

English-Speaking Scholars of
Spanish American Literature

CONTENTS

WORKS OF RICARDO GÜIRALDES

DON SEGUNDO SOMBRA

FOREWORD

Declaro extraordinario este libro de Giovanni Previtali por su admirable comprensión, habiendo sido escrito con tanta precisión, a pesar de no haber conocido el autor a su biografiado y sólo haber sacado sus eficaces conclusiones a través de las obras de Güiraldes y de lo que de ellas y de él se ha publicado hasta la fecha.

Es la obra de un gran amor comprensivo del espíritu de Ricardo Güiraldes, y el haber extraído de él la expresión exacta de lo que amó, pensó, sintió y vivió este gran poeta argentino es loable hazaña.

Auguro un éxito rotundo a este minucioso trabajo, donde estudiantes de literatura hispanoamericana hallarán fiel información para el estudio del hombre y del poeta que fue Ricardo Güiraldes.

Mi gratitud y mi cariño enternecido para Giovanni Previtali.

Adelina del Carril

Bella Vista (Buenos Aires)   Febrero de 1960

PREFACE

El manuscrito de este libro me ha deparado una singular experiencia. Yo he conocido personalmente a Ricardo Güiraldes, quien dejó en mi memoria una imagen muy vívida, que es una de mis felicidades. Puedo recuperar su entonación, su presencia, los hábitos de su voz y de su amistad, pero el número de cosas concretas y comunicables que sé sobre él, es (lo compruebo con melancolía) harto limitado. Como sucede en tales casos, las muchas veces que nos vimos tienden a confundirse en un sola; tardes enteras de minuciosa y agitada conversación forman ahora, en el recuerdo, una sola tarde. Nunca me había atrevido a esperar que esta inevitable simplificación se modificara, pero el libro de Previtali, que tengo el honor de prologar, me devuelve lo que juzgué perdido o inaccesible. Giovanni Previtali sabe mil cosas de Güiraldes que yo he ignorado u olvidado o en las que nunca me fijé; la lectura de esta biografía me las entrega y tengo la curiosa impresión de ir descubriéndolas en mi propia memoria, como si ésta de pronto se profundizara e iluminara y como si yo estuviera ahí.

El autor de *Vida y Obra de Ricardo Güiraldes* ha ejecutado una doble labor de investigación fatigosa y de lúcida recreación y adivinación. Güiraldes poseía el don de la amistad; ese don, más allá de la muerte corporal, le ha ganado hoy este amigo, cuyos ojos nunca lo vieron y que, en 1962, viene a enriquecer y a favorecer a quienes conocimos a Güiraldes, hace más de treinta años.

Todos debemos alegrarnos de que se haya escrito este libro, que será indispensable para el estudio de la vida ejemplar y de la perdurable labor del poeta que cierra y que corona, con una suerte de relato elegíaco, el largo ciclo de la literatura gauchesca.

Jorge Luis Borges

Austin, Texas   Enero de 1962

13

AUTHOR'S NOTE

This book is the result of my effort to produce a comprehensive study of the life and works of Ricardo Güiraldes. It is based in part on my doctoral dissertation at Yale University. I have written it as a tribute to the author of *Don Segundo Sombra*.

To accomplish this task in a manner worthy of the memory of Güiraldes would have been impossible without the collaboration of his widow, doña Adelina del Carril de Güiraldes. Doña Adelina not only checked and corrected my biography of her husband, but she also participated in its writing with new, significant information. Her contribution, given with such warm hearted generosity, has captured my filial devotion.

Similarly I wish to record my indebtedness to don Ismael B. Colombo of San Antonio de Areco for providing much of the material incorporated in the part concerned with the life of Ricardo Güiraldes; to Mr. Herbert Staudt and to Mr. James Sydney Muirden, both of Buenos Aires, for procuring in Argentina transcripts of certain writings of Güiraldes; to Miss Josephine C. Fabilli and her staff at the Columbus Memorial Library of the Organization of American States in Washington, D. C., for supplying valuable references; to Professor Theodore Andersson, Chairman of the Department of Romance Languages at The University of Texas, and to Harriett Andersson, his wife, for the care with which they edited the manuscript and for their encouragement; to Mrs. Helen Pugh Travis, Administrative Assistant for the Institute of Latin American Studies of The University of Texas for her invaluable assistance during a period of three years, especially in typing the manuscript; to my father Professor Giuseppe Previtali, M.D., for providing the means to produce this book; and to my mother Rose Robinson Morrow Previtali for her inspiration.

With grateful recognition to all who have helped me make this study more complete, I dedicate my book to English-speaking scholars of Spanish American literature with a view to casting more light upon Ricardo Güiraldes, as a man and as a poet.

Giovanni Previtali

St. Petersburg, Florida

July, 1962

"This is the portrait of the poet! A photographic reproduction of an oil painting by Arnulfo Testi, done under the direction of Adelina del Carril de Güiraldes from a photograph taken of Ricardo Güiraldes by Bestard in Puerto de Pollensa, Majorca."

(Author's translation of a note written by Adelina del Carril de Güiraldes when she sent him her copy of the portrait in March, 1963).

LIFE OF RICARDO GÜIRALDES

I

Early Childhood

Ricardo Güiraldes was born in Buenos Aires on February 13, 1886.[1] His father, don Manuel,[2] and his mother, doña Dolores Goñi, were staying at the large town house of don Manuel's grandparents, the Guerricos, situated on Calle Corrientes between Avenida San Martín and Calle Florida. His parents, in grateful recognition to Dr. Ricardo Gutiérrez and Dr. Guillermo Udaondo for saving the lives of mother and child during a difficult birth, named their boy Ricardo Guillermo.[3]

When he was a year and a half old, his parents took him and his older brother, Manolo, to live in France. They resided at Saint Cloud. Consequently Ricardo's early childhood impressions were of France. In 1890, a sudden turn in the tide of Argentine prosperity brought the Güiraldes back to Buenos Aires. The two boys were accompanied by a baby brother, Pepito. When Ricardo returned to Argentina he could speak only French.

Soon after arriving in Buenos Aires, the Güiraldes moved to the country. Ricardo saw the old family *estancia,* La Porteña,[4] for the first time. It was a traditional Argentine cattle-

---

[1] ISMAEL B. COLOMBO, *Ricardo Güiraldes; el poeta de la pampa; 1886-1927* (San Antonio de Areco, 1952), p. 13.

[2] For biography of don Manuel J. Güiraldes, father of Ricardo, see "Manuel J. Güiraldes," *La Nación* (Buenos Aires, Jan. 18, 1957).

[3] Colombo, *op. cit.,* p. 19.

[4] Information regarding La Porteña has been derived from the description in Colombo, *op. cit.,* p. 29, and from the description of the *estancia* in Güiraldes' *Raucho* (Bilbao, 1932), pp. 19-21, as well as from recent photographs of the main building.

raising estate, lying in the pampa near the country village of San Antonio de Areco, about 115 kilometers from Buenos Aires. It was to become the center of Ricardo's affections and to influence his life and his writings. The main house was a low spreading building, gleaming in its whitewashed simplicity. Nearby stood the farm buildings, the barns, the farmhands' quarters, their mess hall and kitchen, the bull pen, the corral, and the carriage house with a large, wrought iron replica of La Porteña cattle brand hanging like a standard over the door.

Ricardo and Manolo took to life on the *estancia* and made friends with the kindly disposed ranch hands, among them Victor Taboada, the foreman, Their father encouraged their love for ranch life. He took them to swim in the neighboring Areco River. He supplied them with horses and let them run free to their hearts' content under the watchful eyes of one of the older hands, don Nicasio Cano.[5] During this time the children heard bloodcurdling stories of fierce legendary gauchos and historical figures such as Juan Manuel Rosas, whom Ricardo's great-grandfather had known in his youth as a friend and neighbor.[6] They admired the cattlemen and emulated their ways. Practicing their gaucho skills such as throwing the *boleadoras,*[7] they grew strong in the hardy outdoor life.

The first schooling was provided by a young governess who read to Ricardo and Manolo tales in German by Hans Christian Andersen and the Grimm brothers. Soon, Ricardo was able to speak three languages, French, Spanish, and German. As

[5] An old ranch hand on the *estancia* described by Güiraldes in *Raucho,* pp. 51, 54, and referred to Colombo, *op. cit.,* p. 30, as well as in the dedication of Güiraldes' *Don Segundo Sombra* (Buenos Aires, 1943), p. 9.

[6] Juan Manuel Ortiz de Rosas (1793-1877), Argentine gaucho dictator, of whom Güiraldes' great-grandfather, don José Manuel de Guerrico, was an intimate friend, during their youth in the pampa of Buenos Aires Province. See Colombo, *op. cit.,* p. 19.

[7] A kind of lasso used by gauchos in felling animals from horseback in the pampa. It usually consists of a leather rope with two leather-covered stone balls at the end. See Tito Saubidet, *Vocabulario y refranero criollo* (Buenos Aires, 1943), p. 47.

he grew a little older, he progressed to reading German stories of adventure, among them *Mali der Schlangenbändiger, Durch Urwald und Wüstensand,* and *Im Goldlande Kalifornien.*[8] When the boys outgrew their governess' competence, don Manuel engaged a tutor, don Lorenzo Ceballos, a young Mexican intellectual who had received his degree in civil engineering in Paris and had come to Argentina because, for political reasons, he was unable to return to his native country. Don Lorenzo awakened Ricardo's literary taste. Under his guidance, the boy began a diary of daily occurrences. The tutor turned his pupil's interest to French stories of adventure. Ricardo's imagination was captured by Jules Verne's *Twenty Thousand Leagues under the Sea* and Alexander Dumas' *The Three Musketeers.* Later, Ricardo was introduced to Campoamor, Espronceda, Núñez de Arce, Bécquer, and Jorge Isaacs. But this literature of the end of the nineteenth century held little appeal for him. His heart was elsewhere. It was in the outdoor life of the pampa. Ricardo's boyhood fantasy was alive with dreams of legendary gauchos, about whom he had heard many a tale. He was more interested in acquiring the skills of the gaucho-like cattlemen.

Ricardo's enthusiasm for the life of the cattlemen directed his energy into feats of dexterity and daring. One day, he was seriously hurt.[9] The accident was so severe that it produced, in his semi-conscious mind, a state of uncertainty. He had the impression that he was dreaming he was alive and that in reality he was dead.[10] After he had fully recovered, at the age of twelve he received another blow to his health. He was stricken with asthma. His father sent him for several months to a better climate at Quequén, a barren countryside by the

[8] The facts describing the evolution of Güiraldes' literary tastes from early boyhood are recounted by Güiraldes himself in an autobiographical letter to his friend Guillermo de Torre. See Guillermo de Torre, "Una carta-autobiografía de Ricardo Güiraldes," *Buenos Aires Literaria* (Año I, Nov. 1952), pp. 3-16.

[9] The source of this information, Colombo, *op. cit.,* p. 32, gives no indication of the nature of the accident.

[10] Güiraldes, *El Sendero* (Maestricht, 1932), p. 11.

sea, near Nicochea, about 200 miles south of Buenos Aires. Ricardo was lonely and unhappy away from La Porteña, and found a new pleasure in writing long letters home.[11]

Back home and well again, Ricardo was soon to meet an unknown herdsman who would influence his life.

---

[11] De Torre, *loc. cit.*, p. 7.

II

Don Segundo

When Ricardo was about thirteen years of age, an old cattle driver made his appearance at La Porteña.[1] His name was Segundo Ramírez and he had come from afar to live on the estate. Believed to have been born in Coronda[2] in the province of Santa Fe on July 2, 1852,[3] he was approaching the age of fifty at that time. His father was Patricio. Carmen, his mother, was a full blooded Indian.[4] Both were freed slaves and the servants of don Santiago Ramírez, from whom don Segundo derived his last name.[5] As a boy, he had a life of hardship, especially while working at the *estancia* of the Núñez.[6] When he learned the profession of the cattle driver, he traveled continuously and was said to have fallen into trouble more than once.[7] There is, however, no known record of specific incidents to substantiate this belief. It is more probable that his life of wandering, shrouded as it was in mystery, together with his forbidding aspect merely suggested that he was something of a traditional *gaucho malo*. Worn from years of fatigue and travel, he had come to La Porteña to settle as

[1] Adelina del Carril de Güiraldes, "Nota preliminar," *Don Segundo Sombra* (Buenos Aires, ed. Kraft, 1952), p. 11; also Hebert B. Smith, "El amor y la mujer a través de *Don Segundo Sombra*," *Cuadernos Rioplatenses* (La Plata, 1949), 11; and Ismael B. Colombo, *Ricardo Güiraldes*, p. 95.
[2] Germán Berdiales, "El gaucho en las letras. *Don Segundo Sombra* y su creador: Ricardo Güiraldes," *Pampa Argentina* (Buenos Aires, XXI, Oct. 1947), p. 20.
[3] Eduardo Jorge Bosco, "Un viaje a San Antonio de Areco," *Buenos Aires Literaria* (Año I, No. 2, Nov. 1952), p. 22.
[4] Adelina del Carril de Güiraldes in a letter to the author, dated June 6, 1961, says: "Su madre era india auténtica."
[5] Aristóbulo Echegaray, *Don Segundo Sombra, reminiscencia infantil de Ricardo Güiraldes* (Buenos Aires, 1955), p. 38.
[6] Julián Fernández Hutter, *El alma errante de Don Segundo Sombra* (Santa Fe, 1945).
[7] Juan Carlos Neyra, *El mito gaucho en "Don Segundo Sombra"* (Bahía Blanca, 1952), p. 12.

a *puestero*[8] on the *estancia*.[9] As such, he did not live at the ranch houses with the other personnel but far out in the prairie at the *puesto* called "La Lechuza."[10]

His physical appearance was impressive. His skin was dark and tanned like leather and his little eyes squinted from the habit of scanning the horizon.[11] His narrow forehead, prominent cheek bones, and strong jaw recalled his Indian origin.[12] A large man[13] with short legs in relation to his long torso,[14] he seemed greater in size when mounted on his horse. He wore the traditional *chiripá*[15] which enhanced his resemblance to the legendary gaucho.

Besides the aura of mystery regarding his past, the general esteem in which the hardy cattle drivers were universally held added to his prestige.[16] It has been said that young Güiraldes, looking upon the old *paisano* as the last of the gauchos, admired him for his manliness, courage, self-possession in the face of danger, skill as a herdsman, and affirmative spirit.[17] Don Segundo's taciturn nature only whetted the boy's desire to extract reminiscences from him. At times, don Segundo would speak of the past and, at times, he would invent stories with typical *criollo* roguishness. More frequently, however, he was characteristically uncommunicative.[18]

On the lighter side was his aptitude for regional dances and

[8] A *puestero* is a ranch hand who lives as a kind of keeper on a distant part of the *estancia* to watch over that area.
[9] Silveiro Boj (W. G. Weyland), *Ubicación de Don Segundo Sombra y otros ensayos* (Tucumán, 1940), pp. 26, 27.
[10] Berdiales, *loc. cit.*, p. 20.
[11] Boj, *op. cit.*, p. 26.
[12] Berdiales, "Ramón Subiratz, el pintor que retrató a Don Segundo Sombra," *Pampa Argentina* (Buenos Aires, XXIII, June, 1949), 20, 30.
[13] *Ibid.*

[14] See pictures from original photographs of Segundo Ramírez in Güiraldes' *Don Segundo Sombra* (Buenos Aires, Ed. Pleamar, 1943), p. 32, in Ismael B. Colombo, "Ricardo Güiraldes vecino de Areco," *Farol* (Buenos Aires, Sept. 1953), p. 4, and Augusto Mario Delfino, "Como apareció *Don Segundo Sombra*," *Arte y Plata* (México, III, Feb. 1947), pp. 34-36.
[15] Berdiales, *loc. cit.*, pp. 20, 30.
[16] Neyra, *op. cit.*, p. 12.
[17] Arturo Torres-Rioseco, "Definición de *Don Segundo Sombra*," *La novela iberoamericana* (Albuquerque, N. M., 1951), p. 127.
[18] Boj, *op. cit.*, p. 27.

for improvising couplets in the tradition of the *payadores*.[19]
He was also known for his sense of humor, expressed in
laconic comments.[20]

Contrary to the general impression, don Segundo did not
enjoy an entirely favorable reputation. The wit of his barbed
remarks, spoken in his falsetto tone of voice, was not always
appreciated by his fellow workers on the *estancia*.[21] He was
said to have been a *guapo*,[22] to have been a ready fighter and,
on occasions, to have cut his opponent with his knife not
according to the rules of fair play.[23]

Hence it is apparent that, while Ricardo saw don Segundo
as the personification of the noble gaucho, others had no love
for him. Nevertheless, certain characteristics transcend both
the favorable and unfavorable opinions. They are that don
Segundo was strong, silent, and virile. As a herdsman he was
esteemed for his skill. As an individual he was respected,
either through admiration or from fear.

The colorful figure of don Segundo coming out of the mysterious unknown, and attired in traditional garb, seemed to
Ricardo like the personification of the legendary gaucho. The
friendship between the boy and the old man was to last
through the years and motivate Güiraldes to write, toward
the end of his life, *Don Segundo Sombra.*

[19] Kenneth Porter Kirkwood, "Ricardo Güiraldes and *Don Segundo Sombra*," *Excursion among Books* (Buenos Aires, 1949), pp. 315-329.
[20] Bosco, *loc. cit.,* p. 19.
[21] *Ibid.*
[22] An Argentine term for bully and braggadocio.
[23] Neyra, *op. cit.,* 12.

III

Boyhood

In the same year in which he had met don Segundo, Ricardo left his beloved pampa to go to school in Buenos Aires. The school, Colegio Lacordaire, conducted by Dominican monks, had been an old monastery. Its heavy doors and bare, dark rooms inspired a monastic silence. The halls and courtyards, however, resounded with the hubbub of active Argentine boys, ranging from seven years to youths in their twenties. His father had deposited him there with the advice to study and let no one strike him in the face. "With schooling and dignity," he said, "you can achieve all."[1]

Ricardo left the house on Calle Corrientes at eight o'clock each morning and took the horse-drawn tramway to the school. Playing with the other schoolboys, especially in the ball yard, engaged his attention more than his studies. When the final examination approached in October, he was not prepared. With a word of admonition to his son, Ricardo's father engaged tutors to coach him; the boy surprised his teachers by successfully completing the first scholastic year.

During the summer vacations, Ricardo, with a feeling of liberation, returned to La Porteña for four carefree months of life in the country. At the end of the first summer he went back to school with less regret because he looked forward with anticipation to rejoining his school friends. He spent four succeeding summers on the *estancia,* joining the men in their work, in the round-ups, the branding, and horse-breaking. He grew into a strong, athletic youth, adept in the art of handling horses and cattle.

Ricardo was not a good student. Lacking interest in his school work, he developed a passion for reading books outside

[1] Colombo, *op. cit.,* p. 38.

of his studies. His preference was for French and Russian novels: Hugo, France, Rabelais, Zola, Eugene Sue, Dostoyevsky, Renan, and Flaubert. Reading in French and Spanish, his avid interest spread over a widely varying assortment of writers: the Bible, Dickens, Spencer, Maupassant, Lamartine, Michelet, Samain, Nietzsche, Gorki, Rubén Darío, and Lugones. He devoured with eager lack of discrimination everything within his reach, and his young mind was filled with as odd a collection as that in the gullet of an ostrich.[2]

Amid this confusion, certain books left a vivid impression. They were the works of Renan, Flaubert, Zola and Nietzsche. Carried away by his imagination, he harbored secretly the wish to write.[3]

It was during these schooldays that he read Leconte de Lisle's spirited French translation of the *Illiad* and was first captivated by the enchantment of French verse. The enthusiasm of his discovery led him on to other French writers. He discovered Villiers de l'Isle-Adam, and, delighted, passed on to Baudelaire, and from Baudelaire to Bertrand. In 1893 Rubén Darío arrived in Buenos Aires to help sweep out the cobwebs of romanticism from the Argentine poetic household. Thus Ricardo's poetic consciousness began to unfold in the literary climate of *modernismo*.

During his last school years, Ricardo immersed himself in a world of poetry. Jotting down impressions as they came to him, he had the happy sensation of creating something beautiful and new; he was writing little poems in prose.[4]

Because Ricardo, at the beginning of his reading, had launched himself into an uncharted sea of contemporary literature without map or compass, he had found himself lost among the crowd of authors. Of all the writers Ricardo read at that time, Gustave Flaubert (1821-1880) was the one who most appealed to him. *Salammbô* (1874) was a revelation to

[2] De Torre, *loc. cit.*, p. 9.
[3] Güiraldes, "Carta a Victoria Ocampo," *Sur* (Año I, Verano, 1931), pp. 103-104.
[4] De Torre, *loc. cit.*, p. 9.

him because it, too, was poetry in prose. Its style, he said, had been refined into a series of *"chutes de phrases"* of such poetic cadence that it needed no plot or story.[5] It convinced him that prose could be an even better medium of poetic expression than verse because it was free of the fetters of meter and rime. Inspired by *Salammbô,* he began elaborating his own prose in rhythmic cadences.

His fascination for Flaubert led Ricardo's lyrical inclinations along a well defined course of preference. He sought the poetic in his readings. To his surprise, he found that other writers, Baudelaire, Villiers de l'Isle-Adam, Bertrand, and Poe, also had written poems in prose. The most beautiful seemed to him to be the stories of Oscar Wilde because of their lyrical simplicity. He discovered that the writings of the Bible and of Nietzsche were poetry too. Until then, he had thought that he had been creating something new in his own prose poems. Now he realized that he had "discovered" what had already been done long before.[6]

During his last year in school, Ricardo was so taken up with his world of poetry that he neglected his studies. Consequently, in 1903, he nearly failed to receive his certificate of graduation. He was more interested in becoming a writer.

At seventeen, Ricardo attempted to write his first novel. The subject was young love. He was filled with the romantic inclinations of a youth of his age and poured out his emotions in a style that was more sentimental than poetic. After he had written seventy pages of ecstatic descriptions, without yet having entered into the subject matter of the novel, his enthusiasm waned, and he abandoned his first project of writing a novel.

---

[5] *Ibid.,* p. 10.
[6] *Ibid.,* p. 9.

IV

Youth

In the three years immediately following his school days Ricardo spent a good part of the time at La Porteña. During this period, his fondness for life in the country found expression in music and painting. From his friends among the *peones* he learned how to sing the traditional gaucho songs and play the guitar. Occasionally he took up brush and palette and painted characteristic scenes about the country village of San Antonio de Areco.[1]

When the time came for young Güiraldes to consider the choice of a profession, his leanings seemed to indicate a suitability for architecture. At seventeen, he entered the School of Architecture at the University of Buenos Aires. But his interest in this career was short-lived. His temperament drew him toward more artistic activities. He enjoyed playing his guitar and singing songs in his pleasing baritone voice to his friends in town, among them the Italian baritone Titta Ruffo who, on one of these occasions, exclaimed, *"Canta, canta, Riccardo; sarai un Titta."*[2] The following year, Güiraldes transferred from architecture to law and social sciences at the same university, but he met with no greater success. His love of country life and his passion for other readings distracted his attention from his studies, obliging him to withdraw from the university once and for all.

[1] Colombo, *op. cit.*, pp. 41-43.
[2] *Ibid.*, p. 42. Further information is provided by Güiraldes' widow who in her letter of June 6, 1961 wrote:

Ricardo había heredado su magnífica voz de barítono de su madre y tenía una gran cultura musical. Iba a la ópera y a conciertos en esa época, y se sabía óperas enteras de memoria ... de ahí su amistad con Titta Ruffo. Lo imitaba a Titta a perfección. He oído cantar a los dos el mismo trozo de música y no se sabía cuál era cuál.

La música criolla la cantaba parca, lisa y llanamente como lo hace el gaucho. Ricardo conocía a fondo las dos técnicas: la natural y la cultivada sin mezclar una con otra.

Already at this time his interest was in nativist literature. Several factors contributed to develop his fascination with gauchesque narrations that later were to motivate him to write his *Cuentos de muerte y de sangre* (Buenos Aires, 1915). These were the memory of the tales of gaucho legend he had heard as a child, his love for the traditional in the Argentine pampa so closely associated with his happy days at La Porteña, the existing wave of enthusiasm for Argentine folklore, and the popularity of contemporary gauchesque literature.[3]

Prior to 1900, popular interest in Argentine folklore had been increasing, seemingly in proportion to the disappearance of the genuine gaucho. In 1900, in reality, the gaucho existed only in legend. Nevertheless, the tradition of these men was kept alive in the well known, earlier gauchesque literature.[4] Consequently, the legendary characters of Martín Fierro, Santos Vega, Facundo, Juan Moreira, and their like, had become famous prototypes. In 1884, José T. Podestá, a popular circus impresario, won unprecedented acclaim with his theatrical interpretations of Gutiérrez' *Juan Moreira*. In and about Buenos Aires, Italian immigrants, called *gringos* by the true Argentines, imitated gaucho ways with the passion of enthusiasts. They played cowboy in Argentine style in dead earnest, dressed in gaucho garb, rode *criollo* horses, organized barbecues in the pampa, sipped *mate* and sang *payadas*. They founded clubs to preserve gaucho customs and printed small periodicals filled with stories of gauchos and verse in the style of Martín Fierro. The continued popularity of these regional traditions also is attested by the successful representation in Buenos Aires of three plays of Florencio Sánchez (1875-1910), featuring characteristic gaucho types, *M'hijo el dotor*

---

[3] A most helpful source of information on the fashion for gaucho folklore at this time has been Madeline W. Nichols' "The Gaucho in Literature" in *The Moraga Quarterly* (Winter 1936), pp. 73-82.

[4] Among the most widely read were Hilario Ascasubi's *Santos Vega o los mellizos de "La Flor"* (1815), Bartolomé Mitre's *Santos Vega* (1838), Domingo Faustino Sarmiento's *Facundo* (1845), José Hernández's *Martín Fierro*, Rafael Obligado's *Santos Vega* (1872), and Eduardo Gutiérrez's *Juan Moreira* (1880).

in 1903, *La Gringa* in 1904, and *Barranca abajo* in 1905. Hence, while Güiraldes was still a law student in 1905, the legendary figures of gauchos had captured the imagination of the public, and the folklore of the pampa had become a prevailing popular fashion in Buenos Aires.

Concurrently, this popularity of Argentine folklore set the stage for the recrudescence of a new gauchesque literature, exemplified by an exalted cult of the native land.[5] In 1897 José S. Alvarez (1858-1903), the noted writer of gaucho tales, founded in Buenos Aires the magazine *Caras y Caretas,* which published regional stories for popular consumption. The success of *Caras y Caretas* led to the appearance of two other periodicals, *La Novela Semanal* in 1900 and the *Suplemento Literario* of *La Nación* in 1904, which also published nativist fiction in response to the demand. Encouraged by the periodicals and the fashion, a dozen or more authors wrote stories on gaucho themes.[6] Passengers on the suburban trains could be seen reading gaucho stories as they traveled to and from their occupations in Buenos Aires. In short, during the first decade of the twentieth century, Argentine literature had joined hands with Argentine popular fashion on a common ground: the gaucho tradition.

Accordingly, Güiraldes' appetite for the gauchesque, already strongly planted within him, was favored at this time by the prevailing interest in Argentine folklore. His passion for the traditional motivated him to jot down a few notes outlining the gaucho tales that he had heard as a child. He wrote them down in the most simple language. When he re-read them, he discovered that he had written them in the style most suited to the expression of the gaucho: concision. On a card

[5] For information on the popularity of gauchesque literature in Argentina at this time, see Antonio Pagés Larraya, "Prólogo," *Cuentos de nuestra tierra* (Buenos Aires, 1952).

[6] Most notable among them were Leopoldo Lugones, whose work, *La guerra gaucha* (1905), was a collection of twenty-two campfire-type tales of the gaucho war of independence, Robert J. Payró (1876-1928), famous for his novelette, *El casamiento de Laucha* (1906), the story of a gaucho rogue, and Benito Lynch, born in 1885, whose *Plata dorada* (1909) introduced a realistic psychological analysis of a boy of the gaucho world.

that he kept among his writings he noted with satisfaction:
"I want my stories to be extracts, brief and concise. What I
like best about a man's hand is the fist."[7]

When Güiraldes failed to continue his studies, don Manuel
expressed his disappointment in his son and gave him some
fatherly advice on life. In response to his father's exhortations,
Güiraldes entered a Buenos Aires banking firm. But at the end
of one year, he abandoned the business world because his
artistic temperament was incompatible with numerical calcula-
tions. He wanted to sing gaucho songs, to paint regional
landscapes and, above all, he wanted to be a writer.

Contrary to a malicious legend that has dogged the memory of his youth, young Güiraldes was not a good-for-nothing
playboy. It was not weakness of character that induced him to
change directions; it was his determination to become a writer.
Indeed, it is now known that as early as 1910 he had resolved to
be "the literary disciple of the gaucho." In that year he drew up
the program which was to mark the course of his career. The
following excerpts from a recently disclosed plan of work[8]
attest to the fact that Güiraldes at the age of twenty-four already had set for himself the literary objectives which he
pursued from that time forward:

> Literature does not have to have loud shouting,
> graftings and complicated theories. Quite the
> contrary, it must be as pure as possible—get rid
> of all artifices that are foreign to it and let it
> stand on its own merits.
>
> Nowadays people confuse writers, or better said
> scribblers, with men of letters. They don't draw a
> line between the former, who use language merely

[7] De Torre, *loc. cit* p. 11.
[8] Adelina del Carril de Güiraldes wrote in her letter of June 6, 1961, that
her husband *"en 1910 hizo un plan de trabajo,"* a copy of which she enclosed.
This plan of work, written by Güiraldes when he was twenty-four, is an
unpublished monograph from which the present excerpts have been taken.
(Author's translation.)

as a medium of communication, and the latter, who make language a creation of art. My mission is to look at life from a healthy and intelligent point of view and to translate it into an artistic expression; and by artistic I also mean simple. I shall not seek public approval; I shall be honest with myself. I will polish and continue polishing my language until I will have achieved that simplicity which makes greatness. This is why I have sought out the gaucho and the pampas as my subject matter from among all other themes.

The gaucho is by nature the son of the pampa; both are inseparable from each other; each possesses the simplicity that I have been trying to achieve. In fact, my inclination toward unadorned plainness may well have come from the influence of the gaucho upon me. The gaucho casts out all that is pusillanimous and infirm from his great soul, which is simple and sound, and above pettiness.

.   .   .   .

The beauty of the vast, uniform plain, the great spectacle of those days and nights in the pampa that follow upon each other with equal splendor, but which are never the same, have instilled in me a love for that which is simple and great ...

I have to carry out this work of mine without worrying about the opinions of others ...

My writing can have a literary style without having to use only words approved by the Royal Spanish Academy. Our pampa has its own vocabulary which has come from the need to create new terms. The use of these expressions are as proper—indeed as necessary—as the best.

.   .   .   .

I can write literature with what we may call "gaucho" vocabulary in as pure a style as the most Castilian ...

There is no doubt that already in 1910 Güiraldes had defined his mission to be the literary interpreter of the gaucho.

V

Young Man Abroad

In 1910 Paris was the center of modern culture for many young Argentines. France attracted Güiraldes and his contemporaries through its novels, its poetry. its painting, its sculpture, and its music. Many responded to her appeal and traveled to the French capital. A restless Güiraldes longed to breathe the artistic air of Paris. His father, who had become the *Intendente Municipal* of Buenos Aires,[1] wanted his son to stay at home because the Infanta Isabel of Bourbon was expected to arrive in Buenos Aires for the celebration of the one hundreth anniversary of Argentina's independence, on May 25, 1910. But, when don Manuel escorted the royal princess down the gangplank of the Spanish naval vessel *Alfonso XII,* his son had already departed for Europe.

Güiraldes was twenty-four years of age when he disembarked in Spain. While spending several peaceful days at the Hotel Alhambra in Granada, he began writing the first sketch of a short story of the life of an Argentine playboy in Paris as he imagined it. Later in Paris itself, he would have ample opportunity to compare it with the real thing. What was begun as a short narration, *Los impulsos de Ricardito,* developed later into his first novel, *Raucho* (1917).[2]

At last in the capital of France, Güiraldes looked forward to entering the artistic atmosphere of which he had dreamed when reading Baudelaire and Verlaine. Instead, he was soon caught up in the social whirl of the smart set.[3] Together with Alberto López Buchardo, the Argentine painter and musician, he introduced the tango into the nightlife of that city. His

---

[1] Colombo, *op. cit.,* p. 46. The office of *Intendente Municipal* of Buenos Aires is that of Mayor of the City of Buenos Aires.
[2] De Torre, *loc. cit.,* p. 14.
[3] Alberto Oscar Blasi, "Güiraldes y el ultraísmo," *Estudios* (Buenos Aires, Sept.-Oct. 1953), p. 330.

natural charm won him immediate popularity, and he was a frequent and welcomed guest at the gatherings of distinguished Parisians.

Only a few months had passed when Güiraldes, accompanied by Adán Diehl, a friend with similar inclinations, left Paris on a journey of adventure. This undertaking responded to a basic necessity in Güiraldes: an undefinable longing for new horizons.[4] For nearly two years, Güiraldes and Adán Diehl traveled to different countries of Europe and the East.

The Orient held out a strange fascination beyond its veil of mystery. The passing contact with the people of ancient civilizations, of different races, of varying cultures, and of distinct human characteristics broadened Güiraldes' outlook and helped mature the inclinations of his character. These were his love of beauty,[5] his sense of harmony with the universe,[6] and his esteem of human virtues.[7]

Throughout his travels in strange lands, Ricardo thought of home on the pampa. The farther away and the stranger the people, the more he felt a part of his native soil. His "gauchos" were ever in mind.[8] He compared the different types of humans he met to his beloved men of the Argentine plains. In the light of this comparison, the virtues of the gaucho character stood out in sharp contrast.[9] In Güiraldes' eyes these were the spirit of freedom instead of servility, the pride of

---

[4] Victoria Ocampo, in *Testimonios* (Buenos Aires, 1941), p. 319, describes this characteristic of Güiraldes by saying, "La gioia è sempre all'altra riva."

[5] Victoria Ocampo, speaking of Güiraldes' love of beauty in her "Carta a Ricardo Güiraldes," *Sur* (No. 217-218, Nov.-Dec. 1952), p. 5, said: "Avido de belleza, sea cual fuere su origen, no temías aminorarte haciéndola tuya."

[6] Güiraldes' sense of harmony with the universe is expressed throughout his writing, especially in poetic passages considering nature, the pampa, and infinity. See, for example, in *El cencerro de cristal* (Buenos Aires, 1952), "Tríptico," p. 15, "Solo," p. 19, "Tarde," p. 21, and "Reposo," p. 35. In *El libro bravo* (San Antonio de Areco, 1936), p. 17, he extended his sense of harmony to the people of the pampa: "La armonía delata la existencia de un ser completo y vi que mi pueblo era un ser completo ante el cual mis ojos se anegaron de cariño."

[7] Güiraldes, *El libro bravo, op, cit.*

[8] *Ibid.*, p. 18.

[9] *Ibid.*, p. 16. "Entre extraños aprendí a ver lo que en mí había de nacional, lo que hay en mí no de individual, sino de colectivo y común a todo mi pueblo."

"Los contrastes evidenciaron lo propio de lo extraño."

independence instead of abject humility, aggressive assertive-
ness instead of weak defeatism, loyalty instead of falseness,
and courage instead of fear.[10]

One night in Ceylon, in the fabulous city of Kandy, Güiraldes had a strange experience. In a letter[11] written later to a
friend he related that he and Adán Diehl had entered a native
den of hashish smokers. After having smoked several pipes,
he had a lucid vision which he described as follows:

> Suddenly I saw a large configuration of Argen-
> tina on a map of the world. I could see the land,
> the historical past, and the people of Argentina,
> all at the same time. It was marvelous to behold
> the extension of its territory, stretching from the
> snow covered regions to the tropics in two di-
> mensions; that is to say in its latitudes and in its
> high and low altitudes.
>
> In that expanse, a few aggressive and hardy men
> were fighting against each other in little groups
> like small whirlpools of blood. The land re-
> sounded with their cries of revolt and their shouts
> of confidence in their own strength. I could see
> all this from my knowledge of the entire course
> of different civilizations. Then, looking back in
> retrospect to that time and comparing it with the
> smooth and settled appearance of Argentina in its
> present calmness, I saw that now everything in
> my country was imitation, apprenticeship and
> submission, and that Argentina had no person-
> ality of its own, except in the case of the gaucho
> who still stood upright and firm and who ex-
> pressed himself in a bold, new manner.[12]

Güiraldes returned to Paris in 1911, a wiser young man

[10] *Ibid.*, p. 13.
[11] Güiraldes, "Carta a Valery Larbaud, en la Isla de Elba," *Sur* (No. 233,
March-April, 1955), pp. 110-117.
[12] *Ibid.*, pp. 112-113. (Author's translation.)

and with a greater love for his native land. His purpose had become clear. It was to write about these things that now welled up within him. And writing was within his grasp. He was determined, once and for all, to settle down and become a writer.[13] Seeking a favorable environment in which to do so, he installed himself in the studio of his friend, Alberto Lagos, an Argentine sculptor. There, wrapped in dreams of the pampa, Güiraldes began unfolding his literary talent. It was just a beginning along three different lines, the first steps toward his three later books, *Raucho* (1917), *Cuentos de muerte y de sangre* (1915), and *El cencerro de cristal* (1915).

The idea of *Raucho,* which began taking form in Granada as a short narrative with the title of *Los impulsos de Ricardito,* was further elaborated as *Los comentarios de Ricardito.*[14]

A wave of nostalgia for the happy life at La Porteña revived his passion for Argentine folklore and legend. In this mood, he turned to the notes he had made on the blood-and-thunder gaucho tales he had heard as a boy, and started writing the first gaucho stories of his *Cuentos de muerte y de sangre.*

During this brief period of initial writing activity, in Paris from 1911 to 1912, Güiraldes gave expression to his urge for poetic creation by writing seven poems.[15] They reflected some of the moods that filled his life in the studio. All but one are written entirely in prose, his favorite poetic form. Later he included them in his book *El cencerro de cristal.*

In 1910, Güiraldes had been motivated to leave Buenos Aires by a longing to know Paris. This time his longing was to be away from Paris, it was for Argentina. He loved his native pampa with greater passion now that it was far away. His thoughts flew fondly to the wide open spaces of his homeland. One evening a desperate feeling of homesickness drove him from the studio. Disconsolate, he walked the Paris

---

[13] De Torre, *loc. cit.,* p. 11: "En París, me decidí 'une fois pour toutes' . . . a convertirme en escritor."

[14] *Ibid.,* p. 14.

[15] The poems are discussed under the heading of *"El cencerro de cristal,"* in the part devoted to the works of Ricardo Güiraldes.

streets. They were covered with snow. It seemed such foreign snow to him. Even his own shadow, his own voice seemed foreign to him, foreign to his own race of people. Güiraldes felt more than ever that his real self was gaucho.[16] In that dreary Paris winter of 1912, he packed his bags and took the boat back to Argentina.

---

[16] See Arturo Torres-Rioseco, "Ricardo Güiraldes" in *Atenea* (Concepción, Chile, Sept. 1939), p. 481, in which he quotes Güiraldes as saying to a friend: "Mirá ché, ha sido en París donde comprendí, una noche en que vi solito mi alma, que uno debe ser un árbol de la tierra en que nació. Espinillo arisco o tala pobre. Acababa de dar una vuelta completa al mundo, y esa noche de nieve me corrió por lo despiadado, y lo era más que la escarcha nuestra, porque era nieve extranjera. Me sentí huérfano, guacho y ajeno a mi voz, a mi sombra y a mi raza. Lié mis petates, y ¡hasta la vista!, le dije, ché."

VI

Return to Argentina and Adelina

When Güiraldes disembarked in Buenos Aires in 1912, one of his first acts was to go to the *estancia* and ride out into the open pampa.[1] The joyful sensations experienced on his return to his longed-for country life at La Porteña are best expressed in his own words in "Tríptico,"[2] three short prose poems describing morning, noon, and nightfall in the Argentine countryside. Güiraldes was happy to be back with his beloved people on the ranch, among them don Segundo. He was sadly aware of the passing of the traditional way of life in the pampa, and looked upon his aging friend as the image of a noble race of gauchos that was disappearing before the advance of modern civilization.[3] His sentiment toward don Segundo motivated his idea of capturing the picture of the old *peón* in writing.[4]

At this time two thoughts were uppermost in his youthful mind: Adelina and writing. He would marry Adelina and settle down with firm dedication to writing.[5]

In 1905, five years before his trip abroad, he had met Adelina del Carril at a party given by the Quesada Pachecos in San Miguel, a country village of the province of Buenos Aires.

[1] Torres-Rioseco, *loc. cit.,* p. 481: "Cuando bajé del barco, tomé mi pingo y me entré, como cuando era cachorro, hasta el corazón en la pampa."
[2] Güiraldes, *El cencerro de cristal* (Buenos Aires, 1915), p. 15.
[3] Brito Broca, "Ricardo Güiraldes," *Americanas* (Curitiba - São Paulo - Rio, 1944), pp. 24-25: "Retornando ao campo, aos pagos nativos, o escritor viu no velho peão — personagem real, cuja fotografia ja tivemos ocasião de contemplar — a imagem da clase rural legitimamente argentina, sacrificado pelo espírito de uma civilização que, por desviar-se das tradições nacionais, acarretará série crise económica."
[4] Adelina del Carril de Güiraldes, "Nota preliminar," in *Don Segundo Sombra* (Buenos Aires, Ed. Kraft, 1952), p. 11: "Durante muchos años alentó Ricardo la idea de escribir *Don Segundo Sombra,* cuyo protagonista aparece en uno de los *Cuentos de muerte y sangre.*"
[5] In a lecture in Buenos Aires, Adelina del Carril de Güiraldes said: "De nuevo en Buenos Aires, se dedicó por entero a las letras." See *La Prensa* (June 26, 1956).

Their interest in each other became apparent, when, soon afterwards, he escorted Adelina to an evening reception at the home of his aunt, doña María Güiraldes de Guerrico, in Buenos Aires. During his absence from Argentina, he had kept the memory of Adelina in his affections and, on his return home, they became engaged to be married.[6]

Encouraged by the prospects of a happy future, Güiraldes set to work writing. He took up once more his plan, begun in Paris, to write tales of gaucho life and legend. At the age of twenty-seven, shortly after his engagement, his first story was published in Buenos Aires in Alvarez's *Caras y Caretas.*[7] Alongside the writing of the *cuentos,* he also concentrated on poetry. His urge for poetic creation, however, which had begun to bear fruit in Paris, struggled for expression in the unfavorable environment of Buenos Aires.

When Güiraldes left Buenos Aires in 1910, the dominant trend in poetry was that inaugurated by Rubén Darío. On his return in 1912, the poetic climate was much the same. Argentine poetry lagged behind the artistic evolution of modern letters. The cry of rebellion against *modernismo,* which in 1910 Enrique González Martínez had raised in his famous sonnet,[8] had hardly an echo in conservative Buenos Aires. With a very few exceptions, the literary environment in Argentina was apathetic to the innovations in poetry. Indeed, the situation was even worse; interest in the arts, including literature, was all but dead. Modern world trends in the arts were known only to a very few in Buenos Aires. The great Argentine city, with a population approaching the 900,000 mark at the time, was asleep in an atmosphere of aesthetic lethargy. There were no galleries where new artists could exhibit their art. There were no publishing houses that would accept the works of young writers of worth. Even a recog-

---

[6] Colombo, *op. cit.,* p. 48.
[7] De Torre, *loc. cit.,* p. 12.
[8] Enrique González Martínez, "Tuércele el cuello al cisne...," *Antología poética* (Buenos Aires, 1943), p. 33.

nized writer, Leopoldo Lugones, had to pay for his own publications and wait ten to fifteen years to sell only five hundred copies. This artistically dead environment crushed the spirit of the young artists and writers who sought progress and renovation in the arts. Promising new spirits became impatient and rebellious; then, dejected by the intellectual apathy, they gave up in despair or emigrated.

But, a handful of rebels stood fast in Buenos Aires and defied that bastion of conservatism. They were a group of young artists and writers who became known as "los Pareras" because they met at a studio in a street by that name, where they discussed painting, music and literature. Among them were Carlos Ayerza, Tito Cittadini, Adán Diehl, Alberto Girondo, Alfredo González Garaño, Alberto Lagos, Aníbal Noceti and Güiraldes himself. Like Güiraldes, they were painfully conscious of the mediocrity and stagnation of the Argentine literary environment. Bored to desperation with outworn, monotonous literary tastes, they sensed that there must be something better in the works of the French symbolist poets. But knowledge of the French symbolists, then acclaimed in France, was eclipsed by their abysmal ignorance of modern French poetry. Furthermore, the French symbolists were considered outlaws in the conservative literary circles because they were a flagrant defiance in tone and in form of long established poetic traditions. In Buenos Aires at that time so little was the regard for the new trend in poetry that it was actually a major victory to secure a book of poems or even a single poem of any of the symbolists.[9]

Güiraldes, then, was not alone in his quest for new horizons. These kindred spirits shared his literary preoccupations. They too sought the new, the bold and the modern in poetry. The appeal of the French poets drew them together in a common bond. With the enthusiasm of those who find in each other a sympathetic vibration, they plunged into the obscur-

[9] Güiraldes, "Un libro," *Proa* (Buenos Aires, No. 3, Oct. 1924), p. 35.

ities of the symbolists. Together they traveled down the
strange, new paths of Rimbaud, Mallarmé, Corbière, Laforgue
and Léger, reading to each other and explaining the meanings
of the cryptic passages.[10] This poetry was full of surprising
discoveries and new artistic techniques.[11]

Thus, in the years 1912 and 1913 after his engagement to
Adelina, Güiraldes devoted himself more to exploring and
understanding the French symbolists than to writing. Although at first he fumbled about confusedly in the darkness
of these unfamiliar poetic regions, the innovations of the symbolists gratified his feeling of rebellion against the old and his
thirst for the new. The very disdain in which they were generally held whetted his appetite. He sought out the works
of Rimbaud, Corbière, Mallarmé, Laforgue, and Isidore Du-
casse, and read them with avidity. At this time, not only
were symbolists considered mad and exotic in Buenos Aires,
but so also were they who read them. Consequently, Güiraldes was scorned for his taste and laughed at for his dedicated
reading of these scandalously unpoetic poets. More than that,
he was snubbed into an intellectual isolation. But this only
fanned his enthusiasm for the symbolists and hardened his
determination to know them better. He looked upon them
as his teachers and studied the new techniques of their art.
Rimbaud was so different that he seemed to stand coldly alone
in a greatness of his own. Mallarmé gave him master concepts
by the handful. Laforgue seemed to be the poet who lived,
more than all the rest, in a state of poetic grace, while Corbière was something quite apart: his was an anti-literary literature, a style of fistblows which was an outward expression
of an untamed and bruised interior sensibility. These were
the poets who most appealed to Güiraldes.[12]

In his voyage of discovery among the French symbolists,
Güiraldes found the new poetic world he had sought. At first,

[10] Ocampo, "Carta a Ricardo Güiraldes," p. 5.
[11] Güiraldes, "Un libro," p. 35.
[12] De Torre, loc. cit., p. 12.

it had been a dark unknown. But now he penetrated the obscurity of their poetic subtleties. The wealth of innovations and the discovery of new techniques spurred him into a veritable cult of the new poetic art.

But Güiraldes was not seeking to imitate. He explicitly denied that he followed in the path of the French symbolists.[13] On the contrary, he sought a new poetic expression of his own. Accordingly, among their many artistic innovations and new techniques there was one characteristic that stood out as an example. It was that each one of the French symbolists had the courage to defy convention and give expression to his own individuality in his own way. From Corbière, Mallarmé, and Laforgue, Güiraldes learned the courage to cast aside boldly the garments of imitation and to plunge naked and unashamed into the untrammeled expression of his own artistic personality. He discovered the joy of singing his own spontaneous song.[14] Even though Güiraldes spent most of the year 1913 reading and exploring the hidden recesses of the symbolists, these new-found friends inspired him to break through the barrier of contemporary literary conservatism and to write five more poems, which he included in *El cencerro de cristal*.[15]

Toward the end of the year Güiraldes' literary activities were held in suspense by the approach of his wedding. On October 20, 1913, in the church of Nuestra Señora del Socorro in Buenos Aires,[16] Güiraldes married Adelina del Carril, who, as his life's companion, encouraged him in his work, comforted him in his disillusionments, and shared in his joys.[17]

That same day, after the wedding, the young couple departed for La Porteña. It was already midnight when they ar-

[13] Güiraldes, "Poesía," *Martín Fierro* (Buenos Aires, March, 1927), p. 1.
[14] Güiraldes, "Carta a Guillermo de Torre," *Proa* (Buenos Aires, No. 8, March, 1925), pp. 39-41.
[15] The five poems are "Tríptico," "Leyenda," "Ladrido," "Aconcagua," "Marta," and "Siete verdades y una belleza."
[16] Colombo, *op. cit.*, 49.
[17] Enrique González Tuñón, *Apología de un hombre santo* (Buenos Aires, 1930), pp. 50-52.

rived at San Antonio de Areco. As they drove off in the two-wheeled carriage toward the *estancia,* the light of a full moon flooded the countryside. Riding silently on a large horse alongside them was the majectic figure of an old gaucho, wrapped in the folds of a pale-colored poncho. It was don Segundo, escorting the bride and groom home, ready to pull the carriage out of the mud with his lasso in case the wheels got stuck. Many times Adelina had heard Güiraldes speak fondly of don Segundo, but this was the first time she had seen the loyal old gaucho. Shrouded in the shadows of the moonlight, don Segundo seemed to her like an unreal being.[18]

---

[18] Adelina del Carril de Güiraldes, "Nota preliminar" in *Don Segundo Sombra* (Buenos Aires, Ed. Kraft, 1952), p. 11.

VII

The Birth of *Cuentos* and *El cencerro*

Happily settled with Adelina at La Porteña, Güiraldes found that his urge to write unfolded in a favorable environment. The harmonious atmosphere in which he resumed his work is reflected in his poem "Siesta."[1] It was consequently with renewed determination and high hopes that he took up once more his three original projects: his book of gaucho stories, his book of poems, and his novel *Raucho*.[2] Of the three books, he concentrated on completing the gaucho stories and the poems first, leaving *Raucho* until later. He wrote his *cuentos* at the same time he wrote the poems, alternating his work whenever he tired of one.[3] The rough and virile subject matter of the gaucho was the very antithesis of poetry; and, when Güiraldes felt the need of a respite from his poetic writing, he would submerge himself in writing tales of blood and death. Like twins, both books went through a simultaneous period of gestation and later saw the light at the same time.

During the three years following Güiraldes' marriage in 1913, the continued popularity of gaucho folklore was reflected in the sustained demand for gaucho stories. *Caras y Caretas,* responding to that demand, published fourteen more of his stories.[4] Indeed, the literary climate was favorable to the reception of a book of stories about gauchos. With this in mind, Güiraldes wrote altogether about thirty-seven stories, only a few of which were not directly connected with Argentine country life. In September, 1915, he assembled twenty-six narratives which he published under the title of *Cuentos de muerte y de sangre; seguidos de aventuras grotescas y una*

[1] *El cencerro*, p. 20.
[2] De Torre, *loc. cit.,* p. 12.
[3] Adelina del Carril de Güiraldes. "Nota preliminar" in *El cencerro de cristal,* p. 7.
[4] De Torre, *loc. cit.,* p. 12.

trilogía cristiana.[5] In one of the stories of this book, don Segundo makes his first appearance.[6]

In writing his book of poems, he was motivated by a longing for a new poetic expression. Like his horse, described in "Mi caballo," he was possessed with a "thirsting for new horizons" (*"sed de horizonte"*).[7] The same spirit of adventure that had driven him to travel abroad and that urged him to explore the unfamiliar territory of French symbolism now moved him to pursue new, creative writing. As he clearly expressed in his poem "Viajar,"[8] what he called his "spirit of a ship's prow" (*"alma de proa"*) impelled him to "devour new horizons" (*"asimilar horizontes"*). While working on his poems, he turned for encouragement to the French writers whom he considered his friends and teachers. They were Flaubert, Corbière, Mallarmé, and Laforgue. He consulted them constantly, and he came to look upon them with sincere love.[9] It was their example that emboldened him to liberate his "inner voice"[10] from the forms of literary conservatism. Thus, in 1914 before the first World War, Güiraldes expressed his own aesthetic sensitivity spontaneously and as it moved him. He had found his own voice.[11]

Güiraldes was well on the way to completing his book of poems when the World War broke out in August, 1914. Although Argentina was neutral, he was passionately sympathetic to France. The immensity of the human carnage oppressed his spirit and dissipated his literary creativeness. On August first of that year he wrote in his diary: "The oppressiveness of tragedy has never been so universal... The tumor of hate

[5] The remaining published *cuentos*, not included in *Cuentos de muerte y de Sangre*, appeared in *Seis relatos* (Buenos Aires, 1929) and in *Rosaura (una novela corta) y siete cuentos* (Buenos Aires, 1952).

[6] "Al rescoldo," *Cuentos de muerte y de sangre*, pp. 81-92. Don Segundo makes his second appearance later in "Politiquería," *Plus Ultra* (Buenos Aires, I, No. 8, 1916).

[7] *El cencerro*, p. 13.

[8] *El cencerro*, p. 49.

[9] De Torre, *loc. cit.*, p. 12.

[10] Güiraldes, "Carta a Guillermo de Torre," p. 39.

[11] Alfredo Brandán Caraffa, "La calle de la tarde," *Proa* (Buenos Aires, No. 3, Oct. 1929).

has burst."[12] Later, as the fighting increased in Europe, he abandoned his writing in order to campaign for the intervention of Argentina in the war to end all wars. Together with his brother Pepe, Alfredo González Garaña, and other young men, he founded the Comité Nacional de la Juventud and agitated in street demonstrations and in public addresses to save the national honor of Argentina.[13] When his countrymen failed to respond to his appeal, Güiraldes, saddened, returned to his writing.

By 1915, he had assembled forty-six poems in verse and in prose into one volume. On the cover he wrote the title *El cencerro de cristal. El cencerro* means the horse-bell which is worn by a mare leading a herd of colts. In Güiraldes' memory the cheerful sound of this bell rang crystal clear across the pampa and down the years from his early childhood. Its name on his book of poems suggests a call to follow the new aesthetic note of his poetry.

Completed, *El cencerro* was a profession of Güiraldes' literary beliefs. Even more, it was a confession of his intimate, poetic aspirations. It was his *"alma de proa"* laid bare. He was aware that his poems were far beyond the comprehension of the literary circles of Buenos Aires. Consequently, he was hesitant to expose himself to the criticism of the uninitiated, and sought counsel from a senior poet who had been a rebel in his day, Leopoldo Lugones. With his manuscript under his arm, he called on Lugones at the Biblioteca del Consejo Nacional de Educación and read parts of *El cencerro* aloud to him in his study. The older poet listened until late that afternoon and asked Güiraldes to return and continue reading the next day. At the end, after having suggested the use of more punctuation, Lugones advised the young rebel to publish.[14]

Güiraldes took both *El cencerro* and his *Cuentos* to Impren-

[12] Colombo, *op. cit.,* p. 52.
[13] Alvaro Melián Lafinur, "Discurso en memoria de Ricardo Güiraldes," *Repertorio Americano* (San José de Costa Rica, Nov. 30, 1929), pp. 321-322.
[14] Adelina del Carril de Güiraldes, "Nota preliminar," in *El cencerro*, p. 7.

ta Tragant.[15] Accompanied by Adelina. who shared in the emotion of this moment, he returned many an afternoon to the printers and watched the presses turn out the pages. At last, on September 21, 1915, they witnessed the birth of the twin books. Late that afternoon Güiraldes and Adelina left the printers with the first copies under their arms. They were in a state of exhilaration. Oblivious of his earlier fears, Güiraldes little dreamed of the storm of ridicule that *El cencerro* was to provoke.

The publication of *El cencerro* was a complete failure.[16] Güiraldes' bold innovations, especially in the use of startling imagery,[17] shocked the literary taste that had settled in the poetic climate of *modernismo*.[18] Some readers accused him of being a madman,[19] others called him an unbalanced dreamer and a seeker of the impossible.[20] The few critics who deigned to comment did so with intent to defame him for his audacity, and branded him decadent, symbolist, and futurist, terms which in conservative Buenos Aires carried the connotation of a crackbrain.[21] To them Güiraldes was a Frenchified *poseur,* who affected a foreign attitude,[22] particularly that of the most advanced French poets, of whom they knew little and understood less. Their response to the poems was ridicule and indignant condemnation, even by those in whom Güiraldes expected more intelligence.[23] Lugones himself turned from his young friend.[24] The ridicule reached a point where Güiraldes

---

[15] Colombo, *op. cit.,* p. 59.

[16] De Torre, *loc. cit.,* p. 13.

[17] One of the images that was a principal target of ridicule was "pulcro botón de calzoncillo" in "Luna," *El cencerro,* p. 44. See also Colombo, *op. cit.,* pp.60-61, and an anonymous article in *Síntesis* (Buenos Aires, II, 1927), pp. 383-384.

[18] Ernesto Palacio, "La poesía cristiana de Ricardo Güiraldes" in the Literary Supplement of *La Nación* (May 17, 1928), p. 12.

[19] Adelina del Carril de Güiraldes, "Nota preliminar" in *El cencerro,* p. 8.

[20] González Tuñón, *op. cit.,* 43.

[21] "Era 'raro' para la inercia intelectual y se le acoplaba con lo que en el momento parecía 'raro'." See Güiraldes, "Poesía," *Martín Fierro* (Buenos Aires, March 28, 1927), p. 1.

[22] Ocampo, "Carta a Ricardo Güiraldes," p. 5.

[23] "¡Lástima! Yo creí —por fe en la viveza criolla— ser comprendido a media palabra." See Güiraldes, "Poesía," p. 3.

[24] Lugones expressed his hostility for *El cencerro* by inveighing against what

became the laughing stock of the town. [25] During the entire year after its publication, the bookshops sold only about ninety copies altogether of *El cencerro*.[26] The sale of *Cuentos* fared even worse, since no more than seven copies were sold during the same period.[27]

This indifference and hostility was a blow. Güiraldes had expected better things from the Buenos Aires literary world.[28] Disillusioned in the intellectual capacity of his critics, he withdrew all copies of *El cencerro* from sale and most of the *Cuentos*. Like a man wounded, he returned with his books to La Porteña to destroy them. His first plan was to burn them in a great bonfire. On second thought, he ordered them thrown, to the last copy, into the old well on the place "so that they would rot away" (*"para que se pudran"*).[29] It was his way of saying that his efforts had been wasted on such an unenlightened public.[30]

---

he called "... la trastienda clandestina de las mixturas de ultramar, donde el fraude de la poesía sin verso, la estética sin belleza y las vanguardias sin ejército aderezan el contrabando de la esterilidad, la fealdad y la vanagloria." See Augusto Mario Delfino, "Cómo apareció 'Don Segundo Sombra'," *Arte y Plata* (México, III, Feb., 1947), pp. 34-36.

[25] Colombo, *op. cit.*, p. 61.

[26] Adelina del Carril de Güiraldes, "Nota preliminar," *El cencerro*, p. 8.

[27] De Torre, *loc. cit.*, p. 13.

[28] Colombo, *op. cit.*, p. 62.

[29] Oliverio Girondo, *El periódico Martín Fierro: 1924-1949* (Buenos Aires, 1949), p. 13.

[30] In a letter to the author, dated February 19, 1960, Adelina del Carril de Güiraldes says on this point:

Ricardo era muy consciente, de lo que hacía y del valor que tenía lo que hacía. Sufría de la falta de simpatía humana, de la hostilidad y mala voluntad de la gente. Sufría en el campo afectivo. Prueba de ello lo da esta nota suya de entonces: 'Me daría mucha rabia divertir o entretener, después de muerto, la manada de idiotas que me han disminuido la vida. . . . Si sintiera alrededor mío, no admiración, respeto u otras vaciedades, sino cariño, me triplicaría en poder y en trabajo. La indiferencia me aplasta, pero es inútil, nunca el capón podrá ver...'

No podía aguantar la hostilidad agresiva de los que no comprendían, él que se sentía enriquecido por los dones de sus colegas tanto en literatura como en música o pintura.

VIII

Rosaura and *Raucho*

For a year after the failure of *El cencerro*, Güiraldes retired to the seclusion of the *estancia*. The adverse criticism had injured him deeply; it had killed his joyful spirit of adventure. All desire to write left him. Güiraldes' disillusionment lasted for a long time, as appeared years later when he wrote that it was sheer folly to be a poet in those days when writers had given up their lances for bags of gold.[1] He was disgusted with the materialism he saw about him, and felt a special antipathy for worldly city life.[2] In his reaction against the city where he had been hurt, he sought refuge in the beloved counstryside of happy boyhood memories. La Porteña was an escape from adversity and a comfort in his frustration.[3]

For a while, his feelings were dominated by this sense of injury. Gradually counter influences began healing his spirit. They were several. First of all there was Adelina, who was a source of unfaltering moral encouragement.[4] At the same time, a few colleagues, who also believed in Güiraldes' talent and shared in his literary aspirations, rallied to his side with applause. Among these was Victoria Ocampo, who became Güiraldes' great friend during this time of adverse criticism.[5]

It was also right after the failure of *El cencerro* in 1915 that

[1] Güiraldes, "Un libro," p. 36.
[2] See González Tuñón, *op. cit.*, pp. 31-32: "Las ciudades son prostíbulos más o menos disimulados, con olor a estupro y a riña de borracho."
[3] Colombo, *op. cit.*, p. 67.
[4] In her letter of February 19, 1960, Adelina del Carril de Güiraldes says:
    Ricardo nunca tuvo amargura. Su sufrimiento era sentimental y afectivo. Por eso se sentía herido. Más de una vez me dijo: "Les doy lo mejor de mi sentir y me devuelven patadas de burro." Cuando a esos argumentos me agregó que no publicaría más . . . le contesté: "Dios no te dio el talento para que lo guardes, te lo dio para que lo hagas florecer en los demás. El resultado también pertenece a Dios y no a ti. Tu función es la de darlo sin preocuparte del resultado." Con gran paciencia y coraje así lo hizo, pues, para él, escribir era función tan primordial como la de respirar.
[5] Ocampo, "Carta a Ricardo Güiraldes," p. 3.

Güiraldes found solace in rereading the works of Jules Laforgue. He was moved by the life of that brilliant young man
who, like himself, had struggled against incomprehension, and
who had died so early. He understood so well the young poet's
injured feelings.[6] From a sympathetic sense of companionship
in sorrow with Laforgue, Güiraldes derived strength and inspiration to write his novellette *Rosaura.*

Güiraldes did not write *Rosaura* with the intention of producing a literary work but as a mental escape from the storm
of invectives that raged about him at the time.[7] Shortly before,
his little sister Lolita had complained that she was not allowed
to read Güiraldes' books because they were not fit for young
girls. She urged her brother to write something she could
read. Accordingly, he wrote a sentimental love story, suitable
for young ladies. He said he wrote it a chapter a day, finishing it in twenty days, and enjoyed soaking himself shame-
lessly in tender sentimentality the while.[8] *Rosaura* was first
published in 1918 under the title of *Un idilio de estación* at
the request of Horacio Quiroga, in his weekly magazine, *El
Cuento Ilustrado.*[9] Later, in 1922, it was printed under the
name of *Rosaura* by Francisco A. Colombo at San Antonio
de Areco. He took it to Victoria Ocampo one October spring
day, at her villa in San Isidro, and both entered into the spirit
of the story as he read to her.[10]

After finishing *Rosaura,* Güiraldes rallied sufficiently from
his disappointment to return to writing with serious intent.
At last, he took up his unfinished project of *Raucho,* and
worked at it continuously, until it was completed within the
year. What he had started in 1910 in Granada as a sketch of
a short narrative, under the title of *Los impulsos de Ricardito*

[6] Angel J. Battistessa, "Güiraldes y Laforgue," *Nosotros* (*Epoca* 2, Nov.
1942), pp. 158-159.
[7] De Torre, *loc. cit.,* p. 13.
[8] *Ibid.*
[9] Güiraldes, "Idilio de estación," *El Cuento Ilustrado* (Buenos Aires, Año I,
No. 4, May 3, 1918).
[10] Ocampo, "Carta a Ricardo Güiraldes," p. 2.

and later elaborated in Paris as *Los comentarios de Ricardito,*
now grew into a novel under the name of *Raucho.*[11] The
imagined biography of a profligate Argentine youth in Paris
had already been written. Güiraldes now enlarged the narration to include an account of Raucho's childhood. The introduction of the Argentine scene into the narration reflected the
strong orientation of Güiraldes' sentiments. His thoughts
turned to the memory of his happy childhood days at the
estancia. He completed *Raucho* in this nostalgic mood. From
this time forward, his emotional inclination was directed more
strongly than ever toward his native pampa and, near the
end of his life, it was to guide his hand in writing *Don Segundo Sombra.*

Before *Raucho* appeared in Buenos Aires bookstores, Güiraldes' went on a pleasure trip to the West Indies.[12] He had
traveled to many distant parts of the world, but he had seen
very little of his own America. On December 31, 1916, a party
of four, including Güiraldes, Adelina, their friend Alfredo
González Garaño and his wife, Marietta, left Buenos Aires by
the trans-Andean train for Chile.[13] From Santiago they
boarded the small steamship *Aysen,* and traveled leisurely up
the west coast of South America, stopping at the ports along
the way. After passing through the Panama Canal, they
crossed the Caribbean and visited Jamaica. Although Güiraldes
was on a pleasure trip, he concentrated upon the preparation
of a new book, *Xaimaca* (1923). Instead of viewing the world
before him as a sightseer, he sought to capture the poetic impressions of what he saw by writing them down on small cards.
With one pocket full of blank cards, he would transfer the
written ones to the other. In this way Güiraldes, pleased with
his profitable trip and full of anticipation for his new book,
returned to Argentina with a collection of notes. They were
in the nature of simple poems in prose, strands with which to

[11] De Torre, *loc. cit.,* p. 14.
[12] Colombo, *op. cit.,* pp. 65-66.
[13] Adelina del Carril de Güiraldes, "Valery Larbaud y Ricardo Güiraldes,"
La Nación (Buenos Aires, March 24, 1957), p. 2.

weave a poetic novel. This was the beginning of *Xaimaca*.

On his return to Buenos Aires, in April, 1917, Güiraldes was staggered by another blow to his literary efforts. *Raucho* was a failure. The critical reviews in the press took a humiliatingly patronizing attitude. Among such reviews was one by the editor of *Nosotros,* Roberto Giusti, who, while objecting strongly to Güiraldes' style, encouraged him nevertheless to write in gaucho vernacular.[14]

Victoria Ocampo, however, promptly took her stand at Güiraldes' side. Resenting the shabby treatment *Raucho* had received, she wrote Ricardo a letter of encouragement in which she expressed her approval of his book.[15]

Once again Güiraldes' expectations of contributing to a new literary expression in Argentina ended in disillusionment. As before, his work was not understood. When he realized this, he felt submerged in solitude. "I am as alone as ever," he said.[16]

[14] Roberto Giusti, *"Raucho. Momentos de una juventud contemporánea* por Ricardo Güiraldes," *Nosotros* (XXVII, 1917), pp. 391-394.
[15] Güiraldes, "Carta a Victoria Ocampo," *Sur* (Año I, Verano, 1931), pp. 101-104.
[16] Battistessa, *loc. cit.,* p. 159.

IX

Paris and Valery Larbaud

When World War I ended, Güiraldes had already begun writing *Xaimaca*. But he was restless in Argentina because he felt the need of a more favorable literary climate in which to write.[1] In 1919, believing that the French environment would be more inspiring and therefore more conducive to his writing, Güiraldes, accompanied by Adelina, departed for France. Victoria came to the dock to wish her friends Godspeed.[2]

Before his departure, Güiraldes' friend, Adán Diehl, presented him with a copy of Valery Larbaud's *Barnabooth*.[3] The book was a happy discovery of a new kind of writing.[4] In *Barnabooth,* Güiraldes saw the kind of independent, new expression he was seeking. In its author he believed he had found a writer with an aesthetic sensitivity like his own, a kindred spirit in search of new literary horizons. Valery Larbaud was the writer he most wanted to know in Paris.

His first impression upon arriving in Paris in August, 1919,

[1] Battistessa, *loc. cit.*, p. 158, where Güiraldes is quoted as follows:
Para ser algo vivo, todo esfuerzo de arte necesita caer en un terreno ya labrado por la simpatía. Simpatía es el gesto de hospitalidad que la belleza pide a las almas para poder lograr en ellos su nacimiento.
The quotation is from a prologue written by Güiraldes for a concert conducted in Buenos Aires by his friend Ernest Ansermet.
[2] Ocampo, "Carta a Ricardo Güiraldes," p. 3.
[3] Valery Larbaud, *Barnabooth. Ses Oeuvres Complètes. C'est à dire: Un Conte, ses Poésies et son Journal Intime* (Paris, 1913).
[4] See Güiraldes, "Un libro," *Proa* (No. 3, Oct. 1924), p. 36, in which he wrote about this literary experience as follows:
El cuento me convenció del extraordinario talento de Valerio Larbaud. Los versos me parecieron únicos desde Laforgue, del que encontraba un recuerdo por la intensidad sensitiva y la burla de sus excesos líricos aumentado de un robusto humor. El diario me introducía en las intimidades del más variadamente millonario de los hombres: Extraña feria de todas las grandezas y baratijas del sentir humano.
Aquello era la síntesis del hombre de nuestra época, con su ideología, su lirismo, su sensualidad, su ambiente ...

was one of relief to find the rebirth of artistic creativeness
for which he had hoped. He described this moment in the
following terms:

> I made my first contact with the French literary
> activity of the moment when I read *La Nouvelle
> Revue Française* which had just emerged from
> the war. The periodical appeared to be saddened
> by the recent tragedy; it seemed unable to believe
> that life under a constant cloud of death had really
> come to an end. I grasped at this rebirth of
> beauty, which I needed so badly. When acciden-
> tally I came upon a copy of the first post-war
> issue, I felt like a man who had been saved from
> drowning. With Gide as its editor, it had the
> best assurance for a successful future. Besides, the
> *N. R. F.* had published *Barnabooth.*
>
> Paul Valéry's article on pre-war poetry was most
> remarkable indeed.
>
> But above all, what a relief to feast my eyes upon
> the wonderful clarity of French poetry, when for
> so long a time we had feared that French poetry
> had died.
>
> I was immediately at home with its ideas and
> form. Both Fargue and Romains impressed me,
> each in his own way. My objective, however, was
> still Larbaud. After having read *Barnabooth,*
> which is a universal book, my second find was
> *Fermina Márquez,* which is a South American
> book.[5]

Upon reading *Fermina Márquez.*[6] Güiraldes was delighted
to discover Larbaud's sympatheic view of Latin America. The
short novel treated with understanding the sentiments of Latin
American pupils at a French boarding school. It appeared

[5] Güiraldes, "Un hombre," *Proa* (No. 4, Nov. 1924), p. 24. Author's translation.
[6] Larbaud, *Fermina Márquez* (Paris, n.d.).

providential that Larbaud should be so congenially inclined.
    When Güiraldes met Larbaud, the two were drawn to each
other like old friends.[7] They seemed to speak the same language, the language of poets with common beliefs. Güiraldes
had been right: Larbaud was an enthusiastic friend of Latin
America and of the new expression in modern Hispanic poetry.
He had been following with interest the development of *ultraísmo* in Spain. As early as 1907, in *El Nuevo Mercurio,* he
had predicted what might be expected in Spanish American
poetry. In 1918, in *Hispania,* and, in 1919, in *Littérature,* moved
by the work of Ramón Gómez de La Serna, he had expressed
his admiration for contemporary Spanish poetry.[8] Consequently, Larbaud read with interest Güiraldes' *El cencerro,
Rosaura,* and *Raucho,* and applauded the Argentine poet's
efforts to break away from the old and find a new form of
expression. Having followed vigilantly the influence of French
symbolism in modern Spanish poetry, Larbaud welcomed
Güiraldes with the warm understanding of a *camarade
d'armes.* More than that, he was the first to recognize publicly
the merit of Güiraldes as a modern poet of Argentina. In an
article in *La Nouvelle Revue Française* of July, 1920, he wrote:
"Ricardo Güiraldes is one of the first, perhaps he is the
first, among the poets of the most recent literary generation
in the Argentine Republic."[9] In the same article, Larbaud
praised *Raucho, Rosaura,* and *El cencerro* in terms that showed
his appreciation of Güiraldes' literary purpose.
    Introduced by Larbaud, Güiraldes was cordially received into
the intimate circle of the French *litterati* of the *avant-garde*
in Paris. They met frequently at La Maison des Amis des
Livres in Rue Odéon, near the Théâtre Odéon and the Luxem-
bourg Gardens. It was a little bookshop, run by Adrienne
Monnier, the beloved friend of the writers *("notre amie à
tous").* Here Güiraldes was welcomed as a colleague by Léon

    [7] Colombo, *op. cit.,* p. 70.
    [8] Valery Larbaud, "Poètes Espagnols et Hispano-Américains Contemporains,"
La Nouvelle Revue Française (XV, 1920), p. 141.
    [9] *Ibid.,* p. 145.

Paul Fargue, Jules Romains, Philippe Soupault, Francis de Miomandre, and Adrienne Monnier herself. Mlle. Monnier, long afterwards, kept Güiraldes' portrait hanging in her study together with those of her other literary friends.[10] To Güiraldes' surprise, these distinguished French writers took the trouble to read his poetry. They, Larbaud and Fargue in particular, encouraged him to continue along the difficult, new path of literary expression on which he had started. Güiraldes experienced the comforting sensation of finding himself, at last, in a friendly and congenial literary environment. He was understood and appreciated, and, what was more, by the leaders in modern French literary expression. Joyfully he wrote to his father that, unlike his indifferent and hostile critics in Argentina, the French writers, who indeed were competent to speak with authority on the subject, had approved of his poetry in full measure; that they had strengthened his confidence in the merit of his work; and that he very much needed this demonstration of their friendship to pursue his writing without feeling lost in a vacuum.[11]

With renewed confidence in his ideas, Güiraldes continued his work on *Xaimaca*. His plan was to apply a new style of expression to the native American scene. As he had already tried to do in parts of *Raucho*, it was to be his version of the poetic style he so admired in Flaubert's *Salammbô*.[12]

With each stage of his progress in *Xaimaca*, Güiraldes would show his work to Larbaud, Instead of approving his writing, Larbaud, like a true literary *confrère,* dampened Güiraldes'

---

[10] Battistessa, *loc. cit.* p. 32.

[11] Colombo, *op. cit.*, p. 70, in which he quotes Güiraldes as writing:
... No me ha acostumbrado la vida ni al elogio ajeno o a la ayuda de los colegas, pero hoy tengo de mi parte la autoridad competente, de modo que me siento, en cierta forma, investido de un valor que por otra parte he creído tener siempre, pero que ninguna personalidad del gremio me había reconocido ... La indiferencia o la hostilidad no había modificado mi opinión sobre mí mismo, pero en verdad necesitaba grandemente de ese gesto de un amigo para proseguir trabajando sin sentirme en el vacío. No se hace ningún movimiento sin un punto de apoyo. Ahora lo tengo, y sólido.

[12] De Torre, *loc. cit.,* p. 10.

enthusiasm with his frank opinion. Years later, Larbaud, who regretted what he feared might have been an unintentional injury, wrote Adelina that his criticism of *Xaimaca*, in spite of all, definitely had been helpful to Ricardo.[13]

Through these literary confidences, Larbaud came to know Güiraldes well and to recognize his principal merit. In Larbaud's opinion, Güiraldes' main literary asset was not his ability to create an original style of expression; it was, as he said, something characteristic of Güiraldes and specially of Argentina.[14] Larbaud realized where Güiraldes' talent lay. He had seen it in the poetic passages full of regional, Argentine flavor in both *Rosaura* and *Raucho*. As a friend he advised him to seek out the original and genuine in himself, to recognize his own remarkable Argentine individuality and to express his own gaucho-like personality.[15]

For some time after this, Güiraldes suspended the writing of *Xaimaca*. He was gripped by a wave of homesickness. As years before, he felt like a stranger in Paris. At such moments, the gaucho within him longed desperately for the open spaces of the pampa. During many a wistful hour his thoughts turned back to the memory of his childhood and to the gauchos at the *estancia*. His heart was in Argentina, his being was Argentine, and the gaucho within him clamored for expression. He decided to start work on a book about a gaucho. It was to be about a man he knew, who personified the character of the gaucho, his loyal old *peón*, don Segundo Ramírez. He had long wanted to write about him.[16] He confided his project to Larbaud.[17] In Paris, in 1920, Güiraldes began writing *Don Segundo Sombra*.[18] As he worked on the book, he steeped

[13] Adelina del Carril de Güiraldes, "Valery Larbaud y Ricardo Güiraldes," *La Nación*, 2a. Sección (Buenos Aires, March 24, 1957), p. 2.
[14] See Larbaud, *loc. cit.*, p. 146, who wrote: "Il me semble y découvrir, surtout, une qualité qui ne lui vient que de son auteur: une saveur américaine, et plus spécialement argentine."
[15] Colombo, *op. cit.*, 73-76.
[16] Adelina del Carril de Güiraldes, "Nota preliminar," *Don Segundo Sombra* (Buenos Aires, Ed. Kraft, 1952), p. 11.
[17] Colombo, *op. cit.*, 75.
[18] *Ibid.*, p. 89.

himself in nostalgia for his native land and evoked the atmosphere of the pampa by strumming gaucho songs on his guitar.[19]

In *Don Segundo Sombra* Güiraldes' intention was to express the gaucho personality in a correspondingly characteristic style.[20] His ambition was now to be the interpreter, in all its typical aspects, of what he called an unexpressed race.[21] He believed that the colorful and humorous speech of the gaucho had the elements of a new and lively literary expression.[22] And he set to writing *Don Segundo Sombra* with the avowed purpose of becoming the literary disciple of the gaucho.[23] As he finished the first chapters, he read them to a few Argentine friends who were living in Paris at the time.

When he recovered from his nostalgia, Güiraldes had written the first ten chapters of *Don Segundo Sombra*.[24] He then put them aside and resumed work on *Xaimaca*. The latter was a voluminous manuscript, about which he felt a pride of achievement. Once more he called together his Argentine friends, who had heard the first chapters of *Don Segundo Sombra,* and elatedly read *Xaimaca* to them. When they heard it they told him that *Xaimaca* was of little or no worth and that he should go on writing *Don Segundo Sombra*. That night Güiraldes covered the bulky manuscript with the great silver plaque of his gaucho belt and, turning to Adelina, said, "Well,... anyway, I have you!"[25]

At one of the literary gatherings at La Maison des Amis des Livres, Güiraldes announced his return to Argentina. "I intend to go back to Buenos Aires," he said to his friend Francis de Miomandre, "in order to write the story of a man whom I

[19] Pablo Rojas Paz, "Ricardo Güiraldes," *Síntesis* (II, Nov. 1927), p. 373.
[20] Güiraldes, "Carta a Valery Larbaud," *Sur* (No. 1, Año I, Verano, 1931), p. 106.
[21] *Ibid.,* p. 105-106: "... desentrañar el aspecto poético, filosófico, musical y pictórico de una raza inexpresada."
[22] *Ibid.,* p. 106: "En el lenguaje pulcro y malicioso del gaucho el embrión de una literatura viva y compleja."
[23] Güiraldes, "Carta a Valery Larbaud," *Sur* (No. 2, Año I, Otoño 1931), p. 182.
[24] Adelina del Carril de Güiraldes, "Nota preliminar," *Don Segundo Sombra* (Buenos Aires, Ed. Kraft, 1952), p. 11.
[25] Adelina del Carril de Güiraldes, "Valery Larbaud y Ricardo Güiraldes."

have know since I was a child." He wanted, he explained, to bring back to life a period of Argentina that was disappearing into the past.[26] On Christmas Eve, before his departure, Larbaud, who had applauded his pursuit of a new poetic expression and who had encouraged him to continue his interpretation of the American scene, presented him with a significant farewell gift.[27] It was a copy of Alexis Saint-Léger Léger's ("Saint-John Perse") *Éloges* (1911), a small book of little poems in prose, reminiscences of the author's childhood in the Antilles. After Christmas of 1920, his *Xaimaca* still unpublished, but with a stronger orientation toward his native land, Güiraldes left Paris for Buenos Aires.

[26] Francis de Miomandre, "Recuerdo de Ricardo," *La Nación* (Jan. 7, 1940).
[27] Colombo, *op. cit.*, p. 75.

X

Return to the Pampa

Shortly after his arrival in Argentina, Güiraldes set about steeping himself in the atmosphere of the pampa. Toward the end of June, 1921, he departed with Adelina on a material-gathering trip into the Northern interior of Argentina. Taking the train in Buenos Aires, they traveled to Tucumán and proceeded from there to Salta. In nearby San Lorenzo, Güiraldes was warmly welcomed by Juan Carlos Dávalos, born in 1887, the poet of Indian and mestizo legends of Northeastern Argentina. At home in the latter's spacious study, the two poets soon were communing with each other. Dávalos read his poems to Güiraldes. In a letter from Salta to his mother, Güiraldes wrote that the poet's words seemed to breathe with the emotional climate of the nature about him.[1] His visit was a rewarding experience. He saw how, by suggestion, Dávalos had reflected in his writing the characteristic aspects of the environment and its human types.

His host aided Güiraldes in his pursuit of the colorful and characteristic. Together they rode to the wild Estancia del Rey that spreads across the frontier of Salta and Jujuy. They spent twelve days in the Northern Argentine wilderness, living with the native mestizos and local gauchos, and camping out part of the time with typical rustics, hardly touched by modern civilization.[2] From this trip Güiraldes returned with material for *Don Segundo Sombra*. One chapter of that book is based on the traditional cockfights, staged Sundays as a regular entertainment by the country folk.[3] Also at that time he met the

---

[1] Güiraldes, "De un epistolario," *Sur* (No. 1, Año I, Verano, 1931), p. 112.
[2] Dávalos subsequently wrote *Los Gauchos* (1928), a book of gaucho tales, legends and superstitions of this region, and dedicated it "A Chela, Adelina, Ricardo y Adolfo, en recuerdo de los días que pasamos en 'El Rey'. Hoy somos, mañana no."
[3] Güiraldes, "De un epistolario," *Sur* (No. 1, Año I, Verano, 1931, p. 116.

Ricardo Güiraldes in traditional Gaucho dress. A photograph taken at La Porteña by Adelina del Carril de Güiraldes in summer, 1922.

bearded gaucho, Cruz Guíez, famous in the area for his tall tales of black magic and white magic, and of animals that talked like humans.[4]

In the Argentine summer of the same year, again in the company of Adelina, Güiraldes visited Dolores, in the region south of Buenos Aires. The horrible sight of the mud flats, crawling with carnivorous crabs, reminded him of those lonely days spent as a boy in the barren land of Quequén. The impressions gathered there provided the material for another chapter in *Don Segundo Sombra.*[5]

Back again on the *estancia,* he settled down to resume in an atmosphere of undisturbed tranquility the writing of *Don Segundo Sombra.* He was delighted with his recent experiences in the interior of the country. He felt that at every turn new horizons for artistic expression unfolded before him.[6] He was animated, for example, over the literary possibilities of the regional language. He realized that no one yet had availed himself of the richness of the Argentine vernacular to create a new literary form. It distressed him that the contemporary artists in Argentina ignored the aesthetic treasures of their own land in order to imitate only what was produced in Europe. His enthusiasm prompted him to say that he wanted to be a one-man orchestra to be able to express in music, painting and literature all this wealth of local color.[7]

[4] *Ibid.,* p. 117. Adelina del Carril de Güiraldes, in her letter of June 6, 1961, said that her husband's impression of Cruz Guíez played no part in the character portrayal of don Segundo who also was famous as a storyteller in his own right.

[5] Adelina del Carril de Güiraldes, "Nota preliminar," *Don Segundo Sombra,* pp. 11-12.

[6] See Güiraldes, "De un epistolario," *Sur* (No. 1, Año I, Verano, 1931), pp. 115-116, in which he wrote to his friend, Valery Larbaud:

> ¡Viera lo que es la Estancia del Rey en la frontera de Salta y Jujuy! Un valle de unas setenta mil hectáreas con cerros altos, llanos, ríos, bosques, vacas, tigres, antas, corzuelas, loros, buitres, tábanos, sachamonos, tastás, osos meleros, gauchos, lazos, guardamontes y otras mil cosas diversas, sin contar el cielo que es de todos, según Laforgue.

[7] Adelina del Carril de Güiraldes explained her husband's sentiments at this time in her letter of June 6, 1961. She quotes him with comments as follows:

> "Me paso a veces días con los brazos abiertos temiendo tomar estos tesoros con manos de dilapidador. . . . " He said this be-

With this in mind, he established himself in his large study at La Porteña, amid an array of the gaucho paraphernalia he had collected in his recent travels and over the course of years. The time had now come for him to express in writing the character of the taciturn gaucho and of his environment. He was surrounded, he felt, by so much that was characteristically regional, waiting to be expressed in words. It was now a matter of interpretation, he thought.[8]

Güiraldes' concept of style was that the manner of expression should correspond to the nature of the subject matter.[9] He applied it to his interpretation of the gaucho and his regional environment. He believed the gaucho character should be expressed in the quaint language of the gaucho himself. He had already applied this stylistic principle to reflect the gaucho nature in his *Cuentos.* Now, he would apply it to the speech of don Segundo. In fact, he recorded this intention in so many words when he wrote:

> A whole literary program can be based upon certain characteristics of don Segundo's speech (although not on his storytelling which takes a conventional form). In speaking, don Segundo is sparing of words which he lets fall in the most undeclamatory tone possible; like all gauchos he

---

cause he sees how much can be done with our native lore and indigenous subject matter. He points out that Argentine artists limit themselves to copying what comes from Europe, which is all they can see. Consequently, he said, they are blind to our native treasures which lie untouched. . . . He sees all there is to derive in music, painting and literature from the wealth of our regional material. "Quisiera ser hombre orquesta . . . " He was distressed that he could not do it all himself. (Author's translation.)

[8] See Güiraldes, "De un epistolario" (Verano, 1931), p. 106, in which he writes:

¡Y pensar que en cada una de las formas del arte hay un alma que espera su palabra! En los yaravíes y los estilos está la rudimentaria expresión de la montaña y la pampa. . . . En los tejidos, ponchos y huacos está el criterio interpretativo de la forma y el color. Todo estaría en ser capaz de llevar estas enseñanzas a una forma natural y noble.

[9] Güiraldes, "Poesía," *Martín Fierro* (Año IV, No. 39, March 28, 1927), p. 1.

likes to use well-chosen metaphors; and making witty remarks is one his typical ways of talking.[10]

The style in which Güiraldes proposed to write *Don Segundo Sombra* was a clear-cut departure from the poetic prose which characterized *Xaimaca.* It was also, most decidedly, an intentional separation from the trends of the modern French writers: "In Europe," he said, "many writers take great pains to create novel artistic forms."[11] To produce the desired effect, he explained, the expression of the gaucho must not be vitiated by outside influence; the characters themselves must suggest to the author the best style in which to describe them.[12]

At work at La Porteña his writing gravitated toward the short poem in prose. In February, 1921, his efforts to interpret the nature of the gaucho found expression in the prose poem that began *"Los rostros son inexpresivos."*[13] He was conscious of being the first to express the gaucho in his terms, and he felt that his efforts would not be in vain, if only he could mark the trail.[14] His attitude toward his task of interpreting the gaucho was similar to his attitude toward the writing of poetry, as he wrote in *El cencerro:* "It was a reaching out toward perfection, like a prayer toward Heaven."[15]

In spite of all, he suspended work on *Don Segundo Sombra* for a while and turned to rewriting *Xaimaca,* reworking and polishing its style. By October, 1921, he had almost finished his new version of *Xaimaca.* He also had begun a series of prose poems, which were published after his death by Adelina under the title of *Poemas solitarios* (1928). At that time he wrote to his friend Larbaud that he was enjoying reading Jules Laforgue.[16]

[10] Güiraldes, "De un epistolario," *Sur* (No. 2, Año I, Otoño, 1931), p. 183. Author's translation.
[11] *Ibid.* (Verano, 1931), p. 106.
[12] *Loc. cit.*
[13] Güiraldes, *Poemas solitarios 1921-1927* (San Antonio de Areco, 1928), pp. 16-17.
[14] Güiraldes, "De un epistolario," *Sur* (No. 1, Año I, Verano, 1931), p. 107.
[15] *Cf.* Güiraldes, "De un epistolario," (Verano, 1931) with his poem "Aconcagua" in *El cencerro de cristal,* p. 55.
[16] Güiraldes, "De un epistolario," (Verano, 1931), p. 115.

XI

Back to Friends in Paris

Before leaving Paris in the winter of 1920, Güiraldes had promised Larbaud that he would return the following spring. But, even after having purchased the steamship passage, he put off his trip in order to undertake his excursion into the interior of Argentina which had been so productive of material for his book. *Don Segundo Sombra,* however, had not progressed as hoped, and in the spring of 1922, a year later than originally planned, he returned with Adelina to his friends in Paris.

There he was made welcome by Larbaud and his colleagues at Monnier's with the warmest reception he had ever received in literary circles. Instead of being forgotten, he was fêted. His reputation had increased in his absence. He was sought out by the modern young writers of Paris, with whom he strengthened his ties of friendship. Francis de Miomandre translated into French and published several of his poems from *El cencerro.*[1] The few months spent in Paris during this visit marked a period of recognition and appreciation by advanced French writers of the day. It was also a period of joyous self-expression and of a sense of fulfillment.

Güiraldes' natural charm and ready friendliness made him a popular figure in Paris. He was lionized by the ladies, who contended for his presence at their social functions. On one occasion, Güiraldes agreed to sing gaucho songs to the accompaniment of his guitar. Those present were impressed with his skill. Rarely had they heard anyone who could make the chords of a guitar resound with the harmony of an organ. Among them was the French poetess, Countess de

---

[1] José R. Liberal, "Prólogo," *Don Segundo Sombra, de Ricardo Güiraldes; comentado y anotado estudio del vocabulario y fraseología* (Buenos Aires, 1946), p. 18.

Noailles, who described this experience in her prose poem "La Musique."[2]

Contrary to what may have been expected during a period of so much social activity, Güiraldes did not neglect his literary work. Quite the opposite. He not only gathered the fruits of his popularity by the handfull, but also intensified his writing with greater determination. He worked on his revision of *Xaimaca*. Although he persevered in his intention to write his novel in poetic prose, he was not yet satisfied with his efforts. It was in Paris, in 1922, that he made the final and most drastic changes. He pruned and cut all that he considered superflous, until he felt that he had harmonized the style with the subject matter. At last, during the summer, with *Xaimaca* in its final form, he and Adelina left Paris and took the manuscript to Larbaud in Vichy. The following day Larbaud called on Güiraldes to tell him that he had read the revised *Xaimaca* with joyful satisfaction. He was, beyond doubt, delighted with the way it had turned out. He even quoted from memory the passages that he liked best. Güiraldes had labored on *Xaimaca* more than on any of his other books.[3]

In December, 1922, Güiraldes returned to Buenos Aires. His confidence in his writing had been confirmed. He was full of high expectations for the success of *Xaimaca,* and he anticipated with pleasure the completion of *Don Segundo Sombra.*

---

[2] Battistessa, *loc. cit.,* p. 29; see also Anna Elizabeth de Brancovan, Comtesse de Noailles, *Comtesse de Noailles* (Paris, 1922), p. 244, in which she writes:

> Epaisse et d'aspect maladroit, elle nous surprend, la guitarre fameuse des Espagnes. Elle n'a ni grâce, ni souplesse, mais qu'une main habile la harcèle, et on entendra se becqueter de rageuses colombes. C'est un crépitement si fascinant, si hallucinant, qu'aux accents de ces mélodies ferrailleuses où se provoquent inlassablement de subtiles épées, chevaleresques et vindicatives . . .

[3] Adelina del Carril de Güiraldes, "Valery Larbaud y Ricardo Güiraldes."

XII

The Fate of *Xaimaca*

In Paris, Güiraldes had had the stimulating experience of breathing freely in the congenial company of the new French writers of the *avant-garde*. In Buenos Aires the literary climate was asphyxiating. While new trends were sweeping the arts and letters in post-war Europe, the Argentine world of letters remained unchanged. In Madrid, four years earlier, a small group of young writers already had expressed their intention of carrying forward the existing advanced trends in Spanish literature. They adopted the word "ultra" as their motto, and, in January, 1919, proclaimed their beliefs in their *Manifiesto de Ultraísmo*.[1] In contrast, in Buenos Aires, any sign of a new literary trend withered in the conservative climate. In 1921, Jorge Luis Borges, recently arrived from Spain and full of enthusiasm, founded the periodical *Prisma* to transplant in America the *ultraísmo* he had known in Madrid. After only a few issues, it died for lack of readers.[2] Güiraldes' young friend, Oliverio Girondo, spoke plainly of the backward literary environment of Buenos Aires of this time.[3] He had

[1] Guillermo de Torre, *Literaturas europeas de vanguardia* (Madrid, 1925), p. 46.

[2] Alberto Oscar Blasi, "Güiraldes en el ultraísmo," *Estudios* (Buenos Aires, Sept.-Oct., 1923), pp. 330-335.

[3] See Oliverio Girondo *et al.*, *El periódico Martín Fierro: 1924-1949* (Buenos Aires, 1949), pp. 11-12, in which they wrote:

> . . . vuelve a imperar . . . la misma monotonía fosilante, la misma chatura espiritual . . . mientras en la misma España —con algún retardo y cierta timidez— surge el "ultraísmo" . . . *aquí no sucede nada.* Por increíble que parezca, los eternos figurones gaseosos persisten en una retórica caduca y en un academismo "avant la lettre," a la par que el pésimo "buen gusto" de algunos espíritus marmóreos continúa frecuentando una estética refrigerada o un cierto dandismo tropical. No sólo las casadoras libélulas de Flores son víctimas de la sensibilería más cursi y adulcorada [sic]. El peor Rubén, el de las marquesas liliales y otros pajarracos de "parterre", fomenta el ripio lacrimal y el decoratismo de pacotilla. . . . El personaje de Remy de Gourmont, aludido en el prólogo de las "prosas profanas," "celui qui ne comprend pas," continúa dictando cátedra en universidades, redacciones y cafés.

championed Güiraldes' *El cencerro de cristal* in 1915, and, in 1923, had stirred the complacency of the local atmosphere with the publication of his *Veinte poemas para ser leídos en el tranvía.*[4]

In this unreceptive literary environment of 1923, Güiraldes published *Xaimaca.* The book represented the most advanced literary expression. It was the realization of his concept of applying the modern contemporary European stylistic techniques to the American scene.[5]

Xaimaca fared better than it author's previous works. For the first time Ricardo Güiraldes received the approval of a serious literary critic. In an article published in the June 1924 issue of the *Revista de Occidente,* Enrique Díez-Canedo praised the literary merit of *Xaimaca.*[6] But, in conservative Buenos Aires other critics who, eight years earlier, had expressed such indignation toward the bold innovations of *El cencerro de cristal,* now guarded their comments on *Xaimaca* with non-commital reserve. Their patronizing attitude saddened Güiraldes[7] who, as before, withdrew in solitude to La Porteña.[8]

---

[4] Oliverio Girondo, *Veinte poemas para ser leídos en tranvía* (Argenteuil, 1922).

[5] Pablo Rojas Paz, "Ricardo Güiraldes," *Síntesis* (Buenos Aires, II, 6, Nov., 1927), p. 371.

[6] Adelina del Carril de Güiraldes, letter of June 6, 1961.

[7] Angel J. Battistessa, "Breve historia de una revista de vanguardia," *Verbum* (Buenos Aires, No. 2 y 3, Dec., 1942), pp. 27-28.

[8] See Güiraldes who at that time entered the following observation in *Poemas solitarios* (San Antonio de Areco, 1928):
"Tengo miedo de mirar mi dolor, no vaya que me quede demasiado grande."

XIII

A Period of Transition

Since 1922 Güiraldes had been passing through a period of transition.[1] His sentiments are clearly reflected among the poems and entries which, written during this time, appeared later in *Poemas solitarios* and in *El sendero*.[2] In 1924, after the tepid reception of *Xaimaca,* he was disgusted to the point of turning his back upon the outside world of letters forever. With the intention of isolating himself from all literary contacts about him, he retired to his home in the country and became a recluse from society.[3] He needed to stop to recover from the blow, and to recollect himself. He compared himself to the gaucho cattle driver who, exhausted with fatigue,

[1] This important transition in Güiraldes' life was understood and sympathetically described by Enrique González Tuñón in his book *Apología de un hombre santo* (Buenos Aires, 1930). Furthermore, Adelina del Carril de Güiraldes, in her letter of June 6, 1961, adds the following information regarding Güiraldes' reorientation at this time:
> Entre el año 1922 y 1924 se produce un gran cambio espiritual en Ricardo. Hasta entonces sólo había vivido para su arte. Pero entonces se encuentra con la Filosofía Vedanta que colma sus anhelos espirituales, todavía ocultos en él pero que siempre estuvieron latentes. Al descubrirla se descubre a sí mismo y se le abren nuevos horizontes. Se puede decir que ya no le interesa sino su reino interior. ("Mi alma es un centro que es vigor.")
> Y va con coraje a la "Recherche du temps perdu" en la vida espiritual.
> Esta es una era dolorosa de gestación y descubrimiento. Su sinceridad lo hace ir a fondo de sí mismo y de las cosas todas y ni ceja, ni descansa hasta hallar "por qué" y "para qué" de cuanto investiga.

[2] Güiraldes, *El sendero, notas sobre mi evolución espiritualista en vista de un futuro* (Maestricht, Netherlands, 1932). In a letter to the writer dated Bella Vista, April 20, 1956, Güiraldes' widow said: "...en el sendero... conocerá Vd. la historia de su alma."

[3] Güiraldes, *Poemas solitarios*, p. 24. In addition, Adelina del Carril de Güiraldes, in her letter of June 6, 1961, stresses that at no time did her husband allow his disappointment to defeat him. She describes his attitude at that moment as follows:
> Su dolor no es gazmoño ni cobarde. ("Ignoro la cobardía, cuando me he dicho 'DEBO'.")
> La valentía y el coraje lo acompañan siempre. . . . Era fuerte y viril y jamás se quejaba. Cuando protestaba por alguna injusticia lo hacía con la fiereza del fuerte, pero sin altanería ni petulancia. ¡Era todo un hombre!

stops to rest in order to restore his forces and continue his journey.[4]

Round about him on the *estancia* were the friends of his boyhood, the gaucho *peones*. Their loyalty and affection were a comforting contrast to the sordid and petty ways of the townspeople. Don Segundo was one of them. These simple, strong men of the pampa renewed his faith in mankind. They also restored his morale. There was an aspect of their character that stood out as an example to Güiraldes in his period of frustration. It was their way of facing hardship with fortitude. He admired the silent equanimity with which they accepted fate. They shed no tear of self-pity and showed no sign of complaint in their impassive faces. "We do not complain," he said, "because our way of life is to accept whatever happens."[5] He believed that this attitude was characteristic of the gaucho. He adopted it as a philosophy of life. Henceforth, mindful of the example of his gaucho friends, Güiraldes faced his adversities with courage.[6]

This was a moment of self-evaluation. He turned to silent introspection. In the light of gaucho stoicism, he sought the same hardy fibre within himself. And having found it, he was impelled to justify his existence as a man. Accordingly, he dominated his feeling of injury and resolved to go forward boldly with the task of completing his writing of *Don Segundo Sombra*.[7]

At the same time, in the peaceful surroundings of the *estancia,* Güiraldes experienced, as he had in his boyhood, that sense of harmony with nature. He felt that nature was love and giving, and he responded to the harmony about him with a desire to reciprocate by giving of himself to others. This new feeling toward his fellow man changed his approach to his writing. Heretofore he had created for art's sake alone. Now he rallied to a new cause: to create for others.[8] With

[4] Güiraldes, *Poemas solitarios,* p. 24.
[5] *Ibid.,* pp. 16-17.   [6] *Ibid.,* pp. 12-13.   [7] *Ibid.,* pp. 16-23.
[8] González Tuñón, *op. cit.,* p. 12. See also: *El sendero,* p. 74, in which

renewed confidence in himself and in his mission, Güiraldes began writing again. This time he would be indifferent to public opinion, and he would continue to write as he believed because he had to be himself.[9]

Hence, in 1924, Güiraldes had come through the emotional transition with a new orientation. He was resolved to pursue his work to interpret the silent gaucho, to do so free from other literary influences, to be himself in his manner of expression with complete indifference toward criticism, and, finally, to write, not for art's sake alone, but for others. Thus, toward the beginning of 1925, with his mind at peace and his solitude undisturbed, he was ready to finish *Don Segundo Sombra*. In this spirit he dedicated his work to others, and to the gaucho friends of his childhood in particular. Later, at the beginning of his book, he wrote:

> To you, Don Segundo.
>
> To the memory of the departed: Don Rufino Galván, Don Nicasio Cano and Don José Hernández.
>
> To my friends, the horsebreakers and the herdsmen: Don Víctor Taboada, Ramón Cisneros, Pedro Brandán, Ciriaco Díaz, Dolores Juárez, Pedro Falcón, Gregorio López, Esteban Pereyra, Pablo Ojeda, Victoriano Nogueira y Mariano Ortega.
>
> To the countryfolk back home.
>
> To those whom I do not know but who live in the spirit of this book.
>
> To the Gaucho, whom I hold within me as dearly as the monstrance holds the host.[10]

Güiraldes wrote: "Creo para los otros. Así establezco un guión de armonía. . . . "

[9] See *El sendero*, p. 60, where Güiraldes expresses this decision in the following words:

> Y la diré con la sinceridad de un egotista convencido por los hechos, que no se puede ser sino uno mismo. Así pues, serlo *à outrance* sin temer a los capones.

[10] *Don Segundo Sombra* (Buenos Aires, Ed. Pleamar, 1943), p. 9. (Author's translations).

XIV

Martín Fierro and Recognition

While Güiraldes remained in seclusion at La Porteña, a new development in the field of arts and letters was taking place in Buenos Aires. Cut off from the outside world, Güiraldes knew nothing of the Martín Fierro movement.

"Martinfierrismo" in Buenos Aires was a part of a movement on an international scale for the ultra-modernization of aesthetic expression.[1] It was, in general terms, a state of mind reflecting the spirit of the age, the revolt of the new generation against the artistic taste of the immediate past; it was the restlessness of youth for self-expression in the most advanced manner. In Spain, applied to letters, it had already declared its existence in 1919, in the "Manifiesto de ultraísmo," and soon afterwards became know as the "vanguardia" movement.[2] In Argentina, independently of Spain, a similar phenomenon appeared which also reflected the spirit of revolt and of renovation of the younger generation. Here and there, a scattered number of young intellectuals, who had some knowledge of modern expression and were united in their discontent toward the stifling artistic atmosphere in Argentina, joined forces against the conservative intellectual environment.[3] Among these young men, Evar Méndez and Oliverio Girondo were the two who took the first steps. They proposed to shake Buenos Aires from its artistic and literary lethargy and awaken a new Argentine aesthetic sensibility in all forms of artistic expression. Accordingly, they rallied their colleagues of like mind and, during the month of September, 1923,

---

[1] Pedro Henríquez Ureña, *Las corrientes literarias en la América hispánica* (México-Buenos Aires, 1949), p. 269, Notes 13 and 17.

[2] De Torre, *Literaturas europeas de vanguardia* (Madrid, 1925).

[3] Girondo *et al., El periódico Martín Fierro 1924-1949* (Buenos Aires, 1949). This book is the principal source of information on the Martín Fierro movement in Buenos Aires,

meeting in "La Cosechera" on Avenida de Mayo and in the
"Richmond" on Calle Florida, they decided upon the public
tion of the periodical *Martín Fierro* as their battle standar
Besides Méndez and Girondo, these young men were Pab
Rojas Paz, Ernesto Palacio, Conrado Nalé Roxlo, Luis Fran
and Córdova Iturburu. Although varying widely in the
evaluations and preferences, they were united on the followir
fundamentals: A condemnation of previous American liter
ture that was tainted with the imitation of outmoded Europes
literary styles of writing and which lacked the autochthono
flavor of home soil such as that possessed by José Hernánde
poem *Martín Fierro;* a passion for a refreshing, modern e
pression in all arts; a belief in the value of indigenous Am
ican contributions to the art of writing; the need of intensif
ing and extending the innovations of Rubén Darío; and th
recognition of the value of new foreign literary trends.
the suggestion of Oliverio Girondo, they decided to publi
a manifiesto proclaiming the birth of the *vanguardia* mov
ment in Argentina.[4] Accordingly, on May 14, 1924, numb
four of their periodical carried in bold type the "Manifies
de *Martín Fierro.*" This was the first broadside fired agai
the apathy in Buenos Aires toward modern arts and letter

The publication of the manifiesto not only achieved t
intended effect of shocking literary Buenos Aires from
conservative lethargy and rallying the scattered, forwar
looking young Argentines, but it also roused Güiraldes fro
his self-imposed isolation. In the same number of *Martín Fier*
that carried the manifiesto there appeared a challenge
kindred spirits to come forward and declare themselves.[6]

Joyfully surprised to discover from the clearly express
words of the manifiesto the existence of other young men
like aesthetic sensibilities, Güiraldes, too, rallied with enth
siasm to the call of *Martín Fierro.* He responded to its ch

[4] *Ibid.,* p. 16.
[5] "Manifiesto de 'Martín Fierro'," *Martín Fierro* (Segunda Epoca, Año
Number 4, Buenos Aires, May 15, 1924).
[6] *Ibid.,* p. 4.

lenge in terms that left no doubt as to his belief in their cause. In its issue of June 15, *Martín Fierro* displayed Güiraldes' answer.[7] He declared his affinity with the Martinfierristas on a common ground, namely: A love for the characteristically Argentine, an awareness within himself of being a part of it, and an urge to express it; in a word: a consciousness of an Argentine sensibility. In fact, Güiraldes, who at that moment was about to assert his affinity with the gaucho in *Don Segundo Sombra*, broke through his curtain of silence to extend a friendly hand to the like-minded young writers of *Martín Fierro*.

It was shortly after this time that the two directors of *Martín Fierro*, Evar Méndez and Oliverio Girondo, who were old friends of Güiraldes, succeeded in persuading him to abandon his isolation and to venture out of his retreat into the new intellectual climate. The warm welcome he received from the group of young men, who knew and admired his writings, produced in Güiraldes a feeling of jubilation.[8] Instead of the attitude of incomprehension and hostility, Güiraldes found, for the first time in Argentina, understanding and intellectual congeniality. He was so won over by his new friends and their valiant campaign of literary innovation that he came with Adelina to live in Buenos Aires in order to join them in their battle.

In Buenos Aires, first in their rooms at the hotel Majestic and later in their apartment in Calle Solís, Güiraldes and Adelina invited the "muchachos" to their memorable gatherings. These meetings were veritable mutual admiration reunions. They were popular, lively, and well-attended by the Martinfierristas.[9] Güiraldes opened up to his friends. Often he would speak to them with lyrical inspiration of the latest European literary innovations. At other times he would disclose his vision of Argentina's artistic expression. Better still,

---

[7] *Martín Fierro* (Segunda Epoca, Año I, Numbers 5-6, June 15, 1924), p. 6.
[8] De Torre, "Carta," p. 15.
[9] Francisco Luis Bernárdez, "Ricardo Güiraldes en mi recuerdo," *Criterio* (Buenos Aires, XXVI, 1953), pp. 874-975.

he would illustrate it with a musical interpretation by strumming gaucho songs on his guitar, as all joined in the singing.[10]

Güiraldes felt a very sympathetic affinity with the young men whose struggles for self-expression in the face of hostile incomprehension he knew so well.[11] He felt a sense of obligation to lend the literary fledgelings an encouraging hand.[12] By nature an adventurer in pursuit of new horizons, he became the protector of the young writers who dared risk something new and original.[13]

On their part, the young men of *Martín Fierro* were captivated by Güiraldes as a person and as a poet. They were charmed by his virile and fraternal personality, and inspired by his refreshing sense of the aesthetic. Among those who contributed to the animation of these sessions were Jorge Luis Borges, Pablo Rojas Paz, Alfredo Brandán Caraffa, Francisco Luis Bernárdez, Leopoldo Marechal, Raúl and Enrique González Tuñón, and Augusto Mario Delfino. Their enthusiasm for their new colleague is well reflected by Bernárdez himself in his description of Güiraldes:

> At that time Güiraldes was not quite forty years of age; that is to say he was fifteen years older than the majority of our group. Of medium height and slender build, he was distinguished in appearance and modest in manner. The expression of his fine features was melancholic, although manly. He was a genuinely young man as could be seen not only from his physical appearance (which belied his age) but also from the animation with which he expressed himself. By this, it is not intended to say that he was

[10] Battistessa, "Breve historia de una revista de vanguardia," *Verbum* (Buenos Aires, No. 2 y 3, 1942), p. 29.

[11] Félix Lizaso, "La lección de Güiraldes," *Revista de avance* (La Habana, III, No. 22, 1928), p. 118.

[12] Ana Rovner, "Una entrevista con Adelina del Carril de Güiraldes," *El Hogar* (Buenos Aires, Año LIII, Feb. 24, 1956), p. 4.

[13] Rojas Paz, "Descubrimiento y conquista de la pampa," *El perfil de nuestra expresión* (Buenos Aires, 1929), p. 47.

garrulous. On the contrary, he was usually silent. So much so that he seemed ever to be apologizing for his far-away look by flashing a smile which opened the way to his soul.[14]

Güiraldes won their friendship with his sympathetic comprehension of their aesthetic sensibilities.[15] The devotion of the younger men was such that they looked upon him as an older brother.[16] Besides defending their youthful expression of the new and original, he also championed the innovations of the French authors, with whom he had such direct acquaintanceship. The younger men listened avidly, as he explained with emotion the works of his favorite French writers, among them Larbaud, Fargue, Romains, Henry J. M. Levet, and Saint-Léger.[17] In Güiraldes they recognized the spokesman and the leader of the most advanced literary expression.[18] But the Martinfierristas did not look upon him as a master. To them he was a friend, pointing the way.[19] They responded to his spirit of adventure and to his comradeship.[20]

Associating himself with the literary campaign of the Martinfierristas, Güiraldes contributed to *Martín Fierro* during the succeeding years.[21] In addition, with the purpose of aiding promising young authors of the group who had insufficient means and who could find no publishing houses to accept their works, Güiraldes joined Evar Méndez, Oliverio Girondo, and Sandro Piantanida in founding, in May, 1924, a new publishing house, Editorial Proa. This undertaking, begun with a levy of one hundred pesos from each, well justified its

---

[14] Bernárdez, p. 784. (Author's translation.)
[15] Rojas Paz, p. 33.
[16] Enrique González Tuñón, pp. 11-13, 19.
[17] Rojas Paz, "Ricardo Güiraldes," *Síntesis* (Buenos Aires, II, (6), Nov., 1927), 376; and Félix Lizaso, p. 118.
[18] Bernárdez, *loc. cit.*, pp. 874-875; and Rojas Paz, "Descubrimiento y conquista de la pampa," p. 33.
[19] Anonymous, "Ricardo Güiraldes," *Síntesis* (Buenos Aires, II, 1927), p. 383.
[20] González Tuñón, *op. cit.*, p. 44.
[21] The following are signed contributions of Güiraldes to *Martín Fierro*: "Afecto" (Año II, Núms. 14 y 15, Jan. 24, 1925), p. 4; "Remate," *ibid.*; "Ramón" (Año II, Núm. 19, July 18, 1925), pp. 2-3; "Poesía" (Año IV, Núm. 39, March 28, 1927), pp. 1-3.

existence by publishing, not only the works of the editors of *Martín Fierro,* but, later, also Güiraldes' *Don Segundo Sombra.*

In discovering Güiraldes, the Martinfierristas had found a living exponent of the new aesthetic consciousness, a leader in the movement for modern literary expression in Argentina, and a friend. Although the environment of incomprehension and hostility had not disappeared in Buenos Aires, nevertheless, the years 1924 to 1926 marked the beginning of the recognition of Güiraldes as a literary figure.

XV

The Launching of *Proa*

In August, 1924, a new literary magazine made its appearance in Buenos Aires. It had thirty or forty pages, was about the size of a small notebook, and was issued monthly, each time with a cover of a different color: ochre, green, violet, blue. Its name was *Proa,* and its four directors were Jorge Luis Borges, Alfredo Brandán Caraffa, Ricardo Güiraldes, and Pablo Rojas Paz.[1]

The idea of publishing *Proa* started shortly after Güiraldes had met the Martinfierristas for the first time, when Brandán Caraffa proposed that Güiraldes join him, Jorge Luis Borges and Pablo Rojas Paz in founding a literary periodical. Güiraldes accepted on the spot. Writing of this occasion, he said that he had felt so hurt by the hostility with which his literary efforts had been received that he wanted to revenge himself by helping the young generation as much as he could.[2]

The name "Proa" appealed to Güiraldes because it had a special significance for him. Meaning in Spanish the bow of a ship, it was a metaphorical allusion to an advanced position in an unchartered sea of literature, plowing forward toward the unknown horizon beyond. Güiraldes had used this imagery to express the spirit of adventure in his poem "Viajar," written aboard the SS *Regina Elena* in 1914.

The periodical was the organ of the most forward action in the literary field in Argentina. Its prime object of attack was, like that of *Martín Fierro* in the arts, the indifference and hostility of the public to modern literary expression. It carried out its program along two principal lines. One was the enlightenment of the public with regard to the modern

[1] Evar Méndez, "La nueva revista 'Proa'," *Martín Fierro* (Segunda Epoca, Año I, Núms. 8 y 9, Sept. 6, 1924); p. 9.
[2] De Torre, "Carta," p. 15.

trends of the most advanced Spanish and French writers by
critical articles of their latest works. The other was the publication of the poetry of Argentine and foreign poets whose
bold new writings were theretofore unknown or unappreciated
in Buenos Aires.

Borges, who had been a part of the *ultraísta* movement in
Spain, and who had come to Buenos Aires with the purpose
of implanting the *credo* in Argentina, joined in a happy part-
nership with Güiraldes, who undertook to make known the
works of contemporary French writers. The articles of the
former reflecting the latest literary trends in Spain, and the
articles of the latter, dealing with the most recent literary
expression in France, complemented each other. It appears
from a draft of a letter from Güiraldes to Guillermo de
Torre, dated June 27, 1925, that Güiraldes became acquainted
with the writings of the Spanish *ultraístas* at his time and
not before.[3]

In the first issue of *Proa* appeared three hitherto unpublished
poems from Güiraldes' *Poemas solitarios,* which he was writing at the time.[4] In addition, Güiraldes contributed articles,
giving his impressions of his recent favorites: Fargue, Valery
Larbaud, Romains, Levet, Saint-Léger.[5] Güiraldes' enthusiasm
and contributions were the driving force behind *Proa*'s literary
compaign. For the first time in Buenos Aires eminent figures
of contemporary French letters were discussed intelligently
and appreciated, including, besides those already mentioned,
Supervielle and Soupault.[6]

Proa and Güiraldes received recognition not in Buenos
Aires but in France. In 1925 in Paris, Larbaud wrote, in the
Revue Européenne, that in Argentina a new contact had been
established between the young Spanish-American and the new

[3] *Ibid.*
[4] Five other poems by Güiraldes appear in *Proa* No. 7. They are: "Nubes,"
"Chimango," "Centro," "Mate," and "Concierto."
[5] Lizaso, p. 118.
[6] Battistessa, p. 32.

Spanish literatures, that *Proa* was the mouthpiece of the pioneers (*l'avant-garde*) in Buenos Aires who were battling for the adoption of the latest French and Spanish literary trends, and that Ricardo Güiraldes was their recognized leader.[7]

In Argentina, however, *Proa* struggled to keep afloat in an unfriendly sea of indifference and even hostility. The public responded to *Proa*'s progressive literary campaign with the same negative indifference of which the Martinfierristas had complained. Güiraldes was still looked upon as the mad poet of *El cencerro*.[8] Furthermore, he was accused by others of being so partial to France and to the French authors as to be disloyal to his own country.[9]

The first clear indication that *Proa* was foundering appeared in an S.O.S., sent out in its eleventh issue in June, 1925, in which Güiraldes, Borges, and Rojas Paz, in a last valiant effort to keep it afloat, called for the support of its readers.[10] No response to *Proa*'s call for help came from impassive Buenos Aires. But answers came from abroad, among them one from Alfonso Reyes, dated Paris, May, 1925.[11]

In spite of the continued efforts of its editors and the undiminished quality of its next few issues, *Proa* ceased to exist for lack of readers with the publication of its last number in September, 1925, without so much as a word of regret from the Buenos Aires press. From France, however, the tragic disappearance of the distant literary beacon was

---

[7] Larbaud, "L'Oeuvre et la Situation de Ricardo Güiraldes (1925)," *Revue Européenne* (V, No. 27, 1925), pp. 26-27.

[8] Güiraldes, "Poesía," *Martín Fierro* (Año IV, No. 39, March 28, 1927), p. 2.

[9] Ocampo, "Carta a Ricardo Güiraldes," *Sur* (No. 217-218, Nov.-Dec., 1952), p. 5.

[10] *Proa* (No. 21, June, 1925), p. 47.

[11] See Battistessa, *loc. cit.*, p. 34. Reyes has purposely used imagery similar to that of Güiraldes' poem, "Proa," in *El cencerro*, p. 52. His message reads:

> Amigos, trabajadores de la *Proa*. Soy vuestro, agradezco el llamado, y allá acudo a medio vestir, aunque sea en mangas de camisa, con lo que traigo encima, para reclamar mi puesto en el mascarón de *Proa*, donde más pegue el viento y escupa el mar. Gracias. Pronto me haré presente con prosa y verso.
>
> Las dos manos de
>
> Alfonso Reyes.

mourned by Valery Larbaud, who recorded his dismay in the *Revue Européenne*.[12]

The failure of *Proa* was more than a disappointment to Güiraldes. It was to him the extinction of the small flame of literary enlightenment that he had helped kindle with so much hope. His efforts had been rebuffed and, except in the case of a few kindred spirits, he lost faith in the intellectual acumen of his fellow countrymen.[13] With the end of *Proa* in 1925, Güiraldes received the fourth blow in his literary career.

---

[12] See Larbaud, "Lettres argentines et uruguayennes," *Revue Européenne* (VI, Dec. 1, 1925), p. 70:

> Nous apprenons avec chagrin la disparition de la revue d'avant-garde *Proa* fondée en 1924 par le poète argentin Ricardo Güiraldes.

. . . .

> C'est là qu'ont paru la plupart des études et des notes réunies par J. L. Borges dans "Inquisiciones," des poèmes et des articles de Ricardo Güiraldes et de Brandán Caraffa, des vers . . . (de) Reyes et Pablo Neruda, etc.

[13] Battistessa, *loc. cit.*, p. 35.

XVI

The Completion of *Don Segundo Sombra*

Güiraldes had not worked on *Don Segundo Sombra* since he finished the first ten chapters in Paris in 1920. Finally, in January, 1925, after a period of five years, he returned to writing about the old gaucho. As he progressed he confided his literary aspiration to Jorge Luis Borges. Borges shared his sentiments. In an article in *Proa,* he lauded Güiraldes as the most distinguished man of letters in Argentina for his interpretation of the pampa.[1]

When *Proa* suspended publication in September of that year, Güiraldes did not retire to La Porteña in injured solitude. On the contrary, he remained in Buenos Aires at his post in the management of the publishing house, Editorial Proa. He wanted to be among his young friends. They provided the favorable climate he needed in order to write. As he advanced with his writing, the "muchachos" continued to flock to the lively meetings, at his home, at times in the hotel Majestic, and at others at his father's house in Calle Paraguay and at his apartment in Calle Solís. Even more than providing a friendly atmosphere, these young men, who sincerely harbored a brotherly affection for Güiraldes, rallied round him to encourage him at this moment.[2]

Güiraldes' personality expanded in the congenial atmosphere created by the enthusiasm of the "muchachos". During their gatherings, he communicated to them his feeling for

[1] Borges, "La pampa y el suburbio son dioses," *Proa* (No. 15, Jan., 1925):
  Somos unos dejados de Dios, nuestro corazón no confirma ninguna fe, pero en cuatro cosas sí creemos: en que la pampa es un sagrario, en que el primer paisano es muy hombre, en la reciedumbre de los malevos, en la dulzura generosa del arrabal. Son cuatro puntos cardinales los que señalo, no unas luces perdidas. . . . De la riqueza infatigable del mundo sólo nos queda el arrabal y la pampa. Ricardo Güiraldes, primer decoro de nuestras letras, le está rezando al llano. . . .
[2] González Tuñón, *op. cit.,* p. 20.

the pampa. Being endowed with a remarkable intuition of the Argentine prairie, he was wont to evoke the poetic climate of the gaucho environment by strumming on the guitar and singing gaucho songs. As his voice vibrated with lyrical feeling it struck a sympathetic chord in his listeners. From the musical Güiraldes would pass to the literary interpretation of the pampa.[3]

Thus encouraged by the friendly interests of all who surrounded him, Güiraldes concentrated on completing the book. As he wrote a chapter, he would read passages to the "muchachos." They were witnessing the evolution of *Don Segundo Sombra*. Even more, they attended upon the author's battles with his problems of style and concept. In fact, Güiraldes shared his literary preoccupations with them.[4] Desirous of interpreting the gaucho in a manner true to his image of him, he was at times at a loss to find the fitting presentation. He was also confronted with a stylistic dilemma, seemingly arising from an inconsistency between his inclination toward a poetic form and his wish to express the gaucho personality of don Segundo in terms of his characteristically rustic language.[5] In spite of all, Güiraldes failed to find a solution to what he considered his literary shortcomings. He had been unable to express the gaucho as he envisioned him. He was unsatisfied with *Don Segundo Sombra*.[6]

During the active months spent in Buenos Aires in 1924 and 1925, Güiraldes was struck down by Hodgkin's disease.[7] Behind his cheerful countenance, he kept his illness hidden from his friends.[8] The physical suffering was such that he

---

[3] María Luisa Leguizamón, "Ricardo Güiraldes y algunos aspectos de su obra," *Cuadernos Americanos* (México, XII, May-June, 1923), p. 279; also Bernárdez, "Ricardo Güiraldes en mi recuerdo," p. 875.

[4] Bernárdez, *loc. cit.*, p. 875.

[5] Bernárdez, "La poesía de Güiraldes," *Buenos Aires Literaria* (Año I, No. 2, Nov., 1952), p. 34.

[6] Güiraldes, "De un epistolario," *Sur* (No. 2, Año I, Otoño, 1931), pp. 181-184.

[7] This information was supplied by Adelina del Carril de Güiraldes in her letter of February 2, 1960.

[8] Colombo, *op. cit.*, p. 90.

feared it would prevent his finishing *Don Segundo Sombra*. It was a question of which was stronger: the destructive force of pain, or the will-power to bear it and finish writing.[9] With the true gaucho stoicism he so admired, he dominated his physical ordeal.[10] He welcomed his friends with a smile and a song. In the same spirit, while lying on his back to ease the pain, he wrote page after page of *Don Segundo Sombra*.

As his illness grew in severity, it became apparent that it would be a race between *Don Segundo Sombra* and death. Adelina was his source of strength. By comforting him and fortifiying his morale she kept his spirit alive and helped him to persevere in his writing.[11] But, before the end of 1925, Güiraldes' illness was gaining in its grip and his book was not yet finished. There was only a little more to do, and so little time. At this point Güiraldes and Adelina gave up their apartment in town and retired to La Porteña, so that he might devote his diminishing energies to bringing his work to a close. There on the ranch was the real don Segundo, the aging gaucho who had inspired his novel and served as its protagonist. Conscious of the bonds of affection between them since Güiraldes' childhood, the two friends, silently in true gaucho manner, found strength in each other's company. During these last few months spent at La Porteña, Güiraldes worked steadily among his gaucho trappings in his large study to finish his writing. In March, 1926, his strength depleted but morally victorious, he wrote the last words of *Don Segundo Sombra*: "Me fuí, como quien se desangra".

---

[9] Güiraldes, *Poemas solitarios*, p. 26.
[10] See *El sendero*, No. 26, p. 38.
[11] González Tuñón, *op. cit.*, pp. 49-52.

XVII

Public Reaction to *Don Segundo Sombra*

When Güiraldes gave his manuscript to the printers, he feared that *Don Segundo Sombra* would be another shattering failure, and with good reason.[1] On the very eve of its publication, his critics continued to treat him with a malevolent indifference that shocked his literary friends.[2] Güiraldes anticipated attacks from two opposite directions: one from his colleagues of the "vanguardia movement," who would reproach him for having deserted the ranks of the aesthetic revolution, and the other from his old enemies, the members of conservative literary circles, who would scoff at him for his return to conservative writing. Although he felt both arguments were without foundation, the prospect of adverse criticism gave him considerable concern.[3]

Owing to this premonition, Güiraldes requested only a thousand copies of the book. He had chosen as its printer Francisco A. Colombo, who had produced beautiful editions of *Rosaura* and *Xaimaca*. The elderly printer read, with personal interest, the beginning of *Don Segundo Sombra* and, convinced of the worth of the book, offered to print an additional thousand copies on his own account. Setting the type with old-world craftsmanship, the master printer completed the first two thousand copies of *Don Segundo Sombra* on July 1, 1926. Under the auspices of Editorial Proa, the books, bearing orange colored covers, were shipped in packages of ten to meet their fate on the display shelves of Buenos Aires bookstores.

A month passed with no comment from the press. Meanwhile, the author distributed first copies to his friends, the

[1] Augusto Mario Delfino, "Cómo apareció *Don Segundo Sombra*," *Arte y Plata* (México, III, Feb., 1947), pp. 34-36.
[2] Bernárdez, "Ricardo Güiraldes en mi recuerdo," p. 875.
[3] Güiraldes, "De un epistolario," *Sur* (Año I, Otoño, 1931), p. 181.

"muchachos." At the same time, mindful of the early encouragement of Valery Larbaud, he also sent him a copy with a covering letter dated July, 1926. In the fourth chapter of the book, Güiraldes paid tribute to Larbaud. In this same letter he speaks of it, as follows:

> You will see that the first gaucho who helps little Cáceres, and whose inclinations resemble yours, is named after you. This was done intentionally. It also is no mere coincidence that the name Lares bears the same initial as Larbaud. I did it out of a feeling of great affection and I take as much selfish pleasure in bringing it to your attention.[4]

The first response to *Don Segundo Sombra* appeared in *Martín Fierro* on September 3. The "muchachos" who had witnessed its gestation rallied to help assure its success. Fully aware of the hostility toward their colleague, they, too, were fearful that *Don Segundo Sombra* would fall victim to adverse criticism, especially from Leopoldo Lugones. Unfriendly criticism, from Lugones, whose prestige carried considerable weight in Argentine literary circles at that time, presented a serious threat. Anticipating the accusation that Güiraldes' style was conservative, they warned critics not to make the embarrassing mistake of hastily condemning the book.[5]

The Martinfierristas learned that Lugones was indeed preparing a critical review of *Don Segundo Sombra* and that it would appear soon in *La Nación*. With this knowledge, one of the "muchachos," Augusto Mario Delfino, was commissioned to write a favorable article to be published before the appearance of Lugones' review. Delfino had not yet written his article when he discovered at the very last moment that Lugones' article was about to appear. Hard-pressed to meet

[4] *Ibid.*, p. 182. (Author's translation.)
[5] S. P., "*Don Segundo Sombra*, relato de Ricardo Güiraldes," *Martín Fierro* (Segunda Epoca, Año III, Núm. 33, Sept. 3, 1926), p. 6.

the deadline, he finished his article, "Don Segundo Sombra,"[6] in time for its publication in *El Diario* on Saturday, September 20. The following day Lugones' review, "Don Segundo Sombra," was featured in the literary supplement of the Sunday edition of *La Nación.*[7]

To the surprise of all, Lugones' heavy artillery did not blast at Güiraldes. On the contrary, it boomed a salute to *Don Segundo Sombra* with unprecedented praise. Instead of adverse comments, his lengthy article was a tribute without reservations, full of laudatory expressions. It began by placing *Don Segundo Sombra* in a class with the monuments of national literature, *Facundo* and *Martín Fierro.* It compared don Segundo with Martín Fierro, applauded the artistic presentation, and, it ended acclaiming the success of Güiraldes as a writer.

Lugones' article produced a notable effect upon public opinion in Argentina. It sounded the note in the attitude of the literary circles toward Güiraldes. Immediately following its publication, *Don Segundo Sombra* was hailed as a complete success,[8] as is evidenced by the articles by Roberto Giusti[9] and Juan B. González[10] in the succeeding numbers of *Nosotros.* Indeed, in recognition as the best Argentine literary production in 1926, *Don Segundo Sombra* received the *"Primer Premio Nacional."*

Where Güiraldes had previously been shunned, ridiculed, scorned, and vituperated, now he was congratulated and applauded from all sides. The sudden popularity was so different from his past experiences that it took him by surprise. With characteristic big-heartedness, he shared the credit with

[6] Delfino, *loc. cit.,* pp. 34-36.

[7] Leopoldo Lugones, *"Don Segundo Sombra," La Nación,* Literary Supplement (Buenos Aires, Sept. 21, 1926), p. 4.

[8] Germán Berdiales, "El gaucho en las letras. *Don Segundo Sombra* y su creador: Ricardo Güiraldes," *Pampa Argentina* (Buenos Aires, XXI, Oct. 1947), p. 28.

[9] Roberto F. Giusti, "Dos novelas del campo argentino," *Nosotros* (LIV, Sept., 1926), pp. 125-133.

[10] González, "Un libro significativo, *Don Segundo Sombra*," Nosotros (Nov., 1926), pp. 377-385.

all Argentines. "We all wrote it," he said. "It was within us and we are glad that it has come out in print."[11]

The acclaim of *Don Segundo Sombra* represented a two-fold victory. Güiraldes had triumphed over his physical hardship and he had overcome the indifference and hostility of Argentine literary opinion.[12] The success of his book placed him not only among the leading writers of Argentina but also of Latin America.[13] In Europe, the critics in Spain and France[14] were quick to recognize the literary significance of the novel. In Paris, F. Ortiz Echagüe wrote in *Revue de L'Amérique Latine*:

> The publication of the book won quick recognition for Ricardo Güiraldes. Its success covered the whole of Spanish America. In Madrid, the pontifs of literary criticism, who hardly pay any attention to Argentine literature, had no hesitation in recognizing the relationship of *Don Segundo Sombra* with *Facundo* and *Martín Fierro*.[15]

Before the end came, Ricardo Güiraldes had fulfilled his purpose: the literary interpretation of his concept of the gaucho.

---

[11] Güiraldes, "De un epistolario," *Sur* (Año I, Otoño, 1931), p. 185.
[12] José R. Liberal, "Prólogo," *Don Segundo Sombra, de Ricardo Güiraldes* (Buenos Aires, 1946), p. 18.
[13] Bernárdez, "Ricardo Güiraldes en mi recuerdo," *Criterio* (Buenos Aires, XXVI, 1953), pp. 874-875.
[14] Christiane Fournier, *"Don Segundo Sombra," Revue de L'Amérique Latine* (Paris, LIV, 1927), 365; F. Contreras, "La Littérature d'Avant-garde—Ricardo Güiraldes: *Don Segundo Sombra,* 'Proa', Buenos Aires," *Le Mercure de France* (Paris, April 15, 1927), pp. 489-495.
[15] F. Ortiz Echagüe, "Ricardo Güiraldes," *Revue de L'Amérique Latine* (XIV, 1927), p. 505. (Author's translation).

XVIII

The Last Voyage

At last Güiraldes turned his attention to his health. The gravity of his illness moved him to seek the aid of the foremost physicians in Europe.[1] At the same time the prospect of his return to Paris was a source of joyful anticipation. The thought of rejoining Larbaud and his friends at Adrienne Monnier's was a happy one. Furthermore, he was possessed with a reinvigorated creative urge to write and was full of enthusiasm to carry out his plans. This was his state of mind when he wrote to Larbaud in January, 1927, announcing his departure for Europe on the *S. S. Massilia* on March 15.[2]

The several projects on which Güiraldes looked forward to working were *El libro bravo,*[3] *Poemas solitarios,*[4] *Poemas místicos,*[5] and *El sendero.*[6] *El libro bravo* was still in project form, and was to be, as Adelina later explained, "a book of poems in which he would extol the characteristics of the men of our race."[7] *Poemas solitarios* was a collection of poems that corresponded to Güiraldes' aesthetic and emotional experiences over the years, and which he planned to bring to light in the now more receptive literary environment. *Poemas místicos* were seven poems, also written in his distinctive prose style, but of a religious nature. They were written for his own personal satisfaction and not intended for publication. Neither was *el sendero* intended for publication. It was a series of brief notations, assembled during the more recent

[1] K. P. Kirkwood, "Ricardo Güiraldes and *Don Segundo Sombra,*" *Excursion among Books* (Buenos Aires, 1949), p. 329.
[2] Güiraldes, "De un epistolario," *Sur* (Año I, Otoño, 1931), pp. 185-186.
[3] *Op. cit.*
[4] *Op. cit.*
[5] Güiraldes, *Poemas místicos* (San Antonio de Areco, 1928).
[6] *Op. cit.*
[7] Güiraldes, *El libro bravo* (San Antonio de Areco, 1936), p. 5.

past, in which Güiraldes recorded his thoughts on his spiritual evolution. He jotted them down for himself alone as a method of orientating his inner-most self in view of his approaching end.[8] They reflected his concern for meaning in the unknown, a search for other than material values, and a longing for a more distant horizon beyond this earthly existence. As Güiraldes put these notes in an orderly sequence, they formed an intimate biography, and also an account of the development of his meditations. He called them "Some notes on my spiritual growth in anticipation of a future life."[9]

In *Don Segundo Sombra* Güiraldes had described the restlessness of the herdsman to be ever on the march toward the land beyond.[10] In this same spirit of the gaucho, Güiraldes, having conquered one horizon, now sought a new one farther on.[11]

On the eve of his departure from Buenos Aires, as his friends bade him farewell for the last time, more than one of them noted a certain sadness beneath his usually cheerful manner.[12] It seemed to them that, secretly, he dreaded to leave Argentina because he had a premonition that he would not return.[13] This may explain why, during his last days at La Porteña, he spent the afternoons by the Areco River, gazing into its waters, as he had done so often as a child.[14]

Güiraldes was seriously ill when, in April, he rejoined Larbaud and his other friends in Paris. Soon after his arrival

[8] Adelina del Carril in her letter of June 6, 1961, provides the following information regarding *El sendero*:

    El sendero no lo escribió Ricardo para publicarlo. Era lo más íntimo de su ser espiritual, en el que se ponía frente a frente de sí mismo a fin de hallarse.

    Yo me tomé la atribución de publicarlo porque considero que es un saludable ejemplo de superación para la juventud de nuestra tierra.

[9] "Notas sobre mi evolución espiritualista en vista de un futuro." (Subtitle to *El sendero*.)

[10] *Don Segundo Sombra*, p. 285.

[11] *El sendero*, pp. 34, 102.

[12] Anonymous, "Ricardo Güiraldes," *Síntesis* (Buenos Aires, II, 1927), p. 384.

[13] Alvaro Melián Lafinur, "Discurso en memoria de Ricardo Güiraldes," *Repertorio Americano* (San José de Costa Rica, XIX, Nov. 30, 1929), p. 321.

[14] Colombo, *op. cit.*, p. 95.

he learned that his physicians could not help him.[15] His physical suffering increased in intensity. But instead of being dejected, he continued to write. In *El sendero* he recorded his characteristic attitude in a notation which in substance reads as follows: "If, instead of always seeking to lessen our pain, we could increase our strength to resist it, our sufferings would elevate our moral stature instead of lowering it."[16] Undismayed, he also started work on *El libro bravo*. At no time did he show concern for his physical distress.[17] Instead, with cheerful countenance, he met with his friends at Adrienne Monnier's. There, full of enthusiasm, he spoke of his new ideas and his current literary projects. One of these friends, who remembered Güiraldes' last conversations, said that they turned to three themes.[18] These were his belief in the idealism of young *vanguardista* writers as a salutary reaction against the postwar attitude of despair and materialistic disillusionment, his project of writing a poetic apotheosis of his fellow countrymen which was *El libro bravo*, the book he had just begun, and his interest in the spiritual philosophy of the Orient.

To Güiraldes the appeal of the Oriental concepts of the universe had been increasing for some time.[19] He sought in his readings to learn more about the teachings of Buddha and the beliefs of Brahamanism.[20] As he neared death, he became even more aware of the cosmic.[21] Since childhood he had always been responsive to a sense of harmony with nature in the pampa.[22] This impression of harmony extended from the pampa to the sky and at night to the stars. Throughout his life, he had felt it in his human relationships, most particularly with those who were close to nature, his gaucho

[15] M. S. Noel, "Las últimas páginas de Güiraldes," *Síntesis* (II, 1927), p. 301.
[16] *El sendero*, p. 35.
[17] Bernárdez, "Ricardo Güiraldes en mi recuerdo," p. 875.
[18] Noel, *loc. cit.*, p. 302.
[19] *El sendero*, p. 25.
[20] Juan Carlos Pellegrini, "El sendero olvidado," *Buenos Aires Literaria* (Año I, Nov., 1952), p. 46. See also: *El sendero*, pp. 25, 26, 33.
[21] Noel, *loc. cit.*, p. 303.
[22] *El sendero*, p. 116.

friends. Now he experienced a greater sense of harmony with the universe.[23]

In the spiritual philosophy of the Orient, Güiraldes found an affinity with his longing to reach beyond the limit of his terrestrial existence toward perfection. "The Oriental symbol for perfection," he said, "is the lotus flower: its roots are in the mud, its stem—which reaches upward toward the flower —is in the water, and its flower is in the light."[24]

Four months before his death, he asked Larbaud whether he had ever been attracted toward the Orient. Already a dying man, he wished to share with his friend his thoughts on the future, beyond life. Larbaud, not realizing the gravity of his illness and loath to enter upon so personal a subject, cut him short by expressing no interest.[25] That was the last time the two friends saw each other.

A sudden aggravation of his illness put an end to Güiraldes' stay in Paris only a few weeks after his arrival. Shortly before, Fernando Ortiz Echagüe had given a luncheon in his honor, attended by a number of writers who had not known Güiraldes and who wanted to meet him.[26] Present also was Pío Baroja who, chatting quietly with Adelina, learned of Güiraldes' illness and recommended that his friends go to a village in the French Pyrenees. In May, the Güiraldes left Paris for Arcachon.[27] In September, when it was clear that the end was drawing near, they returned to Paris. There, in moments of respite from the attacks of pain, he rallied his diminishing forces to continue writing. But, having completed only the first few pages of *El libro bravo,* he was unable to continue. He realized he would

[23] *Poemas solitarios,* p. 19:

> Pequeña antena de carne alucinada de imposible, espero en la tensión de todos mis anhelos, que algo grande como un Dios me eleve a la armonía universal.

[24] *El sendero,* p. 116.
[25] Larbaud, "Ricardo Güiraldes," *Le Roseau d'Or* (Paris, 1928), p. 65.
[26] Ortiz Echagüe, "Ricardo Güiraldes," *Revue de L'Amérique Latine* (XIV, 1927), p. 504.
[27] Bernárdez, "Ricardo Güiraldes en mi recuerdo," p. 875.

never again see his beloved pampa.[28] On October 6, two days before his death, he wrote his last words in *El sendero*: "I have had a slight glimmer of what might be called ecstasy!"[29]

He accepted the end with the characteristic stoicism he had attributed to the gaucho.[30] During the moments of physical prostration, and to the very last, he kept his cheerful disposition, and tried to comfort Adelina in her despair. His concern for her was the only visible shadow of sorrow.[31] Güiraldes died at four o'clock in the afternoon, on Saturday, October 8, 1927.[32]

[28] Arturo Torres-Rioseco, "Ricardo Güiraldes," *Atenea* (Concepción, Chile, LVII, Sept., 1939), p. 482.
[29] *El sendero*, p. 116:
     ¿He tenido el más débil vislumbre de lo que se llamaría
     éxtasis?
     ¡Sí!
[30] González Tuñón, *op. cit.*, p. 54.
[31] *Ibid.*, p. 55.
[32] Ortiz Echagüe, "La atribulante noticia," *El Mentor* (San Antonio de Areco, Oct. 14, 1928), p. 1.

XIX

The Last Days of don Segundo

On November 14 of that year, the body of the young *patrón* was brought to San Antonio de Areco for burial.[1] A crowd of "gauchos" were waiting at the station platform when the train arrived.[2] As Güiraldes' white haired father got off the train, the aging don Segundo came forward, hat in hand. For a moment the two old men stood before each other in silence. Returning to his horse, don Segundo mounted and led a procession of three hundred men on horseback to the cemetary.[3] There, Ricardo's father, Leopoldo Lugones, Ricardo Rojas, and don Segundo lowered Güiraldes into the ground.[4] Afterwards, as the old gaucho sat solemnly on this horse, reporters tried to question him. He turned from them sadly and rode away.[5]

In 1936 don Segundo was living with his married daughter in San Antonio de Areco. He was eighty-four, lame with rheumatism, and quite deaf. He still retained some of his traits. He wore his old *chiripá*; his characteristic humor escaped in a few laconic comments; and he disclosed a nostalgic affection for "don Ricardo." On August 20 of that year Don Segundo died. Four "gauchos" escorted his coffin to a field in the pampa.[6] They buried him near Ricardo Güiraldes.[7]

---

[1] Liberal, *loc. cit.*, p. 18.
[2] Anonymous, "El homenaje a Ricardo Güiraldes," *Síntesis* (Buenos Aires, III, 1927), p. 96.
[3] *Ibid.*
[4] Bernárdez, *loc. cit.*, p. 875.
[5] Liberal, *loc cit.*, p. 10.
[6] *Ibid.*
[7] Bosco, *loc. cit.*, p. 22.

"This is the best portrait of Don Segundo Sombra in existence. It is a pen sketch by Alberto Güiraldes (the poet's nephew) drawn for the special edition of *Don Segundo Sombra* which was published by A.A.M. Stols in Maestricht, Holland, in 1928."

(Author's translation of a note written by Adelina del Carril de Güiraldes when she sent him the above drawing in March, 1963.)

WORKS OF
RICARDO GÜIRALDES

XX

Cuentos

Güiraldes published altogether thirty-three short narratives or tales, called *cuentos,* which can be grouped into three categories: gaucho tales, modern anecdotes, and sketches of fantasy.[1]

Gaucho Tales

Twenty-five of the tales are about life in the pampa. They are not short stories in the strict sense but rather sketches of Argentine folklore.[2] The important element in them is not so much the anecdote as it is the portrayal of the disappearing gaucho type, his characteristics, and his environment. The predominant tone is one of fierceness and violence, typical of other gauchesque works with which nearly everyone was familiar.[3] Indeed, as a boy, Güiraldes had heard

---

[1] The editions consulted in this study are *Cuentos de muerte y de sangre, seguidos de aventuras grotescas y una trilogía cristiana* (Madrid, Espasa-Calpe, 1933), and *Rosaura y siete cuentos* (Buenos Aires, Ed. Losada, 1952). In "Nota preliminar" of *Rosaura y siete cuentos,* published in 1952, Adelina del Carril de Güiraldes writes that some of the stories made their appearance earlier as follows: "Colegio," probably Güiraldes' first published *"cuento,"* in *Caras y Caretas,* in 1913 or 1914; "Politiquería" in *Plus Ultra,* in 1916; "Telésforo Altamira" in *La Nota,* in 1914; "Esta noche, nochebuena" included in a book of tales published by a charitable society at about the same time, and "Cuento al caso" in *Leoplán,* in 1937.

[2] In their structure Güiraldes' gaucho tales follow the contemporary trend of the stories of Joaquín González (1863-1923), Martiniano Leguizamón (1853-1935) and José S. Alvarez (1858-1903), whose *"cuentos"* were not short stories at all, but *"tableaux"* or "cuadros de costumbres" of Argentine folklore.

[3] e.g. *Facundo* (1845), *Santos Vega o los mellizos de La Flor* (1851), *Martín Fierro* (1872), and the novels of Eduardo Gutiérrez such as *Juan Moreira* (1880).

similar anecdotes of blood and death.[4] Consequently, in writing his gaucho tales he preserved these characteristics, already established in written and oral legend, and called his stories accordingly *Cuentos de muerte y de sangre.*

He did not, however, limit himself to this aspect. He also represented the gaucho's fearlessness, indomitable character, pride, loyalty, superstition, and "malicia", meaning his mischievous sense of humor. By reading each story in the light of his intention to represent a specific characteristic, one can readily gauge the author's attitude toward the various types. The tales disclose his disapproval of the despotic and cruel *caudillos* and *estancieros,* and of the *"gaucho malo."* They also reveal his sympathy for the underdog and for the humble *peón* in particular. Furthermore, these stories have a characteristic nostalgic charm which springs from his affection for what is typical of Argentine country life.[5] The tale that clearly illustrates this subtle emotional climate is "La estancia vieja."

Two of the narratives are of particular interest because of the appearance of don Segundo Sombra. They are "Al rescoldo" and "Politiquería." In both, Güiraldes has given a brief but striking picture of that well-known gaucho character. He has described only one or two outstanding features of his appearance and of his personality. In "Al rescoldo," for example, the description is limited to a mere outline of an enormous dark man, his small hat pushed back over his forehead as he tries clumsily to strum a guitar with his callous-hardened hands.[6] In the same tale don Segundo is represented as a talented storyteller and teased for his belief in ghosts. In "Politiquería," he is described as a strong, silent man whose opinion is respected by others. He is also full of *"malicia,"* which he expresses in ironic comments.[7] While all of the stories are in the main characterizations of various

[4] *Cuentos de muerte y de sangre,* p. 7.
[5] *Ibid.,* "Cariño a las cosas nuestras."
[6] *Ibid.,* p. 82.
[7] *Rosaura y siete cuentos,* pp. 99-100.

traditional Argentine types, "Al rescoldo" and "Politiquería" are of particular significance in that Güiraldes has sketched the image of the individual whose personality became the basis for his novel *Don Segundo Sombra.*

The style of these stories corresponds to the character of the gaucho and reflects his hard, rough life. Accordingly, Güiraldes' descriptions are contained in a few bold strokes, and the conciseness of his language suggests strength and laconic stoicism. In this regard, he once said: "I want my stories to be extracts that are brief and concise. What I like most about a man's hand is that it can be a fist."[8]

Furthermore, Güiraldes enhances the characterization of the gaucho by representing his vernacular. The narrator's language, however, is a non-vernacular Spanish, although it is full of colloquialisms that might be heard in the speech of an *estanciero,* or used by Güiraldes himself in telling a gaucho tale. The effect is to give the narration a strong regional flavor and to cast the stories in a rustic atmosphere.

A conspicuous feature of Güiraldes' style is the imagery. He uses it for three different purposes. One is to characterize the gaucho, the second is to stylize the narrator's language, and the third is with poetic intent. In all three instances, he discloses his distinctly fertile imagination.

The images with which the gaucho qualifies his speech are notable for their picturesqueness. They are drawn from his surroundings. Consequently, they refer to his domestic animals such as horses, cattle, dogs, and chickens; to wild animals such as jaguar, fox, ostrich, and other birds, and to life in the pampa such as various acts in herding, lassoing and throwing cattle, breaking horses, and skinning animals. Although the gaucho sometimes uses a metaphor, the predominance of the simile gives his expressions a certain charming simplicity. In representing the language of the men of the

[8] De Torre, *loc. cit.,* p. 11: "Quisiera que mis cuentos fueran extractados, breves, concisos; lo que más me gusta de la mano es su capacidad de convertirse en puño."

pampa, Güiraldes has reproduced their imagery with convincing fidelity.[9] This kind of imagery is not, however, limited to the dialogues of the gaucho characters. Güiraldes has also introduced it into the language of the narrator. The intention here is not, as before, to characterize the gaucho, but to give the narrator's speech the country flavor of the pampa.[10] Quite distinct is the imagery used to stylize the narrative prose. His purpose here is solely to enliven the narration with the colorful figments of his imagination.[11] In these instances he sometimes uses metaphors.[12] Güiraldes' imagery of a poetic nature, however, responded to his irrepressible lyrical inclination. In spite of his intention to write these tales in a virile manner he yielded occasionally to his temptation to poetize. Hence, here and there within his prose style are flashes of poetry. Quite unlike the gaucho similes, they are like fine threads of gold woven in the rough material. They consist of a single line, usually reflecting Güiraldes' sensitivity to an aesthetic aspect of nature. The technique is often that of the anthropomorphic metaphor.[13]

In considering the artistic aspect of these stories, special mention should be made of "Nocturno" which ends with the gradual disappearance of the gaucho into the shadows of the night.[14] It is an artistic gradation which Güiraldes was to use later in the conclusion of *Don Segundo Sombra*.

Two significant features stand out in these gaucho tales. One is that, although Güiraldes obviously intended to represent the fierceness and violence so characteristic of the Argentine legendary figure, he also revealed his admiration for the gaucho's praiseworthy traits of character and his love for

---

[9] *Cuentos,* p. 91: "Gritaba como un ternero."

[10] *Ibid.,* p. 40: "Como los mancarrones lunancos."

[11] *Ibid.,* p. 103: "... la boca abierta en aullido prolongado de canto."

[12] *Ibid.,* p. 82: "Una explosión de dientes en el semblante virilmente tostado al aire."

[13] *Ibid.,* p. 102: "... los cardos ... se alzan, rígidos, mirando al cielo con sus flores torturados de espinas."

[14] *Ibid.,* p. 104: "... el matador ... fué desapareciendo como diluído en la obscuridad. Al poco quedaba un movimiento de sombra en la sombra; pronto nada."

his colorful personality. The other feature is that the stylistic trends, which later appear in *Don Segundo Sombra,* are already evident. To recapitulate, these are the conciseness of expression, the combination of the gaucho vernacular of the dialogue with the distinctive style of the narrator, the various uses of imagery, and the introduction of brief poetic expressions.

Modern Anecdotes

The term "modern anecdote" is used here to designate six short narratives that have no connection with the gauchesque and which are told, not as inventions of the imagination, but as accounts of contemporary happenings. Three of them are humorous anecdotes. They are "El capitán Funes," a story of an amusing revenge, "Máscaras," and "Ferroviaria." These last two are stories of seductions with a surprising twist. The other three are moral narratives. They are "Telésforo Altamira," a sketch of the degeneration of a spineless bookworm, "Sexto," a picture of the villification of young love by an evil-minded priest, and "Arrabalera," a description of an over-sentimental romance. Güiraldes has written them in a style commonly used in telling an after-dinner story. Aside from one or two flights of his imagination, he has not made use of his usual imagery. The language in fact offers no notable stylistic feature other than that of a modern anecdote: brevity.

Of more significance than the language are Güiraldes' sentiments toward love, which he discloses in three of the anecdotes. In "Arrabalera" he expresses the same contempt for the swooning mentality of sentimental love affairs which appears later in *Rosaura.* In "Máscaras" he shows a skeptic attitude toward the hypocritic wiles of flirtatious women, and in "Sexto" he defends the unspoiled charm of spontaneous young love. These last two sentiments reappear distinctly in *Don Segundo Sombra.*

Sketches of Fantasy

Three sketches appear under the section called "Trilogía cristiana" in *Cuentos de muerte y de sangre*. All of them are fantasies which reflect a point of view of Güiraldes on some aspect of religion. They are, however, quite distinct from each other in tone and in style.

"El juicio de Dios" is written in a humorous vein and in the natural manner in which one would tell a story of Saint Peter and the gates of Heaven. It is a description of a benevolent God, the Father, sitting in heavenly glory and surrounded by a choir of cherubs. God listens with surprise to several mortals who express widely varying concepts of His nature. The element of humor is evident when a cherub gets his bottom smacked and when each one of the mortals is sent back to earth with a boot in his posterior from the Archangel Michael.

In "San Antonio" Güiraldes shows his contempt for the misguided morality of religious bigots. It is a description of a hermit living in a lonely country hut with an unclean hog. The hermit dreams of an amorous experience of his youth and expiates his evil conscience with masochistic flagellations. The opprobious picture of the hermit is intensified by its close analogy to the grossness of the swine. Although the theme is related to Flaubert's *La Tentation de Saint Antoine* (1878),[15] the style in which Güiraldes has written "San Antonio" differs from Flaubert's in that it is succinct and matter-of-fact. The unreserved frankness of the descriptions taints the story with literary naturalism.

"Güelé" is the story of a fierce *cacique* in the vaguely recorded early days when the Argentine pampa was overrun by Indian hordes. In a raid on a village of white settlers, the *cacique* enters a church. His strange experience at the altar is such that he is miraculously converted and becomes a mystic saint. He expiates his sins by acts of Samaritan charity

---

[15] Gustave Flaubert, *La Tentation de Saint Antoine* (Paris, 1921).

and dies in the pampa amid heavenly visions. The significance of the story appears to be that there is more goodness in a saintly savage like the *cacique* than in a swinish hermit like San Antonio. The language of the narration has a primitive lyrical quality which Güiraldes has achieved by combining an almost biblical manner of expression with colorful imagery.

Although the three sketches are written in three different styles, jocose, factual, and poetic, they all display the distinctive feature of Güiraldes' writing: his imagery. In each story the images properly correspond to the tone of the narration. In "El juicio de Dios" he pictures the cherrubs playfully;[16] in "San Antonio" the amorous spasms of the young girl are described naturalistically;[17] in "Güelé" the narration is ornamented throughout with images that suggest the wild environment of the early pampa.[18]

Although the gaucho tales, the modern anecdotes, and the sketches of fantasy differ in style and subject matter, all have in common a characteristic brevity of expression. The sequence of short, concise sentences gives the language a certain abruptness which nevertheless intensifies the effectiveness of the meaning. The most significant stylistic features, however, are the striking imagery and an occasional line of poetic prose in the gaucho tales and the sketches of fantasy.

[16] *Ibid.*, p. 177: "Como un nimbo de carnes rosadas y puras, una guirnalda de angelitos ... "
[17] *Ibid.*, p. 207: " ... se retorció disparatadamente, como los cadáveres, sobre la plancha hirviente del horno crematorio."
[18] *Ibid.*, pp. 187-188: " ... supercaballos, más ligeros que bolas arrojadizas."

XXI

El cencerro de cristal

El cencerro de cristal[1] contains forty-six poems, some in verse,
some in prose and verse, and the greater part in prose. They
are assembled into five groups, reflecting in general five
different aspects of Güiraldes' sensibilities. First in order
and gathered under the title of "Camperas," are those expressing his love for the pampa and the gauchesque. They begin
affectionately with a poem about his horse and end with
an ode to the ideal gaucho. The second group, called "Plega-
rias astrales," discloses a sense of harmony with the universe.
In four of these poems Güiraldes reaches out for the significance of infinity in the earth, the sun, and the stars. They have
a biblical tone, some seeming like prayers. Within this second
group are also two compositions that contrast with the above
poems in that they express Güiraldes' contempt for romantic
poets who write sentimental verse about the moon. The third
group is assembled under the heading of "Viaje" and represents his longing for new horizons, whether they be physical, such as his travels abroad, or literary, such as his adventures into new fields of poetry. This group is important
because it reflects Güiraldes' spirit of adventurous conquest.
In the fourth group, under the heading of "Ciudadanas," are
collected a disconnected variety of compositions generally
representing his antipathy toward certain aspects of life in
the city. They seem to be in antithesis to his love for the
pampa, expressed in "Camperas." Included in this group is
the poem "Inútil" which describes his creative urge to write.
The title "realidades de ultramundo" fittingly designates the
nature of the fifth and last group. Their main characteristic
is their quality of unworldly fantasy. They illustrate the final

[1] The edition consulted is El cencerro de cristal (Buenos Aires, Ed. Losada,
1952).

achievement of his poetic aspirations: the creation of the poem in prose.

Although Güiraldes designated *El cencerro de cristal* as a book of poetry, it should be made clear that the compositions are not all poems in the sense of lyrical writings in verse. For the most part, they are free from the usual forms of versification. Moreover, they represent many different moods, only some of which are lyrical. Referring to the features that distinguished his poetic expression from the conventional verse at that time, he said that in writing *El cencerro* he plunged right ahead and gave precedence to what was vital over academic considerations. He was not afraid, he added, to represent the grotesque.[2]

The compositions are guided by Güiraldes' concept of poetry. Poetry, as he conceived it, was not a creation of reason. It was not even a human creation, but something toward which man aspired. He believed that it was a part of the harmony of the universe. He identified it with perfection. The writing of poetry therefore was only the poet's reaching out toward perfection.[3] This, in fact, is the significance of the symbolism in his poem "Aconcagua." The lofty mountain rising above the earth toward the heavens, is described as "An aspiration toward perfection" and "A prayer made of stone."[4] Toward the end of his life, Güiraldes summed up this concept of poetry in these few words: "God is beauty. Art, a prayer."[5]

Although poetry was outside the poet, it was a beauty that could be experienced. This was best illustrated, he said, by telling a parable of Ramakrishna: A devout man sent his two sons away to learn the wisdom of Brahma. Upon

[2] Güiraldes, "Poesía," *Martín Fierro* (Año IV, No. 39, March 28, 1927), p. 1: "En el Cencerro me he llevado las cosas por delante, dando la prioridad a lo que es vital, sobre lo que es académico. No he tenido miedo de lo grotesco ... El Cencerro son muchas zapateadas en el aire."

[3] Güiraldes, "A Jules Supervielle," *Sur* (Año I, Otoño, 1931), p. 189: "La poesía es aquello hacia lo cual tiende el poeta."

[4] *El cencerro*, p. 55: "Aspiración hacia lo perfecto" and "Rezo de piedra."

[5] González Tuñón, *op. cit.,* p. 44: "Dios es la belleza. El Arte, un rezo."

their return the father queried them on what they learned. The elder son gave an erudite dissertation on the subject. The younger, when the time came for him to speak, became mute with ecstasy. Whereupon the father said to him, "You are the one who knows what Brahma is."[6] In a poetic allegory, "Siete verdades y una belleza," Güiraldes clearly represents such an experience. He makes the point that, instead of being created by man within himself, poetry "is a thing of beauty . . . which I have plucked from this world to give to my soul."[7] The poet, he said elsewhere, must have what he calls an intuitive perception of harmony.[8] He is like a prism, he wrote in metaphorical terms in another poem.[9] And, like a prism, he spontaneously reflects *"la poesía total."*[10]

The wide variations in the form of Güiraldes' compositions stem in part from his revolt against established poetic molds. "I don't believe in pre-established forms, whatever their names," he said.[11] He believed that conformity produced an unpoetic standardization. "Writing sonnets," he explained by way of illustration, "is an assembly-line production like Ford turns out automobiles."[12] He also added: *"El cencerro* cannot bear orthopaedic wrappings, however perfect they may be."[13] This aversion to standardization came from the desire to liberate his individual expression.[14] In the final analysis, the poetry in *El cencerro* is free from restrictions because, as he put it, "it is a book that wants to breathe as it pleases."[15]

[6] Güiraldes, "Poesía," *Martín Fierro* (Año IV, No. 39, March 28, 1927), p. 1.
[7] *El cencerro*, p. 93: "Una belleza . . . que he arrancado al mundo para dar a mi alma."
[8] Güiraldes, "Carta a Guillermo de Torre," *Proa* (No. 8, March, 1925, p. 39.
[9] *El cencerro*, p. 87.
[10] "A Jules Supervielle," p. 189.
[11] "Poesía," p. 1.
[12] *Ibid.*, p. 2.   [13] *Ibid.*, p. 1.
[14] "Carta a Guillermo Torre," p. 40:
> . . . me rebelo contra la imposición de una actitud transitoria eregida en apostura de eternidad. Dejémosnos mudar, dejémosnos ser varios en los varios momentos y sobre todo dejémosnos ser diferenciados como seres. ¡Fuera el grupo si ha de ser mordaza, y al diablo las escuelas para mayores de edad! ¿Por qué no para mayores de individualidad?
[15] "Poesía," p. 1: "*El cencerro* . . . es un libro que quiere respirar a su antojo."

Withal, Güiraldes' rebellion against the imprisonment of poetic expression in rigid patterns did not prejudice him against them. On the contrary, he makes use of them with the distinguishing characteristic of complete freedom to choose and vary among them at will. In this connection he wrote:

> All poetic forms are good, if we keep adding new ones to those that have been invented in the past. Thus, an academic precept can be useful, and so can a rough tone when there is a call for it.[16]

The choice of the form, however, is explained by his theory of its relation to the subject matter: "Literary form is determined by its inner meaning."[17] He also said that, in his opinion, there is no such thing as a standard form because he felt that in writing one should obey the dictates of one's small, inner voice.[18] It is apparent in Güiraldes thinking that a significant element in poetic expression is the mood and that the form should vary correspondingly.[19]

Because, therefore, Güiraldes was intent upon expressing the inner meaning of his experience, he had no thought of imitating any school of poetry.[20] More than that, he flatly denied that he intentionally imitated.[21] He recognized, nevertheless,

---

[16] *Ibid.*, p. 2: "Toda forma poética es feliz, agregando a las que se han hecho, las que se hacen y se harán ... Ergo: Una regla académica sirve. Un tono burdo también en ocasión."

[17] *Ibid.*: "La forma obedece a lo que el sujeto dicta desde su significado interior."

[18] "Carta a Guillermo de Torre," p. 89: "No hay patrón. Obedecemos a nuestra pequeña voz interior ..."

[19] "Poesía," p. 1:
> No había ... más que leer "Mi caballo" y "Los Filosofantes". El primero escrito en pasión, buscando lo fuerte y lo ideal en un solo impulso de palabras, el segundo escrito para definir lo grotesco, usando el modo chabacano de los remates que se hacían en la Opera.

[20] De Torre, *loc. cit.*, p. 10:
> No creo, . . . que haya yo hecho nada con premeditación. Ignoraba en absoluto lo que pudiera ser una escuela que lleva como propósito exaltar determinadas formas.

[21] *Ibid.*: "Nunca, . . . me propuse hacer algo moderno, ni clásico, ni romántico."

that the had been influenced by certain writers.[22] Thus it appears that, despite his desire for independence from other patterns of poetry and despite his desire for an entirely new and individual poetic expression, there are in *El cencerro* stylistic trends bearing a striking resemblance to those of some of his favorite writers. Among them are Gustave Flaubert (1821-1880), Paul Verlaine (1844-1896), Tristan Corbière (1845-1875), Stéphane Mallarmé (1842-1898), and Jules Laforgue (1860-1887).

Long before writing *El cencerro de cristal* Güiraldes had been charmed by Flaubert's poetic prose. It was free from the sing-song rime of verse and motivated his preference for prose as a medium of poetic expression.[23] Flaubert's language needed only the slightest nudge to push it into a poem, he said.[24] Wishing to reproduce the same artistic effect, Güiraldes sought to follow his technique. The characteristics of Flaubert which he applied to his own composition were the embellishment of his expression with lyrical simplicity, and a conscious effort to elaborate it into the rhythmic cadences that spring from the language itself.[25] As in Flaubert, Güiraldes' poetic treatment of prose is at times more felt than easily identified. At other times, however, this stylization is evident. In the following passage from his "Esfinge" for example, Güiraldes' lyrical simplicity and rhythmic cadences are clearly perceptible:

> La luna riela su acorde quieto sobre la arena, la arena, la arena.
>
> El acorde quieto se alegra en quebraduras luminosas, sobre y dentro del alabastro del templo-joya, apesadumbrado por el avance de la arena

---

[22] *Ibid.:*
   A exigencias personales se juntaban influencias, y naturalmente, como quien escribe sin saberse escritor, fuí colocando los primeros pasos que después me servirían, revisándolos, para atraer de ellos su lógica como *'métier'* y sus méritos como originalidad.
[23] *Ibid.*, p. 12.   [24] *Ibid.*, p. 10.   [25] *Ibid.*

secular, infinitesimal sepultora, inconsciente, des-
tructora, lenta, pesada, en su constancia de vaga-
bundos oleajes muertos.[26]

Some of Güiraldes' poetry has the quality of Verlaine's.
Although there is no conclusive evidence that Güiraldes consciously made use of Verlaine's poetic techniques, the style
of certain of his compositions is so similar to Verlaine's as
to make it appear that he at least unconsciously reflected them.
The principal characteristics of Verlaine's poetry which appear
in Güiraldes' are the following: Verlaine intentionally suffused the subject matter with vagueness. He avoided words
that described with precision, and chose indefinite terms and
metaphors. Shorn of the artificial verbosity of poetic rhetoric,
his language was reduced to a basic economy of expression.
His style was in consequence light and fluid. The concision
of his descriptions seemed to stem from an aesthetic approach
like that of a Chinese artist who paints with exquisite precise-
ness the essentials only. Verlaine's "Simples Fresques"[27] provide a good illustration of his particular poetic treatment.
Correspondingly, Güiraldes' "Simple"[28] (one of his earliest
compositions, written in Beaulieu in 1912) discloses the
Argentine poet's application of these same stylistic techniques
to his prose poem in Spanish. He suffused the physical scene
in vague half-lights:

> Cerca, todo lo que cae bajo la luz borrosa de
> los faroles. Por trechos, agujeros de obscuridad,

---

[26] *Cf.*, the artistic treatment in this passage from *El cencerro*, p. 110, with
the lyrical simplicity and rhythm of the following excerpts from Flaubert's
Salammbô (Paris, 1874), p. 47, and *La tentation de Saint Antoine* (Paris,
1921), p. 2:

> La lune se levait à ras de flots, et, sur la ville encore couverte
> de ténèbres, des points lumineux, des blancheurs brillaient...
> Les boules de verre sur les toits des temples rayonnaient, çà
> et là, comme de gros diamants.
>
> Mais du côté du désert, comme des plages qui se succéderaient,
> d'immenses ondulations parallèles d'un blond cendré s'étirent
> les unes derrières les autres, en montant toujours.

[27] Paul Verlaine, *Poèmes Choisis* (Paris, 1942), pp. 79-80.

[28] *El cencerro*, p. 51.

108 GIOVANNI PREVITALI

pedazos de desconocido, donde la imaginación
puede creerlo todo.[29]

Avoiding words that define with precision, he describes with
indefinite metaphors: "El cielo huyente,"[30] a small path is
pictured in the simplest terms: "Solo, muy solo, va el camino
pequeño."[31] His language is freed from artificial ornamen-
tation and reduced to a basic economy of expression: "Cielo.
Montaña."[32] Furthermore, the concision of his sentences (in
which he has omitted the verbs) are like the delicate strokes
of an artist's brush that give the painting lightness and fluid-
ity: "Aldea modesta, mejillón de la cima."[33] It almost seems
that Güiraldes transposed the style of Verlaine's verse into
poetic prose.

It was Tristan Corbière, however, who set Güiraldes the
example of complete liberation of his expression from lyrical
language.[34] Corbière's poetry bristled with life because he
freed it from the restrictions of propriety and conventional
literary terms to express his rebellious spirit. It was full of
slang, words of the gutter, gross epithets, unexpected neol-
ogisms, and daring imagery. In fact it was unpoetic. Furthermore, corresponding to his impetuous character, his verse was
abrupt and his style often succinct, even telegraphic. The
essence of Corbière's poetic sentiment was not in his language
but in the human emotion that lay behind it. Indeed, his rough
language seemed to intensify by contrast his flashes of human
tenderness. Similarly, Güiraldes' idea of poetry was antithetic
to the lyrical melliflousness of romantic poets as he so clearly
expressed in "Una palabra a los lunáticos."[35] Among Güi-

[29] *Cf., Poèmes Choisis*, p. 79:
> La fuite est verdâtre et rose
> Des collines et des rampes
> Dans un demi-jour de lampes
> Qui vient brouiller toute chose.

[30] *Cf., Poèmes Choisis*, p. 80.
[31] *Cf., Poèmes Choisis*, p. 80.
[32] *Cf., Poèmes Choisis*, p. 80.
[33] *Cf., Poèmes Choisis*, p. 80.
[34] Luis Francisco Bernárdez, "La poesía de Güiraldes," *Buenos Aires Literaria* (Año I, Nov., 1952), p. 35.
[35] *El cencerro*, p. 37.

raldes' poems the one that bears the closest resemblance in style
to Corbière's is "Chacarera."[36] Although he has followed a
pattern of short alternating prose passages and verse, the
notable characteristic of the poem is the spontaneity and
absolute freedom of expression. Both the prose and the verse
are in short, abrupt lines, often without verbs. The style is
clearly elliptical. Even the little commentaries in parentheses
are similar to Corbière's asides in "Hidalgo."[37] Also like
Corbière's, it is free of all aesthetic and poetic artifice. Instead, the language is deliberately commonplace, strong,
slangy, and realistic.[38] The subject matter is merely a poor
farmer's mud-hut, typical in the Argentine pampa, and a
loaded ox-cart on its way to market. Indeed, the poem has
no lyrical quality, at least none in the established tradition.
But, in spite of its unpoetic character, it throbs with human
feeling. This was apparently Güiraldes' design as he confess-
es at the conclusion.[39] In short, Güiraldes had cleared away
all artificial adornment and put his finger upon the essence
of poetic sentiment: the human element. Furthermore, he
found that this emotion expressed itself in the reality of
simple, every-day life and through plain language. As Corbière did, Güiraldes, too, disclosed the truth: *"De l'âme et
pas de violon."*[40]

In Mallarmé, Güiraldes saw a friend and companion in
his own spirit of adventure toward the conquest of new
worlds of poetic expression. He shared with Mallarmé not
only his dislike for the outworn lyrical styles of the past but

---

[36] *Ibid.*, p. 22.
[37] Tristan Corbière, *Les Amours Jaunes* (Berkeley and Los Angeles, 1945),
p. 109.
[38] In "Chacarera," *El cencerro*, p. 24, Güiraldes speaks of a few trees in the
following terms:
    Son por ahora el meadero de la perrada.
Notice also the slang when, speaking of barnyard chickens, he says:
    Y si las pilla el viejo, las cascotea de lo lindo.
[39] *El cencerro*, p. 25:
    No he hecho una descripción poética, lo cual no impide que este
    día sea tan humano como el día de la coronación de Jorge V,
    rey de Inglaterra y emperador de las Indias.
[40] *Les Amours Jaunes*, p. 38.

also his preoccupation with the creation of something beyond the ordinary, for something new. Mallarmé had already expressed it symbolically in his poem "Au Seul Souci de Voyager."[41] In it Mallarmé describes the spirit of the explorer who turns his ship's bows away from the easy riches of known lands of poetry into the hazardous dark unknown beyond. How closely Güiraldes' own spirit of adventure corresponds to that of Mallarmé can be seen best in his poem "Viajar," which ends with the famous phrase *"Tener alma de proa."*[42]

> Asimilar horizontes. ¿Qué importa si el mundo
> es plano o redondo?
> Imaginarse como disgregado en la atmósfera, que
> lo abraza todo. Crear visiones de lugares venideros
> y saber que siempre serán lejanos, inalcanzables
> como todo ideal.
> Huir lo viejo.
> Mirar el filo que corta una [sic] agua espumosa
> y pesada.
> Arrancarse de lo conocido.
> Beber lo que viene.
> **Tener alma de proa.**

In fact, Mallarmé did lead Güiraldes beyond the horizon of ordinary poetry into his dream world of revery which he described in his "Prose pour des Eisseintes."[43] Güiraldes also created this poetic environment of revery. He, too, evoked the dream atmosphere of which the realities of time, place, and clear identities had no part. It was a poetic treament he wished to apply to prose as, in fact, appears in "El verbo":

> ¿En la tierra, por la edad de piedra? ¿En el pa-
> raíso, antes de la expulsión?
> Qué sé yo. Pero lo he visto, como veo mi pluma

---

[41] Stéphane Mallarmé, *Poems* (New York, 1951), p. 114:
  Au seul souci de voyager
  Outre une Inde splendide et trouble
  Ce salut soit le messager
  Du temps, cap que ta poupe double.
[42] *El cencerro,* p. 49.
[43] *Poems,* p. 141.

amar la virginidad blanca, del papel.
Un lago quieto, como espejo, que árboles multi-
formes esmaltan de verde.
¿Ambiente? ... El de una flor en eclosión.[44]

A notable feature of Mallarmé's poetry was his technique
of "sublimation." The process was to dilute the concrete into
the abstract, the fact into the idea. An example of this appears
in "L'Après-midi d'un Faune" where the assault of the fawn
on a naiad is described in vague metaphors.[45] Likewise, Güiraldes in "La hora del milagro" veils a similar human experience in abstract imagery:

> Serás por un momento el eje de las rotaciones,
> omniversales, que por los espacios verifican la pa-
> labra "amor."[46]

Güiraldes applied this technique in the stylistic treament of
other poems. He made use of metaphors that were abstract
and indirect. Not only were the images unclear, but they
were often open to multiple interpretations. On the other
hand, the very multiplicity and vagueness of their meaning
gave them a power of suggestion that reflected a state of
mind or an emotional experience. In "Proa" he humorously
describes his failure to find such a metaphor to express the
billowing ocean:

> El mar arrea cordilleras renovadas, que colum-
> pian al vapor en cuya proa frenetizo de borrasca.
> Busco una metáfora pluriforme e inmensa; algo
> como fijar el alma caótica, que se empenacha de
> pedrería.
> ¿Cómo decir? ... Mar ... mar ... y mientras in-
> sulfo el cráneo de espacio para cantarle mi visión,
> el insolente me escupió la cara.[47]

---

[44] *El cencerro*, p. 126.
[45] *Poems*, p. 80:
> Car a piene j'allais cacher un rire
> Ardent sous les replis d'une seule ...
[46] *El cencerro*, p. 135.
[47] *Ibid.*, p. 52.

But he was more fortunate when he came upon expressions such as,

Sed de horizonte[48]
alma de proa[49]

In "L'Après-midi d'un Faune" Mallarmé recast the theme of man's pursuit of woman into an allegory. The faun is the symbol of man and the nymph that of woman. In "La hora del milagro," Güiraldes, too, transposed the same theme into an allegory. He also symbolized man and woman in the images of faun and nymph. In his poem "Al hombre que pasó" he had already applied this poetic treatment to a native subject matter: the gaucho. Furthermore, he transformed the concrete into the abstract, the gaucho into an idea:

Símbolo pampeano y hombre verdadero,
Generoso guerreo,
Amor, coraje
¡Salvaje![50]

It is not without significance that Güiraldes referred to the gaucho as "Símbolo pampeano." Later, in *Don Segundo Sombra,* he again represented the figure of the gaucho as a symbol.

Of special interest is the conclusion of "L'après-midi d'un Faune." As the naiads disappear, Mallarmé has them fade away into the deepening twilight.[51] Similarly, in the conclusion of "Al hombre que pasó," the spirit of the gaucho disappears into the darkness of the night:

Pero hoy el gaucho, vencido,
Galopando hacia el olvido,
Se perdió.
Su triste ánima en pena
Se fue, una noche serena.[52]

As already indicated, it is an artistic treatment that Güiraldes

[48] *Ibid.,* p. 13.   [49] *Ibid.,* p. 49.   [50] *Ibid.,* p. 29.
[51] *Poems,* p. 88:
          Couple, adieu, je vais voir l'ombre que tu devins.
[52] *El cencerro,* p. 31.

used also at the end of his gaucho tale "Nocturno." It will appear again later at the conclusion of *Don Segundo Sombra*.

Güiraldes read a great deal of Laforgue while writing *El cencerro*.[53] Like Mallarmé, Laforgue also detested the banal in the form and substance of poetry. He, too, was motivated by an urge to seek a new expression and a new subject matter. In other respects, however, he differed widely from Mallarmé. While Mallarmé transformed reality into a dream, Laforgue evoked the reality of the subconscious. Mallarmé's imagery tended toward poetic, abstract metaphors but Laforgue used realistic, concrete imagery of every-day life.

Laforgue's poetry is elliptical in style. It is full of brief descriptions often without verbs, producing the impression of a succession of word paintings in short colorful strokes. His imagery is often obscure and obviously intended to shock. Examples of Laforgue's imagery that appealed to Güiraldes are the epithets and appositions in "L'Imitation de Notre Dame la Lune"[54] with which he vituperates the moon: "Litanies des Premiers Quartiers de la Lune":

> Blanc médaillon
> Astre fossile[55]

"Clair de Lune":

> Oeil stérile comme le suicide
> Crâne glacé
> pillules des léthargies finales[56]

"Litanies des Derniers Quartiers de la Lune":

> Eucharistie
> De l'Arcadie
> Hôtel garni
> De l'infini.[57]

Although they give the impression of an intent to ridicule, they are in reality an expression of Laforgue's bitterness. It is

[53] Angel Battistessa, "Güiraldes y Laforgue," *Nosotros* (XVI, Feb., 1942), p. 159.
[54] Jules Laforgue, *Oeuvres Complètes, Poésie II* (Paris, n.d.), pp. 9-77.
[55] *Ibid.*, p. 12.   [56] *Ibid.*, p. 15.   [57] *Ibid.*, pp. 74, 78.

apparent that this is the direct source both of Lugones' and of Güiraldes's imagery of the moon:

Lugones:

> Ombligo del firmamento
> luminoso huevo
> gran perol[58]

Güiraldes:

> ronda vejiga
> pulcro botón de calzoncillo[59]

The essence of Laforgue's poetry is not the use of eccentric imagery, but the evocation of a mood from the subconscious. He also created a vague emotional climate by means of the technique of the refrain. In "Les Complaintes,"[60] for example, he evoked an atmosphere of childhood reminiscenses by repeating suggestions of French nursery rimes and of the rhithmic tunes of the street hurdy-gurdy. This same technique appeared in Güiraldes' writings for the first time in two of his poems. In "Los filosofantes," Güiraldes ridiculed the pedantry of pedagogues, one of his pet hates, by representing them as elephants. He produces the effect of the heavy, slow, monotonous motion of elephants walking by repeating variations of the same refrain, as follows:

> Los filosofantes
> Elefantes,
> Andantes,
> Se llevan las paredes por delante.
>
> LOS FILOSOFANTES
> SON GENTE IMPORTANTE
> CON PASO ELEFANTE
> EN RITMO DE ANDANTE.[61]

---

[58] Leopoldo Lugones, *Lunario sentimental* (Buenos Aires, 1909), pp. 28, 29, 61.
[59] *El cencerro*, p. 45.
[60] *Oeuvres Complètes. Poésies I* (Paris, n.d.), pp. 55-198.
[61] *El cencerro*, pp. 81, 82.

Similarly, in "Chacarera," the *andante* rhythm of the slow moving ox-cart is maintained throughout the poem by repeating the couplet:

La seria carreta
De bolsas repleta.[62]

Laforgue also applied this technique to his prose. In both "Salomé"[63] and "Pan et la Syrinx"[64] it occurred like a kind of theme song producing a sensation of progressive movement. In "Pan et la Syrinx" in particular, the repetition of "en chasse, en chasse!" charged the whole narrative with the rhythm of an *allure*. Later, as will be seen in *Don Segundo Sombra,* Güiraldes also used the technique of the refrain in prose.

Laforgue recast the old themes of Salomé and of Pan into his own prose style. Güiraldes, too, tried his hand at interpreting them according to his concept of a poetic prose style. His "Salomé" reads as if he were retelling Laforgue's "Salomé". But, he condensed the similar subject matter into an elliptical style that was closer to the style of Laforgue's poetry than to the style of Laforgue's prose:

Un trono.
Púrpura y oropeles,
Niágaras de seda.[65]

And, in describing his impression of the veiled *danseuse,* he wrote with similar brevity:

Desnudeces opacas, a hacer tambolear pilastras.
Es una gasa, una nube.[66]

At the same time, Güiraldes added a pinch of humor to this artistic exercise. He yielded to the temptation of poking fun at Salome and took delight in startling the reader with a succession of bold images: "Un gusanito humano, sin sedas

[62] *Ibid.,* pp. 23, 25.
[63] Laforgue, *Moralités Légendaires* (Paris, 1902), pp. 135-173.
[64] *Ibid.,* pp. 175-212.
[65] *El cencerro,* p. 107.
[66] *Ibid.*

ni oropeles...[67] Finally, with irreverent mischievousness, he
gave the ending a humorous twist from his own fantasy:

> Pero, ¡oh magia! La cabeza, con repentina deci-
> sión, asciende al cielo, con Salomé aferrada a su
> barba.[68]

A remarkable artistic effect in Laforgue's "Pan et la Syrinx"
is the gradation of the daylight from bright morning at the
beginning to dusk at the end. At the conclusion, the nymph
disappears into the gradually increasing darkness of twilight.[69]
Here again is the shadowy fading away that has been seen
previously in Mallarmé's "L'Après-midi d'un Faune." While
in that instance it appeared in poetry, Laforgue applied it to
prose. It is the same artistic treatment which Güiraldes used
in describing the disappearance of the gaucho in "Nocturno,"
in "Al hombre que pasó," and finally in *Don Segundo Sombra*.

Because *El cencerro de cristal* reflects the styles of other
poets, attempts have been made to classify it in relation to
the trends of contemporary poetry. Güiraldes has been described as belonging to *post-modernismo*[70] and as a *"precursor
del ultraísmo porteño."*[71] In general, he has been placed between *modernismo* and *vanguardismo*. Certainly, this designation corresponds to the chronological position of *El cencerro*

---

[67] *Ibid.*, pp. 107-108.
[68] *Ibid.*, p. 109.
[69] *Moralités Légendaires*, pp. 200-206:

> La plaine jusqu'à la colline bleauâtre s'étend, vaste comme une
> après-midi qui finira bien par se fondre dans le soir.
> Et peu à peu, car tout marche, le soleil décline. La pauvre nym-
> phe sent venir le crépuscule qui tisse les invisibles mailles de
> ses filets.
> . . . .
> Ces ébats d'une minute ont ridé à peine les moires crépuscu-
> laires de la rivière lente et mortuaire sous le beau ciel du soir.
> Cela c'est fini sans un mot. C'est fini.
> Et c'est le soir, le soir qui ne porte pas conseil.
> Oh! Là-bas, en face au ras de l'eau, est-ce encore sa tête adorée
> qui regarde encore immobile, ou simplement un bouquet de
> lys d'eau qui jouit dans son genre?
> C'est fini, la rivière s'endort.

[70] Arturo Torres-Rioseco, "Ricardo Güiraldes," *Atenea* (LVII, Sept., 1939),
p. 482.
[71] Guillermo de Torre, *Literaturas europeas de vanguardia* (Madrid, 1925),
p. 80.

(1915) which falls between Rubén Darío's *Prosas profanas*
(1896) and the *Manifiesto de ultraísmo* (1919). Güiraldes
himself, however, made his position clear. It will be recalled
that, commenting on *El cencerro de cristal,* he objected to the
relegation of his poetry to any school or trend. He denied
his style was "*decadente,*" or "*simbolista,*" or "*futurista,*" or
"*ultraísta.*"[72]

The main influence of the French symbolists upon Güiraldes' writing did not stem so much from their particular
techniques as it did from the more fundamental principle of
freely expressing the inner meaning of the subject. In doing
this, Güiraldes availed himself of any stylistic device that he
believed best corresponded to that purpose. For example, he
expressed the virility of the gaucho in forceful, abbreviated
language, and the beauty of nature in more lyrical terms.

In his poems Güiraldes had given free rein to the expression
of himself.[73] The different moods, therefore, reflect various
aspects of Güiraldes' personality. Thus, to understand the
"*significado interior*" of the composition is to understand
Güiraldes. Although there is an occasional element of *rail-
lerie,* there is no bitterness or negativeness. Among the aspects
of his personality that appear in *El cencerro* are (1) the
joyously assertive and optimistic spirit of adventure, his
"*alma de proa,*" (2) his love of the pampa, of nature, and
of the gaucho, (3) his sense of cosmic harmony, (4) his fertile and colorful fantasy, and (5) his humor. In the last regard,
he said: "*Me he reído sobre todo de mí mismo, y a fe que me
ha hecho bien.*"[74]

En *El cencerro,* Güiraldes achieved two ambitions. The
first was the evolution of his poetic style, the second was the
application of his poetic style to prose. For this reason *El
cencerro de cristal* is of significance in understanding Güiraldes' later writings.

[72] "Poesía," p. 1.
[73] Battistessa, "Güiraldes y Laforgue," p. 159: "En el cencerro desfogaba
mi fantasía y mis grandes enviones en una auto-exaltación ritmada."
[74] *Poesía,* p. 2.

XXII

Rosaura

Rosaura[1] is a novelette of eighty-one pages which first was published in book form in 1922 in a non-commercial edition, printed by Francisco A. Colombo at San Antonio de Areco. It is divided into twenty very brief chapters averaging about two and one half pages in length. The theme is the foolishness of sentimental romance and is similar to that in "Arrabalera,"[2] the story in which Güiraldes ridicules melodramatic young lovers. His intention clearly is to make a character sketch of just such a type, Rosaura.

The story is briefly the following: The setting is Lobos, a small town about fifty miles from Buenos Aires, lost to the world in its provincial mentality and boring monotony. Lobos resembles San Antonio de Areco,[3] at about the turn of the century. Rosaura, the principal character, is the product of this environment. She is a pretty girl at the age of incipient womanhood. She is also naïve and romantic. The important daily event in the lives of the inhabitants is the arrival of the six-thirty train from Buenos Aires. Drawn by this attraction, Rosaura and two like-minded maidens, dressed in their Sunday best, proceed daily to the station to parade up and down the platform amid the general excitement of the arrival and departure of the train. One day, as the three girls brashly stare through the train windows at the passengers, they catch the eye of an elegantly dressed young man, who responds to their stares with a polite nod. Rosaura, who is impressed by his distinguished appearance and the cosmopolitan air of the passenger, returns each day to exchange glances with him. He is Carlos Ramallo, the son of a prominent *estanciero*.

---

[1] The edition consulted is *Rosaura (novela corta) y siete cuentos* (Buenos Aires, Editorial Losada, S. A., 1952). The pages indicated in this section refer to the same edition.
[2] *Cuentos de muerte y de sangre*, pp. 149-152.
[3] Ismael B. Colombo, *Ricardo Güiraldes*, p. 76.

When Rosaura learns that he is coming to the next dance at the local social club to meet her, she dreams of an idyllic romance. Clothed in an especially made party dress, Rosaura meets Carlos at the dance and innocently reveals her infatuation. Carlos, the while, with urbane manner and gallant remarks, encourages her illusion. Not unattracted himself by Rosaura, he meets her regularly on Sunday evenings at the station platform and strolls around the town square with her as the young enamoured are wont to do. In due time Carlos tires of Rosaura and casually announces his departure for Europe. He leaves not without assuring her, however, of his early return. Rosaura believes implicitly in his sincerity and clings to the thought of their reunion. But Carlos fails to return. The blow falls when she sees him on the six-thirty train with another woman. Soon afterward, as the train pulls out of Lobos with Carlos and the woman aboard, Rosaura, dressed in the same party gown and clasping the withered flowers of a bouquet he had given her, throws herself before the oncoming locomotive.

The merit of the novelette does not lie in the simple story of this melodramatic infatuation, but in the characterization of Rosaura. With this purpose Güiraldes has made use of several artistic techniques, the most noticeable of which are (1) gradation, (2) symbolism, (3) suggestive imagery, and (4) the technique of the refrain.

Rosaura is not described all at once upon her entry into the narration. She is portrayed gradually as the story unfolds and in a manner in which her personality grows on the reader. Since the characterization is more important than her physical appearance, Güiraldes has concentrated on the representation of her personality through a description of her emotions.

The two conflicting forces in *Rosaura* are the sentiments of the girl and heartless destiny. Güiraldes has represented them in symbols. Rosaura's feelings run parallel to the evolution of the garden from budding springtime to withering fall, with the course of the seasons corresponding to Rosaura's nascent, flowering, fulsome and unrequited love. The mechanical progress of the locomotive which finally passes over the body of Rosaura symbolizes the indifference of destiny.

The narration is ornamented throughout with imagery. In the main the imagery is of two kinds. The first is with the intent to render the description more effective. An instance of this is "Los guantes de abultada costura fingían amputadas manos de indio" (p. 17). The second kind of imagery is intended to evoke an emotional climate by means of suggestion. An example of this is the creation of an atmosphere of amorous entanglement and loving embraces by means of the suggestive descriptions of the clinging vines: "caían como delgadas y largas boas sensuales, complicadas enredaderas voraces de abrazos." (p. 21).

The technique of the refrain is used by Güiraldes to strengthen an impression by reiteration.[4] He makes a lavish use of it to intensify not only one impression but many. The three which Güiraldes emphasizes more than others are the monotony of the environment, the provincial simplicity of the girls, and the inexorability of destiny. The first consists in a repetition of variations of the theme of the uneventful passage of time with such phrases as "Barranca abajo de los días que siempre caminan, repítense las horas." The second is suggested by the reiteration of the analogous descriptions of the girl's simple dresses, as "Tres pasaron del brazo marchando con pausa; una de celeste caramelo, otra de rosa caramelo, otra de amarillo caramelo." And the third impression is intensified by the repetition of the symbol of the train in terms such as "la indiferente máquina viajadora, para cuyo ojo ciclópico el horizonte no es una idea." Each of these impressions is repeated eight times. This stylistic device produces the effect of a refrain in a poem. As will be recalled, it is a technique that appeared in Laforgue and was also used in *El cencerro de cristal.*

[4] Battistessa, "Güiraldes y Laforgue," *Nosotros* (XVI, Feb., 1942), p. 146.

From the exaggeratedly romantic tone of Rosaura it is apparent that Güiraldes wrote the story with his tongue in his cheek. He has not only satirized the type of person represented by Rosaura, he has also ridiculed the genre of the romantic novelette. Almost imperceptibly, however, a serious note appears between the lines. It is the suggestion of Güiraldes' own disillusionment from the failure of his literary aspirations at the time. This throught rises from his words of commiseration for Rosaura in the line that reads "En su fe sencilla por las promesas de un más allá superior estribó toda su desgracia." (p. 72).

XXIII

Raucho

The novel *Raucho, momentos de una juventud contemporánea*[1] is a fictional biography of a young Argentine of the same background as that of Güiraldes. Written in the third person, it describes in eight stages the life of Raucho from early childhood to about twenty-five years of age. The theme is that of the prodigal son, adapted in time and place to Argentina and Paris in the years immediately prior to 1912.

The plot is a follows: Don Leandro, a widower, takes his two small sons to live with him at the *estancia*. The boys are Raucho and his older brother Alberto, who are about five and six years old. Raucho's first impression of the pampa are its silence, its natural beauty, and its serenity. As time passes, the childhood tales he hears and the first books he reads set him dreaming of fabled heroes who perform deeds of courage. The two boys, dressed as little gauchos, accompany their father on horseback as he supervises the estate. They are impressed with the feats of the cattlemen whom they imagine to be traditional gauchos. In their enthusiasm to emulate the ranch hands, the boys ride daily across the pampa, practice the gaucho skills with lassos and *boleadoras,* and become strong, hearty and full of combativeness.

Raucho, at ten years of age, is sent to school in Buenos Aires, where he remains until he is about seventeen. It seemed like an imprisonment to him. He begins his scholastic career asserting his spirit of independence and ends it rebelling against academic authority.

Upon his return to the *estancia* the first sight of the open pampa fills him with a feeling of liberation. He spends the seasons on the ranch learning to be an administrator with

[1] The edition consulted was published in Madrid by Espasa-Calpe in 1932. The pages indicated in this section refer to the same edition.

the help of the head man. His fondness for the cattlemen
motivates him to be not their boss but a fellow gaucho. He
enters into the spirit of their work which is "toda risa, todo
vigor," and participates as one of them in the round-up, the
roping, the branding, and the sheep shearing. In this daily
outdoor life of hard work Raucho fulfills the scope of his
young manhood and is content. Furthermore, his world is
completed with the favors of a country girl, Carmencita.

As work slows down in the winter season, he becomes en-
grossed in reading the works of Lorrain,[2] Maupassant, and
Verlaine among other Freench authors. His imagination carries him away to the Parisian environment of amorous affairs,
and, drawn by the attractions of the city, he moves to Buenos
Aires. After imitating the ways of a Bohemian artist for a
while, he joins the fashionable Jockey Club and becomes a
typical young profligate. He soon discards all thought of
Carmencita for a more sophisticated affair with Jacqueline,
a professional French mistress. Tiring of this existence, he
longs to visit Paris and extracts from his father a reluctant
consent to let him go to France.

In Paris he enters into the night life of the various *rendez-
vous* and *boîtes*. At Maxime's he entices Germaine, a public
dancing partner, away from her protector to become his
mistress. He soon abandons her for Nina, a popular and well-
known actress. Their life together follows the course of the
dreamed Parisian romance until Raucho begins to flirt with
other women. In a drunken bedroom scene Raucho flies into
a rage and beats Nina black and blue, whereupon their re-
lationship degenerates into mutual hatred. Perceiving the
grotesque reality behind his illusion, he wants to free himself
of his degrading existence, but he no longer has the strength
of character to do so.

When his money runs out, he writes to his father, demand-
ing his share of the inheritance, which he receives and

[2] Probably Jean Lorrain, pseudonym of Paul Alexandre Martin Duval (1856-
1906), French novelist and playwright.

squanders in loose living. More spineless than ever and still attached to Nina, he loses all sense of moral decency. Deceiving Nina, he frequents other women while living on her earnings. He degenerates into a state of stupor from constant drunkenness and drug addiction. Nina leaves him for her former lover, and Raucho, despondent and completely demoralized, becomes ill and delirious. He is found in this condition by his friend Rodolfo, who has come from Argentina to bring him home. When the liner docks at Buenos Aires, Raucho, humbled and remforseful, is welcomed by his brother Alberto. The novel ends with a picture of Raucho sitting at dusk under a willow tree by the river, where he falls asleep with a feeling of the serenity of the pampa.

The story of Raucho has been said to be an autobiography of Güiraldes.[3] To some extent this is true. Like Raucho, Güiraldes, as a child, lived with his older brother Manolo on their father's *estancia* near Buenos Aires until he went to school. Similarly, his love for the freedom of the pampa caused him to hate the imprisonment of school. There is no doubt that the picture of the young administrator with a passion for the ranch life of work, vigor and *brío* is a portrait of young Güiraldes at the time he lived at La Porteña bertween graduation from San Ignacio and matriculation at the university. Güiraldes, too, extracted a reluctant consent from his father to live in Paris. Some of the corroborating facts are the following: The description of the *estancia* and its buildings in *Raucho* corresponds in detail to that at La Porteña. The ranch hands are authentic individuals who lived on the estate in Güiraldes' boyhood. Güiraldes even called them by their true names. He mentions them again later in his dedication in *Don Segundo Sombra*. They are Víctor Taboada, Ramón Cisneros, José Hernández, Nicasio

---

[3] Ismael B. Colombo, *Ricardo Güiraldes,* p. 17; Roberto F. Giusti, "Raucho (etc.)," *Nosotros* (XXVII, 1917), pp. 391-394; Valery Larbaud, "Ricardo Güiraldes," *La Nouvelle Revue Française* (XXX, Jan., 1928), p. 134; Antonio Pagés Larraya, "*Don Segundo Sombra* y el retorno," *Buenos Aires Literaria* (Año I, Nov., 1952), pp. 21-32.

Cano, Crisanto Núñez, and don Segundo.

Raucho, however, cannot be called a true biography of Güiraldes.[4] It is in the first place a novel, and, although some of it may correspond to reality, it is largely fictional. Indeed, the chapters devoted to life in Paris are the invention of fantasy. Güiraldes himself indicated this when he said that in writing *Raucho* his intention was to describe the Parisian environment before he knew it and to compare it later with reality.[5]

For the purpose of criticism the narrative will be divided into two parts. The first is that devoted to life in the pampa, and the second to that describing Raucho's experiences in Buenos Aires and in Paris. Each part differs from the other not only in subject matter but also in emotional climate and in style.

Concerned with the pampa are the prologue and the chapters called "Infancia," "Trabajo," and "Solución." Two emotional climates emerge from them. The first stems from Raucho's impressions of nature. Needless to say, Güiraldes attributed to Raucho his own poetic experiences in the Argentine countryside. Most notable among these are its aesthetic effects:

> Oro y acacia y verde compacto (p. 14);

its harmony:

> ¡Oh! vivir en la grande alma serena de aquella
> tierra (p. 16);

its silence:

> ¡Oh! la sorpresa contemplativa del silencio (p. 14);

and the sensory impressions of its seasons:

> Algo como un misterio de eclosión ensopaba el
> aire (p. 39).

The second emotional climate proceeds from the descrip-

---

[4] Larbaud, "Poètes Espagnols et Hispano-Américains Contemporains," *La Nouvelle Revue Française* (XV, July-December, 1920), p. 144.
[5] Guillermo de Torre, "Una carta-autobiografía de Ricardo Güiraldes," *Buenos Aires Literaria* (Nov., 1952), p. 14.

tions of the ranch hands as they work with cattle and horses. In essence, it is an attitude of joy of combat and a determination to conquer, and is transmitted from a series of expressions such as the following:

Moral dominador (p. 90).
Buscador de victorias (p. 90).
Alboroto de alegría y prurito de lucirse en los trabajos (p. 93).
Todo era risa, vigor (p. 95).
Pregusto de lucha (p. 96).

The style corresponding to the representation of nature is poetic. There are, in fact, five descriptions of the pampa at different seasons of the year which are written in the form of brief poems in prose, each printed on a separate page. Conversely, the style of physical combat and *brío* is abrupt and matter-of-fact, creating a continuous staccato effect. The alternation of the contrasting styles produces a refreshing duality. Both, however, have certain common characteristics: brevity and imagery.

In his determination to write concisely, Güiraldes has eliminated all rhetorical embellishments. Sometimes he has omitted verbs and limited the description to word paintings as, for example:

Nubes macizas, chorreantes en su parte inferior
sobre el fondo topacio del cielo. (p. 13).

There are sequences of short expressions, written in brief, strong strokes as, for instance:

Un *torcido* para mayor seguridad de las manos.
Hacer la armada, agregar un rollo y aguantar la
broma que duda . . . (p. 97).

Imagery is the predominant feature in the descriptions of life in the pampa. Güiraldes has used various techniques to represent different aspects of the environment. The activities of the inhabitants and ordinary occurances are pictured in realistic images drawn from the rustic surroundings:

... Caían al lecho pesados y blandos,
como *matras* sudadas (p. 52).

Related to the poetic representation of the pampa is the attribution of human characteristics to nature. Aspects of the
pampa are described in images some of which are physical
and some of which are emotional human attributes:

El campo se estremece de sol (p. 108).
... el tiempo está pensativo (p. 27).

A more subtle technique is the use of abstract imagery to
suggest intangible qualities of an aesthetic or emotional order.
The treatment is applied to material objects:

... la cincha de cuero, blanca como una alegría
p. 27).

It is also applied to human emotions:

Raucho . . . se duerme . .. crucificado de calma
(p. 256).

And the same poetic technique is used to sublimate nature:

Y los mirasoles, blancos más allá del blanco,
insubstanciales como aspiraciones de pureza (p.
148).

The poetic style of Güiraldes' descriptions of nature bears
a close resemblance to the artistic treatment of the same subject in some of the prose poems of *El cencerro de cristal.* In
certain instances the similarity of the imagery is striking. In
the passage on page 147 of *Raucho,* for example, the bird in
flight is described as follows:

Puro y tierno el flamenco se alzaba, como rezago
de aurora . . . y un rojo aletazo de vela trabu-
chando susurraba apenas una tímida explosión de
color fino.

In the prose poem "Amanece," on page 15 of *El cencerro de
cristal,* a bird in flight is pictured in similar terms:

Un churrinche, gota de púrpura, emprende su
viaje azul.

Furthermore, the passage on page 255 of *Raucho* illustrates

Güiraldes' elaboration of his prose in the rhythmic cadenaces
of a poem:

> La tarde, viene, viene. El monte se turba de
> noche . . .

It recalls the artistic treatment of the same subject matter in
the poem "Quietud" on page 26 of *El cencerro de cristal*:

> Tarde, tarde
> Cae la tarde,
> Larga, larga
> Se aletarga
> En derrumbe silencioso
> Como mirada en un pozo.

The criticism of the second part, namely that related to
Raucho's life in the city, refers to the chapters called "Colegio," "París," "Nina," and "Abandono." In sharp contrast
with the emotional climate of the pampa, the atmosphere of
the city is sordid. Three of the environments described are a
house of prostitution in Buenos Aires, the boring existence
at the Jockey Club, and the night life of Paris *rendez-vous*
and *boîtes*. The merit of these passages is the impression of
authenticity produced by the realistic descriptive detail. The
other parts of the narration, however, are unconvincing in
spite of their realistic presentation. Specifically, they are the
liaison with Jacqueline, the affair with Nina, and Raucho's
degeneration. They are reminiscent in subject and in tone of
a similar class of narration, the outstanding examples of which
are Emil Zola's *Nana* (1880) and, in Argentina, Eugenio
Cambeceres' *Sin rumbo* (1885). The melodramatic description
of the drunken bedroom scene in which Raucho beats Nina
seems more inspired by the theme of the traditional *dance
des apaches* in Paris *bistros* than by reality. The degeneration
of Raucho to the point where he becomes delirious from a life
of women, alcohol, and drugs corresponds to fantastic concepts
of depraved Bohemian poets of the *Rive Gauche*. Obviously
Güiraldes viewed such experiences with antipathy. His lack

of nostalgic and affective sentiments toward life in the city accounts for the absence of an emotional climate similar to that in his descriptions of the pampa environment.

The style of the narration of city life is predominantly matter-of-fact. This is due not so much to a difference in stylistic techniques as it is to the unpoetic nature of the subject matter. The expression continues to be characteristically brief and concise. The use of imagery is less frequent and less poetic. Most common are the realistic images which emphasize certain aspects of mundane women:

> ... los senos ... como *tabaqueras de buche* (p. 80).

In this class is Güiraldes' description of Montmartre:

> Odió a Montmartre, que la noche enciende como
> sexo luminoso de ardores lúbricos insaciables, de
> quien había ignorado la lepra (p. 238).

The realism of the imagery in this passage parallels that in his poem "Pierrot," on page 61 of *El cencerro de cristal,* where the same subject is pictured as follows:

> Su dedo, fosforescente, abre en París la herida
> luminosa de Montmartre.

Here and there Güiraldes' intent to poetize a few passages is evident from the occasional use of abstract imagery. An example of this technique is:

> El carruaje corría en la noche como un destino
> (p. 213).

Indeed, the imagery of this subject corresponds to a remarkably similar passage in the prose poem "Verano" on page 59 of *El cencerro de cristal*:

> De tiempo en tiempo, coches pasan, en rectilíneos
> destinos.

Introduced in pages 164 through 169 and differing in tone from the rest of this part of the narration is a prose poem. It is a fantasy in the form of a dream in which Raucho passes in review various classes of women. These are the midinettes, the models, the mannequins, and the temptresses, who parade before him, beckoning and calling him until he is enticed into a passionate involvement. The treament of this passage reveals certain stylistic techniques already seen in *El cencerro de cristal*. Among them are some that are characteristic of Laforgue and Mallarmé. As with Laforgue there is the creation of a lyrical effect by the repetition of a refrain. In the present instance, the refrain consists of the repetition of the beckoning words and of the description of each group of women, and vaguely suggests the sing-song quality of popular music. There is also a conscious use of the technique of abstraction like that in Mallarmé's "L'Après-midi d'un Faune." As has already been seen in "La hora del milagro," here again Güiraldes has described an amorous detail in abstract terms:

> ... su caída al través de todos los precipicios del
> goce (p. 169).

In spite of the abstract imagery Güiraldes has failed to create a dream atmosphere. The weakness in this respect lies in too much realistic detail, an example of which is "... poseyó el fuego de los labios y las valvas" (p. 169).

A comparison of the two parts of *Raucho* discloses Güiraldes' intention to contrast the pampa with the city. His treatment of the former surpasses that of the latter in emotional climate and in poetic style. Indeed, the sordid atmosphere of the mundane world is such an antithesis to the emotional and aesthetic appeal of the pampa that it corresponds to a narrative of a different order. Moreover, the sharpness of the contrast weakens the structure of the novel. Specifically, the sudden change in the personality of Raucho and in the mood with which he is associated produces the effect of a break in continuity. Altogether these differences create the impression that the two parts belong to separate novels, each of a different character. The first part is an example of Güiraldes' best talent. The second is not. The significant literary aspect of *Raucho* is Güiraldes' artistic treatment of life in the pampa. It is a preview of *Don Segundo Sombra*.

XXIV

Xaimaca

Xaimaca,[1] Güiraldes' second novel,[2] is written in the form of a diary. Its thirty-six brief, dated entries and sixteen undated ones covering the period from December 28, 1916 to March 11, 1917, relate the impressions of a trip from Buenos Aires to Jamaica in the British West Indies and part of the return. The voyage corresponds to the trip that Güiraldes and Adelina, together with their friends Alfredo and Marietta González Garaño, took to Jamaica during that same period. The narration begins like a travelogue, but soon develops into an account of a shipboard romance. Therefore, although the book is in the form of a diary of a voyage, it is in reality the story of a love affair. The love described is both moral and physical. It is, however, quite distinct from Güiraldes' other representations of love. It is love on a lofty, idealistic plane. Its exaltation is the theme of the narration. It is described in sentimental and poetic terms. For this reason *Xaimaca* falls heavily into the class of romantic novels.

An outline can give only a misleading impression of the book. This is because the story of the love making, shorn of its wrappings of sentiment, idealism, and poetic treatment loses its character and has little more to offer than other love affairs. The following is a summary of the novel:

There are three characters, Marcos Galván, Clara Ordóñez, and her brother Carlos Peñalba. Marcos is a well-mannered, young Argentine of twenty-five years of age with romantic inclinations. Clara is a lovely young woman who has made an unhappy marriage and longs for affection. A few years

[1] According to the *Encyclopedia Britannica* (Chicago, 1951), XII, p. 873, the Arawak name for Jaimaca was "Xaymaca," meaning the "Isle of Springs."
[2] The edition consulted was published in Buenos Aires by Agencia General de Librería y Publicaciones in 1923. The references to page numbers are from this edition.

older than Clara, her brother Peñalba is an affable companion whose enthusiasm for travel and new climes distracts him from discovering the love affair between Marcos and his sister until toward the end of the narrative.

Marcos meets Clara and her brother on the train as they travel from Buenos Aires to Santiago, Chile. He is taken by the beauty of the young woman. In Chile, Marcos, while accompanying his new friends on several sight-seeing excursions, falls in love with Clara. He conceals this from her. At Valparaíso, all three board the coastal vessel *Aysen*, Marcos bound for Peru and his friends for Jamaica. During the journey along the coast Marcos' infatuation for Clara increases in consonance with the rhythmic progress of the ship and the growing intensity of the heat. From Valparaíso to Jamaica the entries in his diary describe his love on a spiritual plane. The initial phase of the romance develop in two stages: At first Marcos suffers because he believes that his sentiments are not reciprocated. The second stage begins when, in several notes, Clara reveals her gratitude for his affection. Marcos, thereupon, decides to extend his journey in order to accompany her and her brother to Jamaica. During the rest of the ocean voyage he visits her cabin where the lovers profess their sentiments for each other in a progression of endearing expressions, caresses, and embraces. Marcos experiences a sensation of exaltation in the spiritual union of two beings into a single, harmonious identity.

An entirely different phase of the romance develops in Jamaica. After a brief stop-over in Kingston and several excursions in the neighborhood, the three travelers settle in a comfortable hotel at "Port Antonio" in a sub-tropical wood by the sea. That night as Marcos escorts Clara to her room, he is taken with a physical attraction for her. Clara, impelled by a helpless craving for his love, asks him to come in. Dawn finds Marcos with Clara naked in his arms. During the succeeding nights at "Port Antonio" and at the "Monteague"

Hotel in the hills, he revels in the contemplation of Clara asleep at his side. Marcos lives these last few days in Jamaica in a second state of exaltation stemming from a new sensation of joy.

On March 1st, Marcos' dream world comes to an abrupt end when Peñalba, who heretofore has been unaware of the affair, discovers the romance and peremptorily orders him to leave on the next boat. Marcos weakly accedes and, after a pathetic farewell with Clara, embarks for Panamá. Once aboard the ship on the Pacific Coast he submerges himself in gloom, but is rescued momentarily from his depths by Kate, a pretty fair-haired passenger. He reacts to Kate's friendly overtures by forcing his way into her cabin. When he embraces her, however, he realizes it is Clara he wants and retires as quickly as he entered. The narration ends on board ship with Marcos reliving the memory of his romance with Clara. He weeps. The last sensation he records in his diary is that their love is infinite.

The literary climate emerges from two classes of experience. One is related to the physical environment and the other to human relations. In both cases the narrator's emotion seeps through the poetic language. In the descriptions of the environment, the subject is represented in soft lights such as a violent haze or moonlight:

> La luz decrece y las montañas acumulan una den-
> sa atmósfera violeta (p. 25).

In the descriptions of human relations the climate is expressed in terms of emotions and sensations, the sentiment of which is characteristic of *le mal du siècle*. These are anxiety, fainting, suffering, illness, pain, torture, weeping, and dying:

> ¿Por qué no he muerto sobre tu boca? (p. 174).

All together the climate arising from the representations of both the environment and the human relations has given the entire novel its predominantly romantic tone.

The style, with the exception of a few passages, is poetic. It corresponds to the aesthetic descriptions of the scenery and to the romantic character of the love affair. The scenery, however, recedes before the growing preeminence of the romance and becomes an artistic background of the love making. As Marcos' emotions pass through the moral and physical phases, they increase in intensity to a level of exaltation where the narrative ceases to describe the course of events and changes to a eulogy to love.

The most notable stylistic feature is the extensive use of imagery. The principal techniques are the attribution of human aspects to the inanimate, the abstraction of the concrete, and the intensification of emotional and physical sensations. The imagery of human attributes is used to describe the physical environment such as the ship, the sea, mountain scenes, nature, the moon and the stars:

> Las plantas parecen estarse escuchando (p. 166).

The use of abstract imagery is more extensive in that it has been applied to the inanimate and to humans:

> Mar Caribe: inmensa alegría azul (p. 127).
> ...la presencia de Clara es un resplandor nebuloso (p. 168).

Because of the nature of the subject matter, most stress has been placed upon the human sensations, both emotional and physical. The emotional sensations are intensified by the use of imagery of physical sensations, usually of pain:

> ...sus palabras caen en mi carne abierta como una quemadura (p. 165).

Physical sensations are intensified by images of stronger physical sensations:

> Nuestros labios son tajos de nuestra carne que cicatrizan unidos (p. 87).

Furthermore, Güiraldes has intensified the poetic quality of a single subject by describing it in a succession of metaphors.

For example, in the following sentence there are two images, one illustrating the activity of shining, and the other representing light:

Las constelaciones gotean todo su oro (p. 113).

Similarly, the image of Clara's laughter, "Sonar de guijarro," is qualified by the image "cromático":

La risa nítida de Clara es un cromático sonar de
guijarro (p. 151).

Along with the imagery, Güiraldes has combined an extreme simplicity of expression. The entire narration has been stripped of superflous embellishments. There are no involved sentences, and no rhetorical expressions. Indeed, the elimination of unnecessary literary adornment heightens the significance of the essential words. The lines, thus stylized, produce the clear-cut effect of carefully polished gems.

Each sentence frequently encompasses a single thought and no more. In sequence they produce a rapid succession of impressions that are notable for their clarity, and they follow upon each other with a flowing continuity.

The poetic quality of the style gradually increases in parallel ascendancy with Marcos' rising emotions and physical sensations. Accordingly, when from page 171 to page 199 the subject changes from a diary of Marcos' love affair to a eulogy to love, it is no longer a narrative but a series of prose poems. Although the entire section is cast in a lyrical mood and in a correspondingly poetic style, the poems stand out clearly as separate literary units from the rest of the prose. Three of them are the following: (1) The poem describing the serenity of lovers in repose beginning with the word "Pienso" on page 172 and ending on page 173 with "Apenas sé si eres mujer, música o idea," (2) the poem expressing Marcos' sensation of ecstasy beginning on page 173 with the word "Recuerdo" and ending on page 174 with "Ya no sé si eres cuerpo o un delirio, pero el mundo de mis ojos flota para siempre en una aurora," and (3) the poem representing

the highest amorous intensification in a sense of infinity
beginning on page 179 with "Todo duerme" and ending on
page 180 with "Tu boca madura dice apenas: —Hoy es
siempre." The poetic climate of lovers in repose and the sense
of infinity which these poems evoke as well as their stylistic
treatment are similar to "Siesta" and "Reposo" in *El cencerro
de cristal*. Moreover, as Marcos' emotions reach their high
point of exaltation, his language becomes more lyrical and
breaks into verse:

> Paz,
> Suavemente.
> Paz
> Lentamente,
>
> Un ritmo muy lento, un ritmo dormido,
> Esparce indolencia agravada de ideas.
> El ritmo es presencia de un canto fluído;
> Soy nulo en el mundo de paz que me crea (p. 172).

Apart from the style of language, the treatment of the
subject matter is enhanced by several literary techniques.
Among these are Güiraldes' references ot the senses to convey
the presence of the environment. The narration is interspersed
with physical sensations such as the feeling of heat, coolness,
the wind, the sense of smell, and the hearing of sounds, of
which the following is an example:

> Uno que otro susurro en las palmas dice el primer
> sonido, al tiempo que nuestro olfato despierta al
> olor de la naturaleza y nuestra piel al frescor del
> aire (p. 159).

Throughout the narration Güiraldes has created a subtle
sense of rhythmic progress. This is produced by references
to the rhythm of the train and the vessel's engines. There are
seven instances that modulate the course of the journey with
a vague accompaniment like the beat of a march:

> ...compasadamente el barco pulsa los hondos
> porrazos de sus férreas arterias (p. 47).

Güiraldes has also used the technique of the refrain. He
suggests the ponderous movement of the ox-drawn cart in
the mountain village of Curacaví:

> La carreta avanza con ponderosa lenitud de fósil
> que se sobrevive (p. 37).

The same impression is emphasized when the cart's departure
is described in similar terms on pages 39 and 40. It is the
technique that Güiraldes used in "Chacarera" and in "Los
filosofantes" in *El cencerro de cristal*.

The narration contains an example of symbolism. The
steady progress of the ship represents the inexorability of fate
which draws the lovers together. The concept of destiny
becomes apparent when the *Aysen* relentlessly bears down
upon maritime birds:

> Un coro aterrorizado de chirridos subraya el des-
> bande, que a veces se estrella contra el avance in-
> diferente del barco (p. 50).

Güiraldes has also drawn an interesting parallel between
the love affair and the description of the sea. It lies in the
concept of infinity which contributes to the exalted quality
of Marcos' emotions:

> Tengo de pronto la sensación de que el infinito
> está en mí (p. 237).

In the description of the natural surroundings the same concept is repeated like a theme in a minor key:

> ...el mar a nuestros pies habla siempre de infi-
> nito (p. 155).

Special mention should be made of the artistic effect of the
gradation of light. When dawn finds Clara in Marcos' arms,
her nakedness is not described in bold terms. Instead, over
the course of three pages (158 to 1960), her form, first wrapped

in the darkness of the night, is slowly revealed in the gradually increasing early morning light. It is in reverse order the
same technique with which Laforgue pictures the disappearance of the nymph in "Pan et la Syrinx" and which Güiraldes
later applied to the departure of the old gaucho in *Don Segundo Sombra.*

Xaimaca is more like a poem than a novel. Its poetic character lies in the treatment of both the subject matter and
the style. In exalting physical love to the elevated level of
moral love, Güiraldes has represented passion in aesthetic and
idealistic terms. Consequently, the descriptions are at no time
undignified. In this respect they are in direct antithesis to
the realistic and gross pictures of love making in *Raucho.*
The treatment of the subject matter is all the more poetic
because the novel loses its narrative character and becomes
a eulogy to love. This fact, together with the poetic treatment
of the language, transposes the lyrical passages into prose
poems. The literary merit of *Xaimaca,* however, does not
lie in subject matter nor in its romantic sentiment, but in
its poetic style.

DON SEGUNDO SOMBRA

XXV

The Story

A brief review of the story of *Don Segundo Sombra* will facilitate the discussion of its merits. The events narrated take place in the Province of Buenos Aires during the span of years between 1900 and 1908. The principal characters are don Segundo Sombra and Fabio Cáceres. Don Segundo is a cattle herdsman by profession and a traditional gaucho in character. Fabio, at the beginning of the novel, is a parentless boy whose unhappy life in a small country village motivates him to run away and join the herdsman in his travels throughout the pampa. His experience during his wanderings with don Segundo center upon three long cattle drives and constitute the subject matter of the narration. The story is told in the first person by Fabio in the form of memoirs and is divided into three periods. The initial period, in which the first cattle drive takes place, describes Fabio at the age of fourteen. In the second, which includes the other two drives, he is a youth of eighteen. And, in the third, he is a young man of twenty-one.

The portrayal of don Segundo is the primary concern of the novel. In fact it is Fabio's alleged purpose to evoke his recollection of the man who became his adopted father (p. 203).[1] The naration is also concerned with the gradual evolution of Fabio from boyhood to manhood. Consequently, Fabio emerges as the other principal figure and assumes importance as a character in his own right. At first a rascally

[1] The indications of page numbers refer to the edition of *Don Segundo Sombra* published in Buenos Aires by Editorial Pleamar in 1943.

urchin with a cocky self-assurance and an impertinent tongue, he nevertheless is impelled by his admiration for don Segundo to become a gaucho. He soon looses his inflated opinion of himself when he discovers that he has a long way to go before he can be like the physically skilled and morally strong men of the pampa.

Fabio's experiences during the first period illustrate the development of the boy in a battle against physical hardships. They consist of his struggles to master the skills and feats of endurance of the cattlemen. His rough life begins mildly enough when he starts work as a stable boy and sleeps that night on a hard wooden cot. After a good day's work he falls asleep from exhaustion while sitting in his chair and tumbles over backwards. The next morning he faces bravely the rigors of a long cattle drive. During the first day of the journey, he undertakes to ride his unbroken colt, but the bucking colt throws him to the ground and he loses consciousness. Toward the end of the second day, he nearly faints from fatigue. Finally, in the ninth chapter, with the help of don Segundo, he successfully rides his colt. The chapter brings the period to a close as Fabio conquers his bodily suffering in a test of endurance against a raging storm.

In contrast with his physical hardships, Fabio's experiences in the second period are trials of a moral nature. They begin in Chapter XVI when his favorite hourse Comadreja is gored by a bull. In the same chapter he is disheartened when he breaks his collar bone while killing the bull. Following upon this, he is enticed by Paula, a flirtatious country girl, who at the same time has encouraged the attentions of Numa, a slow-witted farmhand. Fabio disgraces himself by provoking Numa into a fight and knifing him. His misfortunes mount when he bets on the races and loses all his heard-earned money and his best horses. The final blow falls when he learns that he is the natural son of a wealthy ranch owner who has died and left him his fortune. Even more than feeling the shame of his illegitimate birth, he is distressed when he realizes that he has become an *estanciero* and thereby has lost his identity as a gaucho.

The third period, which is contained in the twenty-seventh and last chapter of the book, describes Fabio's moral victory over his misfortunes. Now a young man of twenty-one, he has already spent three years on the ranch he inherited. His unwillingness to accept his new life as a rancher was mitigated by the presence of don Segundo. When the moment comes for don Segundo to leave him, Fabio's separation from his adopted father represents his culminating misfortune. As the old herdsman departs, Fabio succeeds in dominating his grief. He bids don Segundo farewell in silence with a handshake and a smile. By accepting fate with gaucho stoicism he has triumphed over moral adversity and achieved the maturity of manhood.

The order of the two aspects of Fabio's evolution is significant. The implication is that the acquisition of the physical strength and the skills of the cattlemen is not enough to become a true gaucho. Fabio must also acquire moral fortitude. In chapter X, Güiraldes identifies the attributes, both physical and moral, of the gaucho. Among the physical skills are the breaking, training, and caring for horses, the use of the lasso and the *boleadoras,* and the various operations of handling cattle. In a word, they make up that quality which Güiraldes designates as "baquía" (pp. 170, 282). The moral attributes on the other hand are described as the will to combat adversity unyieldingly and wholeheartedly, the acceptance of fate without complaint, strength of character with regard to women and drink, reserve with strangers, and loyalty to friends. The essence of these virtues is expressed in the moral sense of the word *hombría.* In sum, all the adversities described in the narration constitute together a schooling in *baquía* and *hombría.*

Throughout Fabio's struggles, don Segundo is ever-present

as an example of physical skill and moral conduct. He is the ideal gaucho in the mind of Fabio who molds his character in the image of the herdsman. Furthermore, he takes the boy under his protection and guides him in the ways of the gaucho by instructing him in horsemanship and in manliness. The essence of his guidance may be summed up in his fatherly counsel to Fabio when he says, "¡Hacete duro muchacho!" (p. 82). After don Segundo has completed his task of making a man of Fabio, he disappears into the pampa as mysteriously as he came.

The concept of destiny underlies the course of Fabio's experiences. It draws him like a magnet to follow don Segundo into the wilderness. Its force impels the two riders to be ever on the march toward the distant horizont. Destiny is also the arbiter in Fabio's journey from boyhood to manhood. His misfortunes are attributed to fate. In this sense his struggles against his moral hardships are a battle with destiny. Here again don Segundo sets the example by his stoic acceptance of the inevitable. At the end of the novel Fabio finally accepts fate's mandate with similar stoicism when destiny ordains that he remain behind in his new role as an *estanciero* and that don Segundo return to his life of wandering.

While the pampa is the background of the narration, it also has human qualities. Like don Segundo, it possesses the attribute of stoicism. It is indifferent to fate, implacable before suffering, it swallows the weak, both animals and men, and imposes its law of the survival of the strong.

Thus *Don Segundo Sombra* has a dual character. It is a portrait of the gaucho herdsman and of the pampa in which he lived. It is also a novel based upon the story of the evolution of a boy to manhood.

XXVI

The Tales

Two tales are introduced into the novel as separate narrative units. They are told by don Segundo. The first, which appears in Chapter XII, is the story of Dolores and the son of the Devil. Dolores, a young *paisano,* fell in love with a beautiful girl, Consuelo, while spying on her as she bathed in the Paraná River. Suddenly a large, red flamingo swooped down, changed her into a midget, and flew off with her. Running away in a daze, Dolores stumbled upon a good witch who took pity on him. She told him that the flamingo was really the dwarf son of the devil Añang, explaining that he had taken the form of a bird to ravish young maidens. She advised him how to rescue Consuelo by breaking the spell with certain holy charms and Indian magic. Carrying out the good witch's instructions, Dolores proceeded to an island where he found an enchanted palace in which the dwarf had imprisoned his victims. When the flamingo alighted and changed into the form of the dwarf, Dolores caught him and castrated him. Whereupon, a flock of little maidens, no bigger than ostrich chicks, rushed from the disappearing palace, among them Consuelo. Dolores returned them to their normal sizes by sprinkling them with holy water. He then embraced Consuelo with whom he lived happily ever after.

The story is in the nature of a fairy tale. Its theme, in fact, is similar to the liberation of the beautiful princess from an evil spell,[1] so familiar to children. Furthermore, the enchantments described are reminiscent of the fantasies of Oriental tales[2] and European popular stories.[3] Withal, Güiraldes'

---

[1] "Dornröschen" in Wilhelm and Jacob Grimm's *Ausgewählte Märchen* (Berlin, 1929), p. 7.

[2] Of the various fantasies of enchantment, the one which strikes the closest resemblance to those of Oriental tales is that of the giant flamingo which recalls the Roc or *Rukh* in "The Story of Es-Sindibad of the Sea and of the

treatment of the tale banishes the impression of any origin
other than that of the native environment. He has achieved
this autochthonous effect by casting the elements of the narration into local terms. Specifically he has regionalized the
setting, the personalities, and the language.

The setting is located on the far reaches of the Paraná River
in Northern Argentina which, though somewhat exotic, is
known to the listeners by hearsay. Its regional aspect is
enhanced by the introduction of indigenous vegetation and
animals. Among the flora are *sombra'e toro*[4] (p. 113), *arboleda
macuca,*[5] and *raíces de flor del aire*[6] (p. 118), while the fauna
are *tigres,*[7] *yarareses,*[8] and *loros* (p. 118). Also natural to the
area are the *caburé*[9] and the flamingo. Although the flamingo,
described as bright red in color like the blood of a bull and
comparable in size to an ostrich, bears a resemblance to the
legendary Roc in the *Arabian Nights Entertainment,* the re-
levant consideration is that Güiraldes has chosen a bird that
is native of the country. Indeed the environment, while un-
common to the pampa, is nevertheless entirely local.

The personalities are familiar countryfolk. Dolores and Consuelo represent ordinary *paisanos* who live in a normal manner until involved in the supernatural. The good witch cor-

---

Land," *Stories of the Thousand and One Nights* (New York, 1910), pp.
256-257.
   [3] María Rosa Lida in *El cuento popular hispano-americano y la literatura*
(Buenos Aires, 1941), on page 68, says that there is evidence that the story
of defeating the devil with the use of charms has entered Argentine folklore
from the European legend of "El velador de la casa hechizada." María Rosa
Lida mentions the origin of an Argentine version as follows: " . . . el cuento del
soldado caritativo que vence al diablo con la ayuda de ciertas prendas mágicas
(Fernán Caballero, *Juan Soldado,* Ramírez de Arellano, No. 126; Cuento Argentino, *Juan Lume,* de Río Hondo, Santiago del Estero; y asociado con prendas mágicas, pero dentro de un argumento distinto, Llano, 5)."
   [4] *Jodina rhombifolium,* an indigenous tree with thorny foliage, known locally
also as *quebracho flojo, quebracho blando,* and *quebracho falso.*
   [5] A grove of umbrella trees.
   [6] *Bromeliácea argentina.*
   [7] Tigre is the Argentine term for jaguar.
   [8] *Yarareses* is a word, derived from Guaraní, designating the poisonous
snakes, natural to the tropics of Argentina and Brazil.
   [9] *Strigiforme,* species of *gladicium nanum,* a small brown South American
bird with a shrill call and an aggressive manner, believed to be rapacious and
sometimes designated as *el rey de los pajaritos.*

responds to a known type, not unlike a *curandera* who possesses a knowledge of magic. The wicked dwarf is described as the son of Añang, who is feared by all good country people.

The vernacular in which the tale is told intensifies the regional atmosphere not only with the rustic form of its expression but also with its imagery. While the discussion of the language is reserved to the subsequent study of the style, it is opportune to observe that Güiraldes has intensified the presence of the environment by introducing into the speech of the narrator such images of local realia as the fox in the following example:

...el corazón le corcoviaba en el pecho como
zorro entrampao (p. 113).

Güiraldes has also cast the magic spells in terms of the local superstitions of the *paisanos*. These are of two classes, *magia negra* and *magia blanca*. To the former belong the Indian beliefs, among which are those related to *Añang* and to the *caburé*. *Añang* is the name given by the aborigines to the Evil One, who has passed from their beliefs to the place of the Devil in the credence of the countryfolk. Similarly derived is the belief that the *caburé* is filled with wickedness and that its feathers, worn as a charm, have the mysterious power of breaking a spell. On the other hand, the charms associated with the religion of more civilized people are considered good and consequently are designated white magic. This is illustrated in the use of holy water to direct Dolores' arrow in killing the *caburé* and to disenchant the maidens. It is interesting to note the power of white magic over the black. In all, it is apparent that the distinct regional quality of the tale flows from the presentation of both the substance and the form of the story from the point of view of the *paisano*.

The second story, which appears in Chapter XXI, is of an entirely different nature. It is a moral tale with a humorous turn. As appears from the following summary, it involves the theme of the Faust legend:

One day when Our Lord was journeying throughout the Holy Land with Saint Peter, the mule on which he was riding lost a shoe. At the next village, the travelers stopped at the shop of a blacksmith. The smith's name was Misery because he was so poor. He had no iron, but gladly fashioned the shoe from a piece of silver. When he refused to accept payment, Our Lord granted him three wishes. Misery, instead of asking for admission to Heaven, foolishly requested, among other wishes, that whosoever should enter his tobacco pouch might not leave without is permission. After Our Lord had left, the smith reproached himself for not having asked for unlimited money and twenty years to enjoy it. Thereupon, the Devil appeared and gave him his wish in exchange of his soul. In time, Misery cleverly tricked all the devils of Hell into his tobacco pouch, thus freeing the world of evil. But, the doctors, lawyers, and rulers, who thrived on the misfortunes of the earth, were deprived of their livelihood and complained to the governor. The governor ordered Misery to release the devils, whereupon the world was set aright. When Misery died he was refused admittance to Heaven, Purgatory, and Hell. As a result he was compelled to wander the earth forever. And that is why there will always be misery and poverty in this world.

In spite of the difference in substance between the two stories the treatment of the second tale is similar to that of the first inasmuch as, here again, Güiraldes has cast the setting, the personalities, and the language into a regional mold. The narration is located in a familiar environment which, as before, is disclosed by the various impressions of the native milieu. The smith's poor shop for instance, though common also in other parts, is typical of the area. Similarly, his *chambergo,* the duck pond and the horse blanket are known local realia. Furthermore, Our Lord and Saint Peter, instead of riding upon asses as might be expected, are pictured traveling on mules in the manner of humble *paisanos.*

Among the personalities, the smith is a familiar type. Not only does he speak in the vernacular, but he possesses the native traits of hospitality and that characteristic astuteness, called *malicia,* which he displays in outwitting the devils. In spite of the fact that the devils, Saint Peter, and Our Lord are not native characters, their conversation in the regional dialect makes them appear like local inhabitants. When, for example, Our Lord also speaks in the vernacular, the odd incongruity, without seeming irreverent, produces a humorous effect: "—Güenas tardes —dijo Nuestro Señor" (p. 221).

Besides the dialect of the characters, the rustic language in which the story is told here again intensifies the impression of the rural environment. As before, this is achieved by reproducing the images of the local realia, which in this instance are associated with the smith's barnyard as, for example, the clucking hen that enlivens the following expression:

... Se puso a gritar como gallina culeca (p. 232).

Although these tales are written in gaucho vernacular, they do not fall within the tradition of gauchesque literature. On the contrary, because of their contemporary subject matter and the humorous tone in which they are told, they represent the art of *criollo* storytelling. Indeed, their significance lies in the characterization of don Segundo as a storyteller.

XXVII

Don Segundo in Fiction

In the creation of the novelistic figure of don Segundo Sombra, Güiraldes was guided by certain motivations. Principal among these was his wish to record the last of a disappearing type of man. He proposed to interpret the aesthetic and moral values of the gaucho. In fact in 1922 he had written to Larbaud that he wanted to reveal the poetic, philosophic, musical, and pictorial aspects of an unexpressed race.[1] Furthermore, his life-long affection for Segundo Ramírez, the old *peón* who lived on the *estancia,* moved him to capture his portrait in a novel. He had already disclosed this intention to his friend Miomandre in Paris in 1920 when he told him that he planned to write the history of a man he had known since his childhood.[2]

Don Segundo is represented as a strong, silent man (p. 26). His speech is characteristically laconic (p. 24). He expresses himself rarely and then only in a minimum of words (p. 44). When he does, his voice is calm (pp. 20, 156), with a sharp clear quality (pp. 20, 23, 156), described as a *falsetto* (p. 45). At times, the tone of his comments have a ring of irony (p. 27).

In considering the artistic aspect of his subject, Güiraldes had also said, "¿Y en cada una de las formas de arte, hay un alma que está esperando su palabra!"[3] Specifically, he wanted to describe the arts of improvising couplets, of *criollo* dances, and of story telling. By ascribing these talents to don Segundo, he attributed to him the picturesqueness of a traditional figure. But Güiraldes has made no mention of the art of *payar.* Indeed, at no time does don Segundo play the guitar, although

[1] Güiraldes, "A Valery Larbaud," *Sur* (No. 1, Verano 1931), p. 105.
[2] Francis de Miomandre, "Recuerdo de Güiraldes," *La Nación* (Jan. 7, 1940).
[3] Güiraldes, "A Valery Larbaud," p. 106.

it is referred to casually: "Con una guitarra por medio." (p. 283). Don Segundo therefore is not portrayed as a *payador,* and, in this respect, he differs from such legendary characters as Santos Vega.

In story telling, however, don Segundo is a master. He had already been pictured in this role in "Al rescoldo."[4] When, in the novel, he again appears as a storyteller, his character changes from what it is in the rest of the book. Contrary to his usual laconic manner of speech, his expression is facile and fluent. Moreover, he has lost the stoicism of the strong, silent man and has acquired the sensibilities of an artist. Before beginning his tales, he hesitates in order to create a suitable atmosphere of anticipation (pp. 112, 220). During the narration he keeps his audience spellbound by creating a climate of credulity. Furthermore, the humorous vein in which he tells the stories differs from the tragic tone that characterizes the narrations of legendary gauchos as, for example, in *Martín Fierro* and *Santos Vega o los mellizos de "La Flor."* He tells them with the optimistic spirit and the sense of *malicia* typical of the Argentine rustic. Thus don Segundo is represented as a *criollo* storyteller and not as a legendary gaucho narrator.

Besides these colorful aspects, Güiraldes' intention was also to represent the noble character of the gaucho as he conceived it. His idea of the moral fibre of this Argentine type had not been fully represented in gauchesque literature. He envisioned an apology of the gaucho distinct from the concepts of Facundo, Martín Fierro, and the *gauchos malos* of Gutiérrez. Accordingly don Segundo does not have the cruelty, the violence, and the despotism of Facundo, nor does he have the pathetic self-commiseration and the defeatism of Martín Fierro, nor the murderous vindictiveness and the elements of tragic fatefulness of Gutiérrez' outlaws. Instead of the negative traits of the gauchos of history and legend, Güiraldes attributed affirmative values to don Segundo. What he

---

[4] *Cuentos de muerte y de sangre,* p. 82.

considered these to be appears in his explanation to *El libro bravo* in which he proposed to exalt "the characteristics of the men of our race."[5] He summarized them as follows:

Mi orgullo	Mi malicia
Mi hombría	Mi sangre
Mi insolencia	Mi hospitalidad
Mi enojo	Mi generosidad
Mi risa	Mi fuerza
Mi amor	Mi pureza
Mi coraje	Mi nobleza
Mi soledad	Mi compadrada
Mi dominio	Mi anarquía

Among these are the moral qualities of the ideal gaucho. In order to represent them more readily, he embodied them in a single model. Thus, by ascribing them to don Segundo Sombra, he made of him an ideal personality.

His purpose, however, went beyond the representation of an ideal character. It was also to express a way of being inherent in the native mentality. As he himself disclosed, his concern was to interpret the philosophy of the men of the pampa:

> ¿Filosofía? Aún no tuvo pensadores que le dieran un libro que fuera tabla de su ley. Pero sí tuvo hombres que a fuerza de ser humanos, dieron fragmentariamente un soplo de grandeza uniforme.[6]

What exactly is this philosophy has not been stated in so many words. But it does transpire from don Segundo's attitude toward life, especially when he is faced with physical and moral adversities.

His character, indeed, is stoic. He accepts fate unwincingly. "The worst that can happen to me is death" (p. 254) is his

---

[5] Güiraldes, *El libro bravo* (San Antonio de Areco, 1936), pp. 5, 9.
[6] *Ibid.*, p. 18.

way of thinking. Having no fear of destiny, he is calm and self-possessesd. When confronted with a physical hardship such as an injury from a fall, his attitude is one of absolute indifference (p. 255). Before adversity of a moral nature he displays the same fortitude. Instances of this are when he is attacked by the *tape*[7] Burgos (p. 27), when he is arrested by the police corporal (p. 134), and when he is provoked by the drunken storekeeper (p. 246). He laughs at his misfortunes with a suggestion of irony (p. 254). There is no tragedy-ridden defeatism in him. On the contrary, he has the affirmative spirit of a strong man who overcomes his troubles (p. 255).

His domineering nature inclines him to being authoritative, so much so that he is prone to give orders to the *estancia* owners who employ him (p. 94). He would have made a great gaucho guerilla leader: "¡Qué caudillo de montonera hubiera sido!" (p. 94). Although he has the reputation of an able fighter of duels (p. 140), he is opposed to violence and killing. He believes in such combats according to the rules of fair play: "Yo he tenido más de muchas de estas diferencias con hombres que eran o se craiban malos y nunca me han cortado ni tampoco he muerto a nadie, porque no he hallao necesidá" (p. 250). Don Segundo is the antithesis of the *gaucho malo*.

Beneath his outward appearance of austerity, he possesses a sense of human values and is moved by affection. An example of this is his characteristic gaucho loyalty to friends regardless of the circumstances into which they had fallen (pp. 140-141). Also typical is his courtesy, especially with humble countryfolk (pp. 41, 246). He has a simpathetic understanding of his fellow men in trouble and, putting aside petty considerations, expresses it generously (pp. 27-28, 151). His paternal affection for Fabio, the boy, and later for Fabio, the youth, appears beneath his severe exterior manner (pp.

---

[7] The Argentine designation for a Guaraní Indian.

84, 153, 220, 234, 266, 268, 271, 285). As the man described in
Güiraldes book, *El libro bravo*,[8] don Segundo possesses a
sensibility that has the quality of greatness.

To wander on horseback across the plains is his life. He
is driven by his restlessness to be ever on the march (p. 94),
and can never remain long in one place: "Llegar no es, para
un resero, más que un pretexto para partir" (p. 285). Freedom is a part of his being (p. 94). He resists the restrictions
of civilized society and flees from the oppressiveness of human congregations (pp. 123, 125). Seeking the solitude of
the prairie, he communes with himself. He is anarchic and
independent (p. 94). From the gaucho of old he has inherited
the spirit of the pampa. All told, don Segundo is also a symbol
of the gaucho philosophy of life.

In his literary treatment of don Segundo, Güiraldes has
revived an image of the traditional gaucho. It is queried how
he has been able to surround his character with an aura of
legend when don Segundo is described as a cattle driver
living in modern times.

The explanation is in part that Güiraldes has represented
don Segundo in the eyes of a small boy and of a youth. It is
evident that Fabio worships the legendary gauchos. Chief
among these heroes are, no doubt, Martín Fierro, Santos Vega,
and the notorious *gauchos malos*. Quite naturally he transfers
their images to don Segundo. So it is that, in the light of
Fabio's imagination, the reader sees the old *peón* as a gaucho
of the past.

Accordingly, it is Fabio, and not Güiraldes, who imagines
the legendary aspects of don Segundo. His descriptions are
few and brief. The initial impression, picturing the dark
figure silhouetted against the sky, conveys the image of a
gaucho horseman:

> El jinete, que me pareció enorme bajo su poncho
> claro ...

. . . .

[8] *Op. cit.*

> Inmóvil, miré alejarse, extrañamente agrandada
> contra el horizonte luminoso, aquella silueta de
> caballo y jinete (pp. 20, 21).

The second impression, which follows immediately upon the first, suffuses the image of the horseman in the half-light of vague terms which suggest a ghost-like apparition from the past:

> Me pareció haber visto un fantasma, una sombra,
> algo que pasa y es más una idea que un ser...
> (pág. 21).

Lastly, Fabio attributes to don Segundo certain qualities of the traditional gaucho. These are the shrouded appearance of the *tapao*,[9] the mysteriousness of a person who has reason to hide his identity and his past, the meaningful silence that typifies a man of few words and violent action, and the faculty of inspiring a sensation of awe in the fantasy of a small boy:

> De golpe, el forastero volvió a crecer en mi ima-
> ginación. Era el "tapao", el misterio, el hombre
> de pocas palabras que inspira en la pampa una
> admiración interrogante (p. 26).

Once Don Segundo's mysterious personality is established upon his entry at the beginning of the book, it is retained throughout by describing him as little as possible. Moreover, it is important to note in this connection that Güiraldes has represented don Segundo from a distant perspective. There is no close-up view of his character that allows the reader to penetrate into his emotions and into the working of his mind. On the contrary, the description of don Segundo is limited to wholly external impressions while his inner being is hidden in silence or implied from his conduct. It is apparent that Güiraldes deliberately clouded the intimate features of his

---

[9] The word *tapao* in this context means a mysterious person who covers his features with a cloak or other garment.

character in order to envelope him in mystery as, indeed, Fabio affirms:

> Pero, ¡qué hombre que no concluía nunca de
> conocer! (p. 153).

Güiraldes intensifies the legendary character of don Segundo at the end of his novel. In the same manner as at the beginning of the narration he again pictures the dark figure of the gaucho horseman silhouetted against the sky:

> Un momento la silueta doble se perfiló nítida
> sobre el cielo (p. 285).

And, once more he describes him in the vague terms which give him the quality of a ghost from the past:

> Aquello que se alejaba era más una idea que un
> hombre.

It will be observed that Güiraldes has recalled the first impressions of don Segundo by reiterating the same images in similar language. In this way he has created an evocative effect which strengthens the illusion of the shadowy apparition. Besides, he represents Fabio experiencing this sensation himself:

> Mis ojos dormían en lo familiar de sus actitudes.
> Un rato ignoré si veía o evocaba (p. 285).

The conclusion of the novel leaves the reader with a lasting impression of don Segundo. This is produced by the artistic treatment of the old gaucho as he disappears riding away into the shadows of the pampa. The dilution of the concrete image of the horseman into an abstraction is achieved in a gradual fading away. It is a fading away in two dimensions. One is in distance, and the other is in the failing light of dusk. In both instances, the progressive disappearance is contained in a succession of brief *tableaux vivants*. In the dimension of distance, each impression of don Segundo's diminishing figure is followed by a short eclipse. All together they emphasize the separate steps of his disappearance as set out below:

Impression 1:
>Lo vi alejarse al tranco.

Eclipse 1:
>... caballo y jinete repecharon la loma ...

Impression 2:
>Un momento la silueta doble se perfiló nítida sobre el cielo ...

Eclipse 2:
>Y bruscamente desapareció ...

Impression 3:
>La silueta reducida de mi padrino apareció en la lomada.

Eclipse 3:
>Mi vista se ceñía enérgicamente sobre aquel pequeño movimiento en la pampa somnolente.

Impression 4:
>Se fue reduciendo como si lo cortaran de abajo en repetidos tajos.

Eclipse 4:
>Sobre el punto negro del chambergo mis ojos se aferraron con afán de hacer perdurar aquel rezago. Inútil ...

Concurrently the failing light of nightfall is graded in the following steps:

1. Caballo y jinete . . . difundidos en el cardal.
2. ... el cielo, sesgado por un verdoso rayo de atardecer.
3. El anochecer vencía lento ... Unas nubes tenues hacían largas estrías de luz.
4. ... aquel pequeño movimiento en la pampa somnolente.

At this point the gradually disappearing figure has evaporated into an abstraction:

>No sé qué extraña sugestión me proponía la presencia ilimitada de un alma.

In a final impression, Güiraldes has represented don Segundo as a spirit. He had done this, not by description, but
by the power of suggestion of a single word. It is *Sombra*.
By ascribing it as a surname to don Segundo, Güiraldes has
stressed the horseman's quality of a shade from the past:

"Sombra," me repetí.

A comparison of the fictional character with the living don
Segundo shows a striking likeness. The obvious resemblance
leaves no doubt that Güiraldes reproduced the portait of the
old *peón de estancia*. As has been seen, the similarities between
the two are, in the main, the following: In both cases, the
time of the setting is about 1900. Their past was veiled in
mystery. Like Sombra, Ramírez was a cattle driver, adept
in the skills of his profession, but neither was a true gaucho.
There is no question of the identity of their physical aspects.
Both had the same familiar build and the same fierce, dark-
skinned countenance. Their traditional dress contributed to
the impression of a gaucho of old. Moreover, the reputation
of each as a fighter of duels and of having been involved
in troubles suggested the unsubstantiated illusion of a *gaucho
malo*. In action, they paralleled one another in courage and
affirmative spirit. Each was equally taciturn and expressed
his views in brief comments charged with a characteristic
humor known as *malicia*. They spoke in the same *falsetto*
voice. Neither played the guitar. On the other hand, Ramírez,
like his counterpart, was said to compose couplets and to
delight in folk dancing. But more than all this, both don
Segundo's were masters of the art of story telling. Significant
also was the fondness of the old *peón* for an admiring boy
of fourteen, namely young Ricardo.

Although they resemble each other in these respects, they
differ in others. In the novel don Segundo is respected for
his imposing character and dignified conduct, but in life his
humor and his propensity for fighting were a cause for some
unpopularity among his fellow cowhands on the *estancia*.

In this regard, the fictional personality of don Segundo is distinct from the real. While, therefore, the similarities indicate that Güiraldes availed himself of the physical features, the manner, and the talents of don Segundo Ramírez as a model for don Segundo Sombra, the differences disclose the author's purpose of recording the moral characteristics of the gauchos in an ideal image.

XXVIII

Fabio

Since Fabio emerges as the other principal figure, his character deserves special attention. As he develops from boyhood to manhood within the course of the eight years encompassing the period of the novel, his personality changes. In fact, in each of the three stages of his evolution he is to a degree different.

At the beginning of the first stage Fabio describes himself from about six to fourteen years of age. Ignorant of his own name, he is known as *Guacho,* meaning a parentless waif. Taking to the streets of the village, he is given to entertaining spectators with displays of impertinence at the expense of others. In a word, Fabio begins his career assuming the truculent mannerism of a young rogue.

Following upon this initial portrait, Fabio's combat with life in the pampa gradually alters his personality. As a result of the reprimands he receives he discards his impertinence and, in his struggle with physical hardship, he loses his unbecoming self-assurance. At the end of the ninth chapter he is a changed boy. His character is completely divested of the attributes of a street urchin. On the other hand, he has gained in idealism and in the spirit of conquest.

A new Fabio is represented at the beginning of the second stage. A youth of eighteen, he is pictured fully formed in the skills of the herdsman. His character, however, is still immature. This appears when he is confronted with the misadventures consisting of the injury of his horse Comadreja, the affair with Paula, the loss of his earnings, and finally his disillusionment upon discovering he is no longer a gaucho. In each instance he is afflicted by his misfortune. During this period, in spite of the example and encouragment of don

Segundo, Fabio has not yet acquired the strength of character to overcome his moral hardships.

A third Fabio is described in the final stage. A young man of twenty-one, he has acquired a sense of true values and has learned to face his adversities with fortitude. He shows a depth of discernment in his preference for the herdsman's life of freedom and combat over the wealthy ranch owner's material posseessions and sheltered existence (pp. 281-282). This is also revealed in his contempt for his friend Raucho's inclination toward amorous adventures (p. 284). Finally, he displays his moral calibre in the stoic acceptance of his separation from don Segundo. With this he has achieved maturity.

It is apparent, therefore, that Fabio's personality has passed through three distinct phases. At the same time, each phase is a step toward fulfillment. When, finally, Güiraldes completes the evolution of Fabio's character, he has indicated that to become a gaucho is to be a man.

Besides the attention given to Fabio's character in terms of universal human values, Güiraldes has also ascribed to him certain traits which are characteristic of the gaucho in particular. That Fabio possesses the combative spirit of the pampa herdsman is evinced by the courage with which he rides his bucking horse and with which, on two occasions, he battles wild bulls. Furthermore, like the notorious *gaucho matrero,* Fabio is impelled by violent aggressiveness, when he engages in a fight with Numa and when he attempts to attack his friend Pedro Barrales.

Contrasting with the gaucho's courage, is his fear of the supernatural. Likewise Fabio's imagination is full of the superstitions of black and white magic. The famed loyalty of the gaucho is exemplified by the devotion of the two companions to each other and in particular when Fabio forgoes a lucrative offer in order to remain with his protector.

It is perhaps, in part, because the men of the pampa give greater importance to other values that they are improvident with money. Typically, Fabio loses all his earnings at the races. At the same time, his horse is characteristically his most treasured possession as shown by his love for Comadreja on page 91 and page 176. Similarly on page 147 he expresses his affection for his mare Garúa, calling her "Linda madrinita baqueana."

True to type, Fabio also cherishes the freedom to roam the pampa. "Si hubiera seguido mi sentir," he says on page 282, "andaría aún dejando el rastro de mi tropilla por tierras de eterna novedad." This is the concept that freedom is as dear as life itself and is expressed on page 285 when he says "huella y vida eran una sola cosa." Accordingly, Fabio possesses that notable mental attitude which Güiraldes calls, on page 62, "alma de horizonte."

Though garrulous while still a street urchin, he acquires taciturnity. It is, in a sense, the outward expression of gaucho stoicism. Instead of "largar el brulote" as he puts it on page 14, he learns to hold his tongue: "Me guardé bien de desembuchar mis sinsabores" (page 205). When, at last on page 285, he takes leave of don Segundo, he does so in silence: "No hablábamos. ¿Para qué? ... Bajo el tacto de su mano ruda, recibí un mandato de silencio."

In ascribing these attributes to Fabio, Güiraldes has implied that aggression is a negative feature of the gaucho. Don Segundo, on the other hand, does not have this characteristic. When, finally, Fabio is patterned in the image of his model, he discards this quality and emerges with the positive traits of the ideal gaucho.

At the conclusion of the novel Güiraldes represents Fabio as being transformed into "un hombre culto." After so much stress on the worthy qualities of the rustic men of the pampa, the representation of Fabio in a more civilized role clashes with his previous bucolic characterization. It is evident, however, that it was not Güiraldes' intention to change his personality but merely to give the reader an explanation of how an uneducated herdsman had acquired the ability to write memoirs. Furthermore, Güiraldes stresses the point that clothes do not make the man. Don Segundo clearly expresses this thought when he says: "Si sos gaucho en de veras, no has de mudar, porque andequiera que vayas, irás con tu alma por delante como madrina 'e tropilla." (p. 271). It follows, therefore, that Fabio's transformation into an "hombre culto" is only an external change, and that his character remains the same.

The literary treatment of Fabio contrasts with that of don Segundo. The primary distinction stems from the fact that Fabio is the narrator of his own biography. Consequently his portrayal of himself is more personal. It is to be noted, however, that the approach contains two different perspectives. The first is subjective in which Fabio sees himself from his own point of view, namely that of the boy, the youth, and the young man. The second perspective is objective. It pictures Fabio from the distance of the writer, Mr. Fabio Cáceres, an "hombre culto" and an author whose point of view coincides with that of Güiraldes himself.

The following moods and sensibilities correspond to the subjective characterization of Fabio. There are, in broad lines, three principal moods, representing a high, low, and even state of his morale. When at the beginning Fabio sets out across the pampa to join don Segundo, he enters his life of adventure elated by a feeling of optimism. No sooner is he confronted with the realities of his new existence than his high spirits are deflated by a series of sobering experiences. When at the end of the first cattle drive he successfully overcomes his hardships, his achievement fills him with a cheering feeling of satisfaction. Then again, when he his eighteen, Fabio begins the second period in a state of elation. Not only is he pleased with himself in the role of a young gaucho, but he is also full of animation as he participates in the Christmas festivities. He is rapidly demoralized, however, by the succeeding misfortunes. His morale rallies only in the end when he learns to accept the adversities of fate with equanimity.

It is apparent that, as Fabio passes through a series of changing scenes, the predominant influence upon his moods is nature. He is responsive to the poetic aspects of the pampa and is inclined to expressing them in lyrical terms. He speaks, for example, of the open countryside: "De grande y tranquilo que era el campo, algo nos regalaba de su grandeza y su indiferencia" (p. 220). In this respect, Güiraldes has attributed to Fabio, the narrator, his own sensibility of a poet: "Yo sufría por todo, como un agua en declive, al viento, al sol y a la hojita del sauce llorón que tajea el lomo" (p. 255).

Offset against this subjective portrayal of Fabio is his representation from the objective view of the author. As previously observed, Güiraldes, at the beginning of the novel, pictures Fabio in the role of a rascally street urchin. He describes him as mischievous, self-assured, impertinent, and motivated by a malicious sense of humor. By ascribing these qualities to his character, he has recalled the manner, the behavior, and the mentality of the traditional boy rogue of Hispanic literature represented by Lazarillo de Tormes.[1]

While Fabio unmistakably resembles a young *pícaro,* Güiraldes has not carried the treatment beyond an initial suggestion. Soon, in fact, elements appear in the boy's character that distingish him from that literary prototype. One is the absence of that amoral quality characteristic of the typical rogue. This is apparent on page 17 where Fabio is repelled by the immorality of a house of prostitution. Another is his idealism, a quality notably lacking in the character of the rogue.[2]

[1] *Cf.* T. B. Irving, "Myth and Reality in *Don Segundo Sombra,"* Hispania, XI, No. 1, March 1957, p. 46, in which the author designates Fabio as a *pícaro* in the following terms: "His aimless pranks are reminiscent ,to be sure, of those of Lazarillo de Tormes, . . . for the waif steals many a page in Spanish literature from the time of Lazarillo on . . . "

[2] *Cf.* Edwin S. Morby, "Es *Don Segundo Sombra* novela picaresca?" *Revista Iberoamericana,* I, Nov. 1939, p. 377, in which the author questions the picaresque character of Fabio because of the boy's idealism; "Falta saber hasta qué punto se admiten en las novelas del género [i.e. picaresque novels] elementos de idealismo; nada, por cierto, más esencial a este libro que el idealismo que respira, ni nada menos picaresco . . . "

From the very beginning Fabio is impelled by the image of the ideal gaucho, personified in don Segundo. His respect for the noble attributes of the herdsman appears at the outset when he admires his magnanimous conduct toward his would-be assassin, the drunken Burgos. Besides these, a more fundamental difference is Fabio's attitude toward life. It distinguishes him from the *pícaro* in that, instead of circumventing hardships by the use of his wits and ruses, he faces them squarely in a determined spirit to overcome them:

> En fin, había que hinchar la panza y aguantar la cincha... y si mi cuerpo no me daba, mi voluntad le serviría de impulso. ¿No quería huir de la vida mansa para hacerme más capáz? (p. 53).

After shedding the features of a rogue, Fabio gradually acquires the semblance of another literary image. Inherent throughout the course of Fabio's career is the concept of chivalry. Although it is at no time expressed in specific terms, his adventurous wanderings suggest an epic in the Arthurian tradition of the *Chansons de Gestes*.[3] Indeed, Fabio sets forth in his quest to become a gaucho much like a squire in search of knighthood. The analogy lies on two planes, one physical and the other moral. In the first instance the young horseman rides throughout the land encountering a series of physical trials which he overcomes by deeds of strength and valor. In the second, before he can be considered to have won his spurs, he must also demonstrate that his character is worthy and beyond reproach. Furthermore, in the same tradition he passes through an apprenticeship under the tutelage of his protector who schools him in the corresponding art of combat and in honorable conduct.[4] When at last he completes his education in *baquía* and *hombría*, his achievement is comparable to the fulfillment of the requirements of *caballería*. Thus, by this subtle suggestion of an epic of chivalry, Güiral-

---

[3] *Cf.* Chrestien de Troyes, *Yvain (Le Chevalier au Lion)* (Manchester, 1942).
[4] *Cf.* Don Juan Manuel, "Libro del cavallero et del escudero," in *Obras de Don Juan Manuel* (Barcelona, 1955).

des has reflected the figure of Fabio in the light of a knight-errant of the pampas.

In addition to these two literary treatments of Fabio, there is a third. It is pictorial. Of this there are three instances which occur at the beginning of the separate stages of his life. In each Fabio's image is offset by the background of water. The total impression produces the effect of artistic canvasses. The first of these pictures depicts the small boy sitting beneath the stone arch of a bridge, fishing in the river. The second portrays him as a young gaucho, dressed in the traditional manner, and standing by another river while his horse, decked in typical saddlery, drinks from the water. The third represents him as a young man, sitting by a pond in the prairie, his horse standing beside him. Silhouetted against this artistic landscape in a static posture as if posing for a portrait, Fabio is caught in the frame of a literary painting.

The pictorial treatment of Fabio, however, differs from that of don Segundo. The principal distinction is that the image of the old gaucho is diluted into an abstraction, both visually and conceptually, while that of Fabio is delineated in clear-cut features. The separate artistic techniques can be compared to different styles of painting in which the subject of one is suffused in the half-light of nightfall and that of the other is reflected in the bright light of day.

XXIX

The Country Folk

The lesser characters, with the possible exception of Raucho, are all typical inhabitants of the pampa. They are barely described. On the other hand, Güiraldes has recorded their mental attitudes, occupations, habits, and speech. In short, he has portrayed them by representing their personalities more than their physical appearance. Their particular sense of humor, for example, which is qualified by a dry wit and colorful imagery, is illustrated in the comment of an old *paisano* who remarks to Fabio, "Sos muy cachorro para miar como los perros grandes" (p. 36). Another attitude, shyness, proceeds from the awkward manner of the countryfolk assembled for the Christmas celebration:

> Sufrí la ilusión de que la paisanada no tenía más razón de ser que la de sus manos, inhábiles para el ocio. Eran aquéllos unos bultos pesados y fuertes, que las mujeres dejaban muertos sobre las faldas y que los hombres llevaban colgados de los brazos, como un estorbo (p. 100).

Contrasting with this is the horse-trainer Valerio's joy in combat and will to conquer, expressed in every movement as he breaks-in a bucking bronco:

> Valerio, de cuerpo pequeño y ágil, seguía a maravilla los lazos de una "bellaqueada" sabia en vueltas, sentadas, alabanzos y cimbrones. Su poncho acompasaba el hermoso enojo del bruto, que en cada corcovo lucía la esbeltez de un salto de dorado. Sus ijares se encogían temblorosos de vigor. Su cabeza rayaba casi el suelo en signos negativos y su lomo, encorvado, sostenía muy arriba la sonriente dominación del jinete (p. 71).

Similarly, each of the following personalities is described in terms of characteristic attitudes: The farm youths Pedro, Goyo, Horacio, Patrocinio and Antenor, hearty goodhumor; an un-named cow-hand who is badly hurt in a round-up, stoicism; the *puestero* don Sixto, superstitious fear; the *puestero* don Candelario, the spirit of hospitality; the *estanciero* don Leandro and the two other *estancieros,* paternally patriarchal authority; the tavern keeper don Pedro, convivial sociability; Burgos, Numa, the drunken pulpero, and the *forastero,* quarrelsome aggressiveness; the *curandera,* maternal solicitude.

Inseparable from the description of the inhabitants are their occupational activities. As the handling of cattle is the chief of these, Güiraldes has represented its various aspects. Besides the three cattle drives, he has also described many others that are typical of their profession. Among them are the round-up in Chapter XVI, the horse breaking by Valerio in Chapter VII, the skinning of a lamb in Chapter VIII, and of a horse in Chapter XXIV.

Principle among the habits that are common to the countryfolk is drinking *mate* tea, which is sucked from small gourds through thin tubes called *bombillas.* To offer *mate* to a visitor is a requisite of hospitality as is seen when Valerio orders it upon the arrival of don Segundo. It is also customary to pass a gourd of *mate,* like a peace pipe, round the circle of friends as a gesture of amicability: "...desde había un rato chupábamos por turno la bombilla..." (p. 270). By picturing the *paisanos* sipping their favorite beverages in seventeen instances Güiraldes has evoked their moments of friendly conviviality.

Equally typical of those who live and work in the open country is their manner of eating. The men squat round the campfire and cut slices from a roasting cow with their work knives: "...abajo de los sauces, ardían los fogones lamiendo la carne de los asadores. ¡Lindo olorcito!" On seven occasions, the cattlemen are described eating round a *fogón,* which plays so important a part in their daily lives. Not to be overlooked is his mention of their practice of rolling their own cigarettes: "... tranquilos armamos un par de cigarrillos de la guayaca ..." (p. 220). Because these various habits are a part of the native's way of life, their introduction adds a typical aspect to their portrayal.

Three revelant features stand out in the regional vernacular in which the countryfolk speak. The one that generally impresses the reader first is the terminology of their provincial dialect. The second is the colorful imagery that discloses the *paisanos'* vivid fantasy. The third feature is the impression of the sound of their speech that is transmitted from the written representation of their pronunciation. It produces upon the reader the effect of hearing the native voices. In all, Güiraldes' reproduction of the typical aspects of their language has given their oral expression a quality of authenticity.

Therefore, although Güiraldes hardly described the physical appearance of the countryfolk, nevertheless he has conveyed a sense of their presence by portraying the distinguishing features of their personalities.

Of particular interest are two incidents. In each of them a lesser character is cast in the image of a legendary gaucho personality. The first occurs in Chapter XIV where the police corporal recalls the figure of Sergeant Navarro in Gutiérrez's novel *Juan Moreira*. In Gutiérrez's novel the sergeant seeks to arrest Juan Moreira and commands him: "... dése preso."[1] In like manner, the corporal commands don Segundo: "¡Dése preso, amigo!" (p. 143). The second incident takes place in Chapter XXIII when Antenor engages in the tragic duel with the *forastero*. The manner in which Antenor deals the final blow recalls the figure of Martín Fierro in a similar plight. Fierro stabs the lunging savage and lifts him in the air on the blade of his knife:

Al fin de tanto lidiar

[1] Eduardo Gutiérrez, *Juan Moreira* (Buenos Aires, c. 1881), p. 146.

> En el cuchillo lo alcé
> En peso lo levanté
> A aquel hijo del desierto;[2]

Antenor dispatches his adversary in the same fashion:

> Un encontrón y vimos al forastero levantado hasta
> la misma altura de Antenor, para ser tirado de
> espalda como trapo (p. 50).

There is a still more significant aspect in the characterization of the native types: the features of the pampa reappear as moral attributes of its inhabitants. Specifically, the distant horizon, the impassivity, and the silence of the pampa are transferred to the men. The herdsmen, for example, are moved by the call of the wide open prairie to be ever on the march toward its distant horizon:

> Todos me parecían más grandes, más robustos,
> y en sus ojos se adivinaban los caminos del maña-
> na. De peones de estancia habían pasado a ser
> hombres de pampa. Tenían alma de resero, que
> es tener alma de horizonte (p. 62).

Furthermore, the impassive expression on their faces reflects the stoic indifference of the countryside to hardship:

> En sus rostros indiferentes el agua resbalaba como
> sobre el ñandubay[3] de los postes y no parecían más
> heridos que el campo mismo (p. 89).

And their silence seems to be a mute echo of the soundlessness of the grasslands:

> Cada cual se esforzaba en lucir su crédito, su
> conocimiento, su audacia, con ese silencio del
> gaucho, enemigo de los ruidos inútiles (p. 170).

The equation of the character of the pampa with that of its inhabitants points to Güiraldes' intention of representing the influence of nature in their personalities.

---

[2] José Hernández, *Martín Fierro* (edited by Eleutorio Tiscornia), (Buenos Aires, 1925), p. 188.
[3] Ñandubay is an Argentine hardwood.

Deserving of special attention is Raucho. He appears only briefly in the last two chapters as Fabio's new friend who helps him make the transition from *resero* to "hombre culto" (p. 284). But more important is the fact that he is the same *cajetilla agachao* (p. 278)[4] as in the author's previous novel *Raucho*. Indeed, in both novels his description coincides not only in name but also in identity as the son of don Leandro Galván. In *Raucho,* as has been indicated earlier, he is the figure the author himself at that age. When he appears again in *Don Segundo Sombra,* he once more represents Güiraldes.

[4] A city dandy who affects the appearance of a gaucho.

XXX

The Customs

Certainly one of the most picturesque aspects of life in the pampa is provided by the customs of the countryfolk. Some of them, such as *las payadas* and *las corridas de la sortija,* which are more closely associated with gaucho tradition are merely alluded to as reminiscenses of the past. Described, however, are *el juego del dedo tiznao,* a cockfight, horse races, and the country dances.

El juego del dedo tiznao is a game feigning a gaucho duel, commonly played among farm youths. It is described briefly in Chapter IV when Goyo and Horacio engage in a contest to mark each other with a finger, blackened with soot, instead of a knife.

The cockfight in Chapter XIII is given considerable attention. The battle between the feathered combatants is made to live with convincing reality because Fabio describes it, not as a mere spectator, but as an interested party. His sympathies are for the speckled cock with the broken beak. In fact during a running account of the fight, he involves the reader in his anxiety for the bird by making it seem human. Furthermore Güiraldes has given the contest the impact of a drama. He has presented it as a miniature theatrical performance. The dramatic steps are the introduction of the protogonists (the modest speckled cock and its opponente, a truculent fowl of a tortoise-shell color), the development of the conflict to the point of suspense when the antagonist is gaining, and the sudden happy solution when the speckled cock finishes off its adversary in a single blow.

The horse races, described in Chapter XX, are typical of the rural environment. They take place near a *boliche*[1] in the

---

[1] In Argentina *boliche* carries the connotation of a poor country tavern.

pampa where the local inhabitants compete with their *criollo* horses. The description of the horses and the excitement of the events are communicated to the reader from the dialogue when don Segundo and Fabio converse with several *paisanos* on the merits of the various entries. The races themselves are represented also from the point of view of Fabio whose betting fever passes through the stages of anticipation, enthusiasm, recklessness, and frustration as he watches his choices run down the track and lose.

Most picturesque of all is the description in Chapter XI of the country dances. It is an artistic *cuadro de costumbres*. The countryfolk begin with the more common steps of the waltz, the mazurka, and the polka and soon proceed to the traditional *gato cantado, gato con relación, triunfo* and *prado*. The dances are described with a gradual crescendo of their tempo from a slow beginning to a high pitch of animation. When the first notes of the more formal dances are played, the *paisanos* begin to move stiffly. But their animation increases gradually during the traditional dances until the strumming of the guitars fills the air with vigor. Finally, two couples, "que sepan floriarse," launch themselves into the evolutions of the *gato cantado*. The scene is enlivened with music, movement, and emotion. Güiraldes has produced the effect by a special treament of these three elements. The sensation of the music is transmitted by the suggestion of its sounds and its rhythm. The guitars, for example, seem nearly audible:

> El latigazo intermitente de acento iba irradiando
> valentías de tambor en el ambiente (pp. 104-105).

The movement of the dancers is coordinated with the rhythm and is described in terms of sight and sound. The couples respond to the accelerated pace of the chords:

> Un apuro repentino enojó los cuerpos viriles
> (p. 106).

The sound of their feet keeps time with the beat:

> Tras el leve siseo de las botas de potro trabajando

> un escobilleo de preludio, los talones y las plantas
> traquetearon un ritmo, que multiplicó de impa-
> ciencia el amplio acento de las guitarras esmeradas
> en marcar el compás (p. 106).

A sense of harmonious motion is conveyed by the description
of the waving folds of the men's gaucho trousers:

> Agitábanse como breves aguas los pliegues de los
> chiripases (p. 106).

And the dance ends with a colorful flourish of skirts and
petticoats:

> Las faldas femeninas se abrieron, más suntuosas,
> y el percal lució como pequeños campos de trébol
> florido, la fina tonalidad de su lujo agreste p, 106).

Furthermore the emotions of the *paisanos* infuse the dancers
with the breath of life. Their initial shyness is revealed at the
beginning in the descriptions of their immobility. When they
begin to dance, they hold each other rigidly at arms' length.
As the tense atmosphere dissolves, the couples express their
festive emotion in the artistic postures of the traditional *gato*:

> Los hombres con ágiles galanteos de gallo que
> arrastran el ala . . .
> Las mujeres tomaron entre sus dedos las faldas,
> que abrieron en abanico, como queriendo recibir
> una dádiva o proteger algo (p. 105).

Finally all are moved by the spirit of the dance:

> . . . pero una alegría involuntaria era dueña de
> todos nosotros, pues sentíamos que aquélla era la
> mímica de nuestros amores y contentos (p. 106).

Of course, the introduction of these customs, including don
Segundo's *criollo* storytelling, has embellished the novel with
a pageant of folklore. But, more than this, Güiraldes also
has interpreted the artistic expression of the countryfolk.

XXXI

The Pampa

The pampa in the novel is no longer the wild, open prairie roamed by the gauchos of old. The numerous references to *callejones* (p. 234), along which the riders travel, and to the wire fences (p. 219), that enclose the grasslands, as well as the mention of farm machinery (p. 97), all indicate that Güiraldes has represented the Argentine countryside of the twentieth century.

The setting in which the novel begins is San Antonio de Areco,[1] a country village that lies in the pampa a little more than eighty miles from Buenos Aires. This community is the nearest to "La Porteña," the Güiraldes *estancia,* situated a few miles away. While the town is not named in the book, two references are sufficient to establish its identity. One is the mention of the *pulpería "La Blanqueada"* (pp. 11, 17, 21, 273) which is located there. The other is the description of the bridge,[2] the old stone structure that spans the Areco River (p. 11). The region throughout which the riders travel is specifically designated as the Province of Buenos Aires:

> Llevados por nuestro oficio, habíamos corrido gran
> parte de la provincia, Ranchos, Matanzas, Perga-
> mino, Rojas, Baradero, Lobos, el Azul, Las Flo-
> res, Chascomús, Dolores, el Tuyú, Tapalqué y
> muchos otros partidos... (p. 94).

Also identifying the area is the mention of the towns of Navarro (p. 123) and Luján (p. 273).

Within this region are its typical places. Some of these are the *Boliches* and *pulperías* such as "La Blanqueada," the

---

[1] Federico Ernst, "Recuerdo de Don Segundo," *El Hogar* (Buenos Aires, Oct. 18, 1957), p. 3.
[2] The location of the bridge is described in an anonymous article, "El Puente Viejo," in *El Hogar* (Buenos Aires, Oct. 18, 1957), p. 3.

almacenes, and the *ranchos* of the *puesteros.* There is no attempt, however, to picture them in the light of quaint local landmarks as seen by an outsider. On the contrary, they are approached from the point of view of the rural inhabitant who is already familiar with them. Their description therefore is limited to the minimum necessary to identify them to the native reader who needs no further explanation.

The landscape of the pampa rises forcefully from the background of the narration. Its most outstanding aspect is its personality. Like a human countenance it expresses feelings. Some of these are:

Joy

> Los postes, los alambrados, los cardos, lloraron su alegría (p. 90).

Sleep

> ...el campo que nada quería saber fuera de su reposo (p. 105).

Suffering

> La pampa debía sufrir por ese lado... (p. 148).

Fear

> ¡Qué amabilidad la de esos pagos, que se divertían en poner cara de susto! (p. 160).

Ruthlessness

> ...la pampa al que anda trastabillando muy pronto se lo traga... (p. 165).

Death

> Pobre campo sufridor el de estos pagos y tan guacho como yo de cariño. Tenía cara de muerto (p. 204).

Impassivity

> Y salimos al galope corto, rumbo al campo, que poco a poco nos fue tragando en su indiferencia (p. 217).

The humanization of nature does not carry a symbolic significance. It is quite simply a poetic interpretation of the pampa. It also serves as an artistic background to the representation of the characters. Indeed, as has been observed, the human features of the pampa parallel the attributes of its inhabitants. The most notable of these, which Güiraldes has ascribed to both the men and their setting, is stoicism.

The essence of the pampa envelopes the novel in a regional atmosphere. Güiraldes has produced this effect, not by presenting the landscape as an object of description *per se,* but by reproducing the fleeting impressions he mentions in the following passage:

> En la pampa las impresiones son rápidas, espasmódicas, para luego borrarse en la amplitud del ambiente sin dejar huella (p. 75).

In fact, by interspering them throughout the narration like a succession of glimpses, he conveys the presence of the pampa. Furthermore, in doing so, he has not represented the environment objectively, but has interpreted it through Fabio's subjective experiences. Of these there are two kinds: the physical and the mental. Both are often combined in the treatment of the same impression.

Fabio's physical experiences cover the various aspects of his environment, including the landscape, the sky, the weather, the animals, the cattle drives, and his daily life. They are conveyed in terms of his five senses. Frequently, the representation of several sensations in a single passage is used to communicate the awareness of the moment, as in the following instance:

Feeling
> Respiré hondamente el aliento de los campos dormidos.

Sight
> Era una oscuridad serena, alegrada de luminares lucientes como chispas de un fuego ruidoso.

Hearing
> A lo lejos oí tintinear un cencerro.

Smell

> Los novillos no daban aún señales de su vida tosca,
> pero yo sentía el olor de la presencia de sus qui-
> nientos cuerpos gruesos (p. 60).

The sense of taste appears in only two instances, one of which is the following:

> Con mi padrino, nos arrimamos a un cordero de
> pella dorada por el fuego. ¡Carnecita sabrosa y
> tierna! (p. 137).

Related to the sounds of the pampa is its silence. Because of the contrast the effect is impressive:

> Ya muy lejos, la montonera de hacienda iba alar-
> gándose y eran los gritos un eco muy reducido ...
> ¡Qué silencio! (p. 172).

Singly, each mention of Fabio's physical experiences transmits to the readers the feeling of that moment. But more than that, Güiraldes has reproduced also sensations of a prolonged nature. He has done this by repeating certain of these single impressions like a theme throughout the narration. Thus, for example, the varying hues of sunlight, twilight, and darkness reproduce a constant picture of the surroundings, particularly of the prairie and of the sky. The continuous lowing of the cattle strengthens the consciousness of their presence. During the first cattle drive, Fabio's increasing fatigue and aches intensify the whole long trial. The sway of his horse's pace, equated with the plodding motion of the cattle, suggests the perduring rhythm of the herd on the march. The tinkling of the lead mares' bells punctuates the journey with a musical note against the background of the pampa's infinite silence. All together, these brief glimpses of the landscape, the sky, the animals, and the herdsman's daily life produce a total awareness of the pampa. Because they are represented as physical experiences, they have a quality of reality.

Güiraldes has combined such experiences of the senses with

projections of Fabio's state of mind or mood. At the beginning
of the novel, for example, when Fabio sets out across the
countryside on a new life of adventure, his feeling of exhilira-
tion is associated with the fields, sparkling in the morning
sunshine.

> Sentíame en poder de un contento indescriptible.
> Una luz fresca chorreaba de oro el campo. Mis
> petizos parecían esmaltados de color nuevo. En-
> derredor, los pastizales renacían en silencio, chis-
> peantes de rocío; . . . (p. 33).

It is to be noted for future reference that the passage ends
with tears of joy:

> . . . y me reí de inmenso contento, me reí de liber-
> tad, mientras mis ojos se llenaban de cristales co-
> mo si también ellos se renovaran en el sereno
> matinal (p. 33).

Also expressive of Fabio's moods are the descriptions of the
stars. When, for instance, he leaves Paula and rides dolefully
away into the night, the stars communicate his unhappiness:

> Y había tantas estrellas, que se me caían en los
> ojos como lágrimas que debiera llorar para aden-
> tro (p. 204).

Other examples in which Güiraldes has described the pampa
in the light of Fabio's moods are the following:

Satisfaction

> Respiré hondamente el aliento de los campos
> dormidos. Era una oscuridad serena, alegrada de
> luminares lucientes como chispas de un fuego rui-
> doso. Al dejar que entrara en mí aquel silencio
> me sentí más fuerte y más grande (p. 60).

A sense of infinity

> La puerta pegaba con energía sus cuatro golpes
> rígidos en el muro, abriéndolo a la noche hecha
> de infinito y astros, sobre el campo que nada
> quería saber fuera de su reposo (p. 105).

A sense of the vastness of the world
> Perdido en la noche, cantó un gallo, despertando
> la simpatía de unos teros. Solitarias expresiones
> de vida, que simplificaban la inmensidad del
> mundo (p. 61).

Loneliness
> Atardecía. El cielo tendió unas nubes sobre el
> horizonte, como un paisano acomoda sus colorea-
> das matras para dormir. Sentí que la soledad me
> corría por el espinazo como un chorrito de agua.
> La noche nos perdió en su oscuridad (p. 148).

Moral strength and impassivity
> De grande y tranquilo que era el campo, algo nos
> regalaba de su grandeza y su indiferencia (p. 233).

Serenity
> Como un arroyo que se encuentra en un remanso,
> daba vueltas y me sentía profundo, lleno de una
> pesada quietud.
>
> . . . .
>
> Ahí estaba la noche, de quien me sentía imagen
> (p. 280).

Finally, as the novel comes to an end, the increasing darkness
in which the landscape is steeped reflects Fabio's sadness:

> El anochecer vencía lento, seguro, como no está
> turbada por un resultado dudoso (p. 285).

Then, in contrast with the tears of joy that mark Fabio's ex-
hiliration at the beginning of the novel, the reader receives
a last glimpse of the darkening plain through Fabio's tears
of sorrow:

> ...algo nublaba mi vista, tal vez el esfuerzo, y
> una luz llena de pequeñas vibraciones se extendió
> sobre la llanura (p. 286).

As has been seen in the descriptions of the landscape,
Güiraldes has combined Fabio's emotions with impressions

of light. Sunlight is joyous, starlight is mediative, and darkness imparts somber moods. Furthermore, it will be observed that throughout the novel the variations in light, which start with the glimmer of dawn and close with the shadow of dusk, are coordinated with the changing climate of Fabio's emotions, which begin with joy and end with sorrow.

This dual approach from the senses as well as from the sentiments of Fabio conveys the impression of living not only the physical but also the emotional experiences of the pampa. By the same measure, Fabio's sensitivity to nature, which is Güiraldes', is largely accountable for the poetic character of the novel.

XXXII

Symbolism in *Don Segundo Sombra*

Certain concepts underlie the narration. Principal among these are the course of life, destiny, adversity, and the particular spirit of the gaucho. They have been represented in terms of aspects of the pampa. As will appear in the following illustrations, the imagery, while used to describe poetically, also carries a symbolical significance.

The Course of Life

Water is the symbol of life. It appears in three different combinations. The first is with rivers and ponds, the second with the image of don Segundo and with the trails of the pampa, and the third with sleep. In rivers and ponds the varying degrees of running and still water represent Fabio's past years:

> Está visto que en mi vida el agua es como un
> espejo en que desfilan las imágenes del pasado
> (p. 281).

At the beginning of the story, the fast flowing stream that carries away the cork of Fabio's fishing line suggests the course of events that is about to change the life of an aimless boy:

> Pareciéndome la pesca misma un gesto superfluo
> dejé que el corcho de mi aparejo, llevado por la
> corriente, viniera a recostarse contra la orilla
> (p. 11).

Later, in the slow moving river, the little whirlpool, so like the dimple in a child's cheek, brings back recollections of Fabio's childhood:

> Mi vista cayó sobre el río, cuya corriente apenas
> perceptible hacía cerca mío un hoyuelo, como la
> risa en la mejilla tersa de un niño (p. 92).

Lastly, the calm water of a pond reflects Fabio's steady character as a man:

> La laguna hacía en las orillas unos flequitos cribados (p. 281).

The course of human existence is carried forward in the poetic image of don Segundo. The metaphor "río" stands for Fabio's life as he follows in the trail of the mysterious gaucho:

> Me parecía haber visto . . . algo que me atraía con la fuerza de un remanso, cuya hondura sorbe la corriente del río (p. 21).

Once the metaphor "río" is established as the symbol of life, when it is subsequently applied to poetize the aspect of the pampa trails, it continues to convey the suggestion of the progress of Fabio's existence. Thus, when the trails are compared to flowing streams, they too acquire the symbolical significance of the road of life:

> . . . el callejón se ensanchó como un río que llega a la laguna (p. 82).

> Por trechos la tierra dura parecía tan barnizada, que reflejaba el cielo como un arroyo (p. 89).

> Por el camino, que fingía un arroyo de tierra, caballo y jinete repecharon la loma . . .

> . . . .

> Demasiado sentía yo en mí la sorbente sugestión de todo camino para no comprender que en don Segundo huella y vida eran una sola cosa (p. 285).

The images of streams which are associated with sleep also have a multiple force. One is the pictorial description of sleep itself, another is the suggestion of the qualities of oblivion and peacefulness, and the third is the symbolization of the end of the journey:

> Y esperamos con calma que se nos fuera acercando la noche, poco a poco, como una cosa grande

y mansa en la que nos íbamos a ir suavecito, de
costillas, como un río que va gozando su carrerita
de olvido y comodidad (p. 261).

Como un arroyo que se encuentra con un reman-
so, daba vueltas y me sentía profundo, lleno de
una pesada quietud (p. 280).

Destiny

It has been noted that destiny is a governing force in
guiding Fabio's career:

¿No se es dueño entonces de nada en la propia
persona? ¿Un encuentro inesperado puede pre-
sentarse, así, en forma de destino...? (p. 253).

¡Suerte! ¡Suerte! ¡No hay más que mirarte en la
cara y aceptarte linda o fea, como se te da la gana!
(p. 254).

One of the lessons don Segundo teaches his ward is to accept
it unflinchingly:

También supe por él . . . el fatalismo en aceptar
sin rezongos lo sucedido . . . (p. 93).

While Güiraldes has described destiny in plain terms, he has
also represented it in symbols. Because it affects the course
of Fabio's life, the images of destiny and life are pictured
together in two instances. In the first, the insignificant cork
of Fabio's fishing tackle carried by the stream symbolizes
both the boy's life and the force of destiny which sweeps him
along in its current:

...corcho, llevado por la corriente... (p. 11).

The concept reappears in the description of don Segundo in
which the river again represents Fabio's life. Here too, the
power of fate draws Fabio into its course:

... algo que me atraía con la fuerza de un reman-
so ... (p. 21).

In a subsequent passage the fortuitous change in Fabio's career is pictured in the image of a bur which has attached itself by chance to don Segundo's trousers and is carried away:

> Pensé en don Segundo, que en su paso por mi pueblo me llevó tras él, como podía haber llevado un abrojo de los cercos en el chiripá (p. 92).

At the end of the novel, destiny, which separates Fabio from don Segundo, is symbolized in the image of the diverging paths of the two riders:

> El caballo de don Segundo, dió el anca al mío y realicé, en aquella divergencia, todo lo que iba a separar nuestros destinos (p. 265).

The Falls

In his boyhood struggles against physical adversity, Fabio's defeats are symbolized in a series of falls. For instance, he falls from his chair because of fatigue in Chapter IV, from his horse in Chapter VII, and from exhaustion at the end of the first day's cattle drive in Chapter VIII. Conversely, after he has achieved the stature and the dexterity of a young gaucho, his triumph over his physical hardships is represented in the fact that he is able to keep his saddle and to fall on his feet. It is illustrated in Chapter XVI when his horse falls beneath him and he lands in a standing position. Also symbolized in the image of the fall are his failures of a moral nature. When, in Chapter XXV, Fabio is about to disgrace himself again by fighting his friend Pedro Barrales, don Segundo restrains him and says meaningfully, "Si es que te has caído, yo te puedo ayudar a subir" (p. 267).

The Spirit of The Gaucho

Reference is made to that elusive attribute in the gaucho character which Güiraldes describes as "alma de horizonte." More than the urge to travel toward the distant horizon, it is a mental attitude best expressed in the similar metaphor "alma

de proa." It appears throughout the novel in the spirit of
optimism with which don Segundo tempers his stoic acceptance of adversity. Its presence introduces a cheerful note, not
unlike the sound of the lead mare's bells. Indeed, besides its
aesthetic effect, the crystal-like ring of the *cencerros* that ac-
companies the progress of the horsemen's journey subtly
acquires the significance of this moral quality of the gaucho.
The first suggestion of its symbolic meaning appears in the
following passage:

> Goyo y yo abrimos la tranquera del corral, dejando
> salir las tropillas que pronto hicieron familia cada
> cual con su madrina, cuyo cencerro les sirve de
> voluntad (p. 63).

The same concept lies beneath the description in two subsequent passages:

> Las tropillas que iban delante llamaban siempre
> con sus cencerros claros (p. 75).

> Guiado por los cencerros caminé hasta ver la gran
> silueta del paisano, abultado en la noche (p. 84).

Finally, Güiraldes clearly reveals the symbolism of the lead
mare's bell when he represents don Segundo using the word
"alma" instead of "cencerro" in the imagery of the following
statement:

> —Si sos gaucho en de veras, no has de mudar,
> porque andequiera que vayas, irás con tu alma
> por delante como madrina's tropilla (p. 271).

Don Segundo Sombra

Don Segundo is also a symbol. The concept he represents
is contained in the image of the shadow. Because of the vagueness of the word, its meaning is not at first clear. Indeed, it
merely suggests a symbolic significance, motivating the reader
to seek an interpretation. A possible explanation seems to lie
in the similarity of the old gaucho's character with the per-

sonified aspects of nature. This would lead to the supposition
that don Segundo is a symbol of the pampa. The thought is
supported by the image in Güiraldes' poem "Al hombre que
pasó," in which the gaucho is described as "símbolo pampeano." The impression, however, is misleading. Don Segundo
is not the symbol of the pampa itself, but of certain aspects
of its inhabitants. As already shown, the image of the shadow,
associated with that of an apparition, carries the suggestion of
a gaucho of the past. It evokes the semblance of Martín Fierro
and of other legendary figures. As don Segundo's personality
unfolds during the narration, he discloses the positive attributes of the men of the pampa. When finally at the end of
the novel he is again abstracted into a shadow and then into
"un alma," he clearly symbolizes the noble qualities in the
character of the gauchos of all time.

The symbols of water, its current, Fabio's falls, and the ring
of the horse-bells provide the narration with a suggestive
background that colors the journey of the two horsemen
with deeper meaning. More, subtle, however, is the symbolism
in the figure of don Segundo, because it represents human
character in the image of a fictional personality.

XXXIII

The Style

There are three variations in style in *Don Segundo Sombra*. The first is in the utterances of the rustics, the second in the tales told by don Segundo, and the third is in the narration proper. In all of them the Argentine vernacular is present to a degree. In fact, its significance in each of the differing styles warrants a good look at the regional dialect before proceeding further.

The vernacular in the novel is comparable to that in *Martín Fierro* and other gauchesque poems. It is also spoken by the rural inhabitants of the Province of Buenos Aires. Güiraldes has captured the language by reproducing its principal features. These are its pronounciation, its parts of speech, its terminology, and its imagery.

The sounds of the pronounciation are represented in the spelling as in the expression "naides haiga." Similarly reproduced are the vernacular variation in the parts of speech. Among them are the verbal as "querés dirte," the adverbial as "en torno mío," the exclamations such as "¡Jué pucha!" and the epithets as "¡Negro indino!" Altogether these written forms produce upon the reader, who is familiar with the dialect, the impression of hearing it spoken.

The terminology[1] of the vernacular can be divided into three categories, each corresponding to a distinct aspect of the rustic atmosphere. One group of words is of Indian origin; other expressions are in Spanish but have a particular regional meaning; and the last are terms associated with horses

---

[1] The vernacular terminology in *Don Segundo Sombra* with its corresponding meanings in Spanish is the subject of a learned study by Horacio Jorge Becco in his *Don Segundo Sombra y su vocabulario* (Buenos Aires, 1952), and has been listed in a glossary by Pablo Rojas Paz in his "Caudal lexicográfico de Ricardo Güiraldes" in the edition of *Don Segundo Sombra*, published by Editorial Pleamar (Buenos Aires, 1943), pp. 237-291.

and cattle. Most of the Indian words refer to indigenous flora and fauna as for example *caburé*, a small native bird; *charabón*, an ostrich chick; *mamboretá*, a mantis; *mangangá*, a variety of wild bee; *ñandu*, an ostrich; *ñandubay*, a local hardwood, *yaguareté*, a large jaguar; and *yararás*, a large snake. Others are *gualicho*, an evil charm or talisman, and *guayaca*, a tobacco pouch usually made from the craw of an ostrich. Not to be forgotten are the native words for a parentless waif, *guacho*, and the Indian name for the Devil, *Añang*. The aboriginal terms not only recall the partly Indian origin of the gauchos and their descendants but they also introduce an exotic touch into the speech of the *paisanos*.

More frequent, however, are those expressions which, although in Spanish, carry a particular meaning in the vernacular. Some of them are *bicho-feo*, a native bird; *estar en pedo*, to be drunk; *fiero*, ugly; *ganar el lado de las casas*, to win a person's confidence; *hace una ponchada de años*, many years ago; *hacer sebo*, to loaf; *largar el brulote*, to speak out of turn; *pitar el juerte*, to have a disagreeable experience; *saber venir*, to use to come; *sombra'e toro*, an indigenous tree. Their appearance in the languages of the characters reproduces the quaintness of the countryfolk's way speaking and, along with it, a certain rustic charm of the speakers.

Horses, which are ever present, are referred to in local terms of their color and merits as for instance *crédito*, a horse to be proud of; *malacara*, a horse with a white streak down the front of its head; *mancarrón*, a lame and almost useless horse; *petiso*, a small horse; *pingo*, a fast and spirited horse; and *rodomón*, a half wild horse. There are many other expressions common to the cattlemen's profession. Some of these are *bajar los cueros*, to unsaddle; *bellaqueada*, the rearing of a horse; *echar a verijas*, the act of pulling a rope in lassoing; *entablar una tropilla*, to train horses to follow a lead mare; *lao del lazo*, the right side of a horse; *lloronas*, spurs; *recado*, saddle and trappings; *rienda abajo*, leaving a docile horse standing untied;

tendida, the galloping spurt of a frightened horse; and *tranco,* a horse's walking pace. This equestrian terminology, which is typical of the parlance of the inhabitants of the pampa, conveys the atmosphere of a world of horses and cattle.

Imagery is the colorful feature that characterizes the expression of the *paisanos.* Since it is in terms of the surrounding realia, it refers mostly to animals. Besides providing an element of caricature when applied to the description of humans, it qualifies their speech with picturesqueness:

> Un paisano... quedó como borrego que ha perdido el rumbo de un golpe (p. 101).

Furthermore, conforming to the usage of the vernacular, the most frequent form in which the images are expressed is the simile as in the following illustration:

> Los brazos se me cayeron como alones de avestruz cansado (p. 193).

The other common form in which the images are expressed is the adverb of comparison that appears in the following example:

> ...el pobre muchacho ... quedó más estirao que cuero en las estacas (p. 114).

Equally typical, although represented less frequently, are the images occurring in analogies. In these instances, they appear in metaphorical terms. For example, an old paisano, modestly protesting that he is too old and ugly to dance with a pretty farm girl, says:

> ... a una madrinita como ésta no se le acollara mancarrón tan fiero (p. 102).

All together, by recording the sounds, the structural forms, and the terminology of the vernacular, Güiraldes has reproduced the regional language with the naturalness of the spoken word. He has also captured in the imagery the colorful fantasy and the humor of the countryfolk.

Of the several styles the one in the utterances of the characters wholly conforms to the vernacular. Besides this, the speech of the rustics reflects their laconic nature. Their remarks are therefore few and expressed in a curt manner. In great part they are limited to brief comments, sayings, proverbs and exclamatory statements. Nevertheless, because they are full of humor and imagery, they introduce a note of animation. True to life, Güiraldes has represented the countryfolk's delight in illustrating their expression with imaginative analogies as, for example, in the comment:

> No te fíes de los gallos que entran dando el anca
> (p. 156).;

in the saying:

> ...al que tiene mala entraña no le conviene mostrar la hilacha (p. 208);

in the proverb:

> No hay taba sin culo (p. 170).

and in the exclamatory statement:

> ¡Qué cotorra pa' mi jaula! (p. 101).

Though colorful, they are not poetic. On the contrary, their style is prosaic. This is necessarily so, since the manner in which the countryfolk speak is an expression of their down-to-earth personality. In fact, there is a total lack of cultural refinements which, by contrast with the literary quality of don Segundo's stories and of the narrative part of the novel, emphasizes the rusticity of the utterances of the characters.

Although don Segundo tells his stories in the same vernacular, his style as a raconteur differs from that of the utterances of the other countryfolk. His language preserves the previously described features of the dialect, but at the same time it is molded into a literary form. This is seen in the elegant turn of phrase and in the balanced absolute constructions which reveal the hand of a skilled writer:

> Compadecida, la vieja le dijo que ella sabía de brujerías y que le ayudaría, dándole unas virtudes

> pa rescatar la prenda, que el hijo'el Diablo le ha-
> bía robao con tan malas leyes (p. 116).

Furthermore, the polished elaboration of the sentences is such that they follow each other in a flowing sequence. In all, the literary structure of the language of the tales becomes apparent by translating its passages from the vernacular into current Spanish. Shorn thus of its regional mask, it will reveal itself to be Güiraldes' own narrative style.

In determining the style in which Fabio narrates the novel, Güiraldes faced a problem of choice. His purpose was to interpret don Segundo and the pampa artistically. On the other hand, he wished to represent the rustic personality of the narrator. Thus, there was the possibility of one of two approaches. The first was that of the novelist which lent itself to the refinements of a literary treatment. The second was that of Fabio who, as one of the rustics in the novel, would express himself only in the vernacular. Güiraldes resolved this inconsistency by combining both approaches within the form of memoirs of Fabio, who had since learned to write. The style, therefore, conforms to the literary expression of "un hombre culto," interwoven with the regionalism of "un alma sencilla." Accordingly, the narration is written in Güiraldes' carefully worked literary style, the characteristics of which are its concision and the absence of rhetorical embellishments. The following example is typical of many in which he has fused the extreme simplicity of his expression with a vernacular form:

> Cerca nuestro había un rosal florecido (p. 184).

Since Güiraldes was concerned principally with the interpretation of the aesthetic, emotive and metaphysical features of the pampa and its inhabitants, his style is predominantly poetic. The poetry in it is derived in the main from the imagery.

It is recalled that images are also a characteristic feature of the vernacular. As was said, they are colorful or humorous but they are not aesthetic. Indeed, like the speakers of the regional dialect they are rustic. Now it appears that Güiraldes has introduced just such rustic images into his narrative style:

> ...la tormenta había pasado como vuelo de hal-
> cón sobre el gallinero (p. 257).

Gallinero certainly is a prosaic word. Nevertheless the total effect is poetic. The poetry however, lies in the idea. What Güiraldes has done is to dress a poetic thought in refreshingly bold images. In doing so he has somehow sharpened the whole picture.

He has also made an extensive use of more aesthetic images. They are of three kinds, visual, suggestive, and abstract. The visual images produce striking pictorial effects:

> Su poncho acompasaba el hermoso enojo del bruto
> que en cada corcovo lucía la esbeltez de un salto
> de dorado (p. 71).

Among the suggestive are those that communicate a special quality of sound:

> ...las lechuzas empezaron a jugar a las escon-
> didas, llamándose con gargantas de terciopelo
> (p. 82).

Others which suggest the human features of nature are the basis of Güiraldes' description of the pampa:

> El pasto y los cardos esperaban con pasión segura.
> El campo entero escuchaba (p. 87).

The most subtle are the abstractions in which he has sublimated certain intangibles aspects of the characters and of nature. The following illustrates his treatment of the cattlemen's spirit of adventure:

> Tenían alma de reseros, que es alma de horizonte
> (p. 62).

Similarly, an indefinable aspect of the pampa is expressed in another abstraction:

Y el campo había vuelto a su calidad de desierto.
... vació que tenía algo de eternidad (p. 176).

The intangible aspects of don Segundo are also described in abstract images. The increasing indefiniteness of each image suggests the progressively evanescent quality of the mysterious horseman.

A ghost-like apparition:

Me pareció haber visto un fantasma (p. 21).

A shade:

... algo que pasa y es más una idea que un hombre (p. 21).

And finally, a spirit:

No sé qué extraña sugestión me proponía la presencia de un alma (p. 286).

By reiterating at the end of the novel the same images that appeared at the beginning, Güiraldes gives them added poetic force:

Aquello que se alejaba era más una idea que un hombre (p. 285).

"Sombra", me repetí (p. 286).

Regarding the form in which the images are cast it is interesting to observe the prevalence of the simile in the visual figures, of which the following is one of many:

El cielo tendió unas nubes sobre el horizonte,
como paisano acomoda sus coloreadas matras
para dormir (p. 148).

On the other hand, because of their more literary character, the images of suggestion are expressed mainly in verbal metaphors:

Los postes, los alambrados, los cardos lloraron su alegría (p. 90).

Not a few, however, are also represented in similes:

¡ ... Qué gusto moverse en el aire que me caía de todos lados, como cariño! (p. 233).

In the case of abstractions, the delicate quality of their concepts calls for a polished literary form. Consequently they are found most frequently in a metaphor contained in a prepositional phrase:

> ...La noche hecha de infinito (p. 105).

But, here again, some images, though abstract, are expressed in similes:

> Breves palabras caían como cenizas de pensamientos internos (p. 111).

The outstanding feature about the forms in which the images are cast is the abundance of similes. In a poetic style one would expected a greater use of metaphors as a more sophisticated device. But Güiraldes leaned toward the simile precisely because of its simplicity. In fact, by consciously availing himself of this elementary form of the vernacular, he succeeded in giving his narrative style something of that naïve charm which characterizes the speech of the rustics.

In review, the illustrations have not only shown that the images and their various treatments are the basis of the poetic style. They have also disclosed the stylized introduction of rustic images and form. Indeed, Güiraldes' poetization of these features of the vernacular constitutes an artistic literary innovation.

Besides the aspects just discussed, still another qualifies the poetic style. Güiraldes' expression is tempered with a flowing continuity. This is achieved by a careful elaboration of the sentences into the natural cadences of the language. The effect is to give the passages the rhythm of poetry, as can be ascertained by reading the following aloud:

> Inmóvil
> miré alejarse,
> extrañamente agrandada contra el horizonte luminoso,
> aquella silueta de caballo y jinete.
> Me pareció haber visto un fantasma,
> una sombra;

>   algo que pasa y es más una idea que un ser;
>   algo que me atraía con la fuerza de un remanso,
>   cuya hondura sorbe la corriente de un río (p. 21).

The passage has the quality of a poem in prose. Its rhythm, imagery and polished form are the elements which together distinguish the prevailing style in *Don Segundo Sombra*.

The technique of the refrain adds to the poetic quality of the style. It consists in the repetition of a single aspect of the environment. In this way, Güiraldes intensifies the impression and produces the effect of a refrain like that in a poem or in music. His application of it to several subject matters can be seen in the following illustrations:

The pitchfork

In the first example, the reader receives an impression of the sound of the pitchfork rattling on the bare boards of the little cart driven by Fabio when employed as a boy helper at don Leandro's *estancia*:

>   En los zanjones esgrimía yo el instrumento, que
>   luego venía matraqueando de una manera ensor-
>   decedora sobre las tablas del carro vacío (p. 36).

When the description is repeated, it acquires the significance of a familiar sound, similar in effect to a refrain:

>   ...un susto me hizo castigar al pobre bichoco,
>   tomando rumbo a las casas al compás del férreo
>   canto de la horquilla, que se temblequeaba sobre
>   las planchas del carrito (p. 45).

The March

The technique is used to greater advantage to mark the progress of the first cattle drive with an impression of rhythmic movement. The cadence of the marching animals is described initially in the following passages:

>   ...la marcha seguía pausada, sin cansancio (p. 67)
>
>   Absorto en el movimiento de las paletas fuertes y
>   el cabeceo rítmico, esperé a los troperos (p. 68).

It gathers intensity in succesive repetitions until it qualifies the description with a rhythmic beat:

> Animales y gente se movían como una idea fija:
> caminar, caminar, caminar (p. 75).

> Influído por el colectivo balanceo de aquella marcha, me dejé andar al ritmo general... (p. 76).

> ... sufría la ilusión de que el suelo todo se movía como una uniforme masa carnosa (p. 82).

> ... atrás todo iba quedando trillado por dos mil patas, cuyas pisadas sonaban en el barrial como masticación de rumiante (p. 89).

> ... volvimos a caer en nuestro ritmo contenido y voluntarioso: Caminar, caminar, caminar (p. 90).

The "Cencerros"

When the technique of the refrain is applied to the sound of the lead mares' bells, the reiteration of their tinkling embellishes the already poetic style with the aesthetic note of a musical accompaniment:

> A lo lejos oí tintenear un cencerro (p. 60).

> ... un cencerro agitó sus notas con precipitación de gotera (p. 60).

> Todo era quietud, salvo el leve cantar de los cencerros... (p. 81).

> La yegua madrina alzó la cabeza, desparramando un tropel de notas de su cencerro (p. 145).

In the novel as a whole, the stylistic elements, which have just been indicated, can also be identified in Güiraldes' previous works. They deserve a parting glance in the light of their origin in order fully to evaluate their contribution to the style in *Don Segundo Sombra*.

The language of the novel is poetic. Withal, it is simple in the extreme. Stripped of rhetorical adornments and reduced to the bare essentials, it is refined to a purity characteristic of the polished sentences in *Xaimaca*. The simplicity produces a concision of expression observed in those compositions of *El cencerro de cristal* which are reminiscent of Verlaine. Furthermore, the poetic content is transmitted through the naturalness of the spoken word with a spontaneity described by Corbière as "de l'âme et pas de violon."

The plainness of the expression is only an outward appearance. The sentences are carefully wrought into the natural cadence of the language. They follow upon each other with the meter of Güiraldes' poems in prose in which he sought to capture the rhythm of Flaubert's *chute de phrases*.

Like Mallarmé, Güiraldes used the technique of sublimating the subject matter in abstract images. This has been seen in metaphors like "alma de horizonte" in *Don Segundo Sombra*. They are remarkably similar in poetic treatment and concept to "sed de horizonte" and "alma de proa" in *El cencerro de cristal*. They differ, however, from the imagery of Mallarmé in that their significance is clear and they do not produce a climate of revery. It will be recalled, moreover, that in his poem "Al hombre que pasó" Güiraldes also sublimated the figure of the gaucho in the abstract metaphors "amor" and "coraje." When in a similar manner Güiraldes abstracts the human form of don Segundo into an idea, he, like Mallarmé, veils his subject in vague images which create a dreamlike impression.

Güiraldes' symbolism, however, is in the main unlike Mallarmé's Its meaning is not shrouded in cryptic metaphors like the French poet's. The contrary is true: water (which is the course of life), Fabio's falls (which represent adversity), and the ringing of the horse-bell (which echoes the gaucho's spirit of optimism) provide an artistic accompaniment to the travels of the riders in the same manner as, in *Rosaura,* the changing aspects of the garden underscore the girl's infatuation, and, in *Xaimaca,* the progress of the ship parallels the inevitability of the lovers' passion. But, the more subtle symbolic significance of the shadowy figure of don Segundo, who is the fictional incarnation of gaucho character, is the product of a poetic treatment which Güiraldes already had applied in "La hora del milagro" when he followed Mallarmé's "L'Après-midi d'un Faune."

Unquestionably Güiraldes adopted Laforgue's technique of the refrain. In like manner, he intensifies an impression of the environment by reiterating it. Examples appear first in *El cencerro de cristal* where the effect is created by the repetition of the *andante* motion of elephants in "Los filosofantes" and of "seria careta de bolsas repleta" in "Chacarera." Other instances appear in *Rosaura,* among them the different colors of the girls' dresses. In *Xaimaca,* they are the slow-moving ox-cart and the rhythm of the ship's engines. In *Don Segundo Sombra* the repetition of the sound of the pitchfork rattling in the little cart has a similar effect. Likewise, the reiteration of the motion of the cattle march produces a sense of rhythm comparable to that in "Los filosofantes" and to the throb of the ship's engines in *Xaimaca.* The treatment of the sounds of the horse-bells is closer to Laforgue's technique. It conveys a musical quality in a manner not unlike that in those poems of Laforgue in which he suggests the sounds of a hurdy-gurdy and of children's songs. It differs, however, in one respect: The French poet evokes the rhythm and the music by suggestion only, while Güiraldes also describes the sound. Regardless of this difference, the significant consideration is that it is a technique of Laforgue's poetry which Güiraldes has applied to his prose.

Beginning with *El cencerro de cristal* and ending with *Don Segundo Sombra,* the influence of French writers is apparent. It is in no sense an imitation of style. Indeed, apart from the use of their poetic techniques, the style in *Don Segundo Sombra* is entirely distinct, as can be observed alone from the nearly complete absence of elliptic language and obscure imagery. The explanation lies in Güiraldes' guiding principle that the form of the expression must correspond to the significance of the subject matter. As his intent was to represent the poetic, he availed himself of the devices which best suited his purpose. Among them are those which have no connection with the symbolists. The total contribution of all the poetic techniques has given the style in *Don Segundo Sombra* the quality of a poem in prose.

Within the poetic treatment is the rustic element provided by the vernacular speech of the characters. It introduces the flavor of the gauchesque that characterizes *Cuentos de muerte y de sangre*. The expression of the countryfolk, because it is unliterary, emphasizes by contrast the polished expression of the narrator. Nevertheless, it contains stylistically significant features. These are its well-known colorful imagery and the simple form in which it is expressed. Güiraldes exploited their artistic value to advantage when he transferred them to his own narrative style. By combining rustic images with poetic techniques he poetized the vernacular. Furthermore, by casting artistic images into simple forms, he qualified his literary style with the picturesqueness and natural charm of the language of the gaucho.

With the sensitivity of a poet, Güiraldes sought beauty everywhere, particularly in the objects of his affection. Viewing the pampa in this light, he interpreted its emotional and aesthetic aspects as he saw them. Indeed, he represented it in three different ways. It will be recalled that these are the sensory experiences of Fabio, his emotional sensations, and the pictorial descriptions. The reality of the environment rises from the first, the intangible presence of nature from the second, and its aesthetic appearance from the third. Each is but a mere glimpse of a different aspect and is conveyed in a few words or a brief line. Güiraldes has combined all three impressions to describe a single experience. Thus with the skill of an impressionist painter he captured the essence of the moment and communicated the spell of the pampa.

XXXIV

The Stature of *Don Segundo Sombra* among Novels

Because its subject matter is concerned with the Argentine pampa and its native types, *Don Segundo Sombra* falls within the class of Spanish American regional novels of which *La vorágine* (1924) by José Eustasio Rivera and *Doña Bárbara* (1929) by Rómulo Gallegos are the outstanding examples. Aside from the differences in style in these three works which have already been discussed by eminent critics,[1] certain aspects of the Argentine novel set it apart from the others. The chief distinction lies in Güiraldes' approach. While the other authors have also concentrated their attention upon descriptions of the native scene, the tropical forest in one and the Venezuelan plains in the other, they view the wilderness as city dwellers who are foreign to the environment. Thus nature appears exotic and hostile. Güiraldes, on the contrary, has approached the pampa, not as an outsider, but from the point of view of a native. By representing it through the impressions of the *gauchito,* he has produced a more authentic description of an American region.

Furthermore, the principal figures in *Don Segundo Sombra* differ from those in the other novels in that their character and their daily life are entirely regional. Don Segundo is a

[1] Fernando Alegría, *Breve historia de la novela hispanoamericana* (México, 1959); Enrique Anderson Imbert, *Historia de la literatura americana* (México-Buenos Aires, 1949); John A. Crow, "A Critical Appraisal of the Spanish American Novel," *Hispania* (XXIV, 1951), p. 155; Lowell Dunham, *Rómulo Gallegos, Vida y obra* (México, 1956); Pedro Henríquez Ureña, *Las corrientes literarias en la América hispánica* (México-Buenos Aires, 1949); Juan Marinello, "Tres novelas de la naturaleza americana, *Don Segundo Sombra, La vorágine, Doña Bárbara,*" *Revista Bimestre Cubana* (XXVIII, 1931), pp. 82-93; Eduardo Neale-Silva, *Horizonte Humano, vida de José Eustasio Rivera* (Madison, 1960); Jefferson Rea Spell, *Contemporary Spanish American Fiction* (Chapel Hill, 1944); Arturo Torres-Rioseco, *La novela en la América hispánica* (México-Buenos Aires, 1949).

typical *resero* of the region. Fabio's impressions and emotions
are common to an Argentine country boy. Altogether their
outlook on life is that of the *paisano*.

Besides this, don Segundo's resemblance to the traditional
gaucho and his moral character elevate his personality to
an unusual literary stature. By giving him the features of
Martín Fierro, Güiraldes has cast his image in an aura of
legend that has no equal in contemporary Spanish American
fiction. In attributing to him the noble qualities of the
gaucho, he has created a symbol of a philosophy of life, the
moral significance of which surpasses the characterizations
in the other novels.

Although certain features in *Don Segundo Sombra* have
been compared with those in *Don Quijote*,[2] there is little
in common between the two novels other than nostalgia and
the moral significance contained in the figures of both horsemen. Like the Caballero de la Triste Figura, the wandering
herdsman stands for the ideals of a disappearing race of men.
As don Quijote continues to travel down the centuries from
his journeys across La Mancha, the image of don Segundo
carries a lasting memory of the pampa.

The writer of this study has endeavored to indicate, over
and above the stylistic merits of the novel, the universal
human values that give *Don Segundo Sombra* its perennial
character in the literature of Argentina.

---

[2] See Eunice Joiner Gates, "A Note on the Resemblances between Don Segundo Sombra and Don Quijote," *Hispanic Review* (XIV, 1946), pp. 342-
343; also T. B. Irving, "Myth and Reality in *Don Segundo Sombra*," *Hispania*
(XL, March, 1957), pp. 44-48; Arturo Torres-Rioseco, *Novelas contemporá-
neas de América* (Santiago, 1939), pp. 142-143.

BIBLIOGRAPHY

Within existing limitations an attempt has been made to assemble a comprehensive bibliography of the writings of Ricardo Güiraldes and of the material which concerns his life and works. The following listing is classified into (I) the works of Ricardo Güiraldes, (II) translations, (III) critical and biographical material, and (IV) other bibliographies.

Under the heading of the works of Ricardo Güiraldes, the titles are divided into (1) the first editions of his books and (2) his other writings. Under translations, the listings have been separated into (1) translations of *Don Segundo Sombra* and (2) translations from his other books.

In view of the numerous printings of *Don Segundo Sombra*, reference is made to the first edition only. Suffice it to say that to date the publishing houses of Argentina and Spain have printed more than one hundred and twenty-five thousand copies of the novel. In the United States an edition, prepared by Ethel W. Plimpton and María Fernández for English speaking students of Spanish, was published by Henry Holt and Company in 1945. At the date of this writing the latest edition is being prepared for publication in Buenos Aires.[1] The book used in the present study was printed in Buenos Aires by Editorial Pleamar in 1943 from a first edition copy, corrected in Güiraldes' hand.

Don Segundo Sombra has been translated into twelve other languages. The first translation was made into French in 1932 by Marcelle Auclair. A German translation appeared in 1934. In 1935, Harriet de Onís translated the book into English under the title of *Don Segundo Sombra, Shadows on the Pampas.* The English translation was published simul-

---

[1] Güiraldes' widow, Adelina del Carril, in a letter to the writer, dated April 20, 1956, advised, "Ya están imprimiéndose sus 'Obras Completas', que espero saldrán este año entre junio y agosto."

taneously in two editions, one in England and one in the United States. The other translations[2] are in Czech, Danish, Dutch, Italian, Japanese,[3] Portuguese,[4] Swedish, Ukranian, and Yiddish. Of all the translations the most successful has been the French, which, by 1962, entered its twelfth edition. The extensive translations into foreign languages bespeak the universal appeal of *Don Segundo Sombra.*

Since some of the critical material has not been available in the United States, missing citations have been added from the bibliographies of María Teresa Beláustegui and Horacio Jorge Becco. Any merit that this compilation may have for completeness is in good measure due to these distinguished Argentine bibliographers of Ricardo Güiraldes. Their works are listed here under classification IV.

Not included in this bibliography is the Spanish language edition of the present book, which has been translated into Spanish by Professor Pablo Max Ynsfran of The University of Texas and will be published in Buenos Aires under the title of *Vida y Obra de Ricardo Güiraldes.*

[2] See María Teresa Beláustegui, "Contribución para el conocimiento de la bibliografía de Ricardo Güiraldes," in *Buenos Aires Literaria* (Año I, No. 2, Nov., 1952); pp. 48-55.

[3] See Harriet de Onís, *Spanish Stories and Tales* (New York, 1954), note on p. 165.

[4] Besides the edition mentioned by Beláustegui, Daniel Wogan, in "A literatura argentina no Brasil," *Revista Iberoamericana* (Feb., 1947), pp. 135-141, says that Hermes da Fonseca Filho has made an unpublished translation into Portuguese of *Don Segundo Sombra.*

I. Works of Ricardo Güiraldes

1. Books

El cencerro de cristal. Buenos Aires, Imprenta de José Tragant, Librería la Facultad, 1915.

Cuentos de muerte y de sangre; seguidos de aventuras grotescas y una trilogía cristiana. Buenos Aires, Imprenta de José Tragant, Librería la Facultad, 1915.

Raucho; momentos de una juventud contemporánea. Imprenta de José Tragant, Librería la Facultad, 1917.

Rosaura (Novela corta). San Antonio de Areco, Establecimiento Gráfico Colón, de F. A. Colombo, 1922.

Xaimaca. San Antonio de Areco, Establecimiento Gráfico Colón, de F. A. Colombo, 1923.

Don Segundo Sombra. Buenos Aires, Editorial Proa, 1926 (1 ed.).

Poemas místicos (Edición póstuma de Adelina del Carril de Güiraldes.) San Antonio de Areco, Imprenta Colón, de F. A. Colombo, 1928.

Poemas solitarios 1921-1927 (Edición póstuma de Adelina del Carril de Güiraldes.) San Antonio de Areco, Imprenta Colón, de F. A. Colombo, 1928.

Seis relatos. Buenos Aires, Editorial Proa, 1929.

El sendero. Notas sobre mi evolución espiritualista en vista de un futuro. (Edición póstuma de Adelina del Carril de Güiraldes.) Maestricht, Master Printer A. A. M. Stols, 1932.

El libro bravo. San Antonio de Areco. Establecimiento Gráfico Colón, de Francisco A. Colombo, 1936.

Rosaura (Novela corta) y siete cuentos. Buenos Aires, Editorial Losada, 1952.

Pampa (Poemas inéditos). Buenos Aires, Editorial Ollantay, 1954.

2. Other Writings

"Esta noche, Nochebuena," in *Cuentos de Navidad inéditos de distinguidos autores.* Buenos Aires, Editorial Proa, c. 1917.

"Telesforo Altamira," *La Nota* (Buenos Aires), 10 enero de 1919, p. 32.

"Un libro," *Proa*, No. 3, 1924, pp. 35-40.

"Un Hombre," *Ibid.*, No. 4, 1924, pp. 24-32.

"Un poeta," *Ibid.*, No. 5, 1924, pp. 12-15.

"Contestaciones a la encuesta de Martín Fierro," *Martín Fierro*, Segunda época, año I, Nos. 5 and 6, 1924, p. 6.

"Nota," *Proa*, No. 6, 1925, p. 71.

"Un prólogo," *loc. cit.*, pp. 41-47.

"Poemas" (including "Nubes," "Chimango," Centro," "Mate," and "Concierto"), *Proa*, No. 7, 1925, pp. 9-16.

"Carta a Guillermo de Torre," *ibid.*, No. 8, 1925, pp. 39-45.

"Un canto," *ibid.*, No. 9, 1925, pp. 31-34.

"Grafomanía," *ibid.*, No. 11, 1925, pp. 8-12.

"De mi hemorragia del No. XI," *ibid.*, No. 12, 1925, pp. 35-41.

"Afecto," *Martín Fierro*, Segunda época, año II, Nos. 14 and 15, 1925, p. 4.

"Remate," *loc. cit.*, p. 4.

"Ramón," *Martín Fierro*, Segunda época, año II, No. 19, 1925, p. 2.
"Poesía," *ibid.*, año IV, No. 39, 1927, pp. 1-3.
"Una carta inédita," *Síntesis* (Buenos Aires), V, 1928, pp. 155-157.
Mi caballo y el hombre que pasó. San Antonio de Areco, Talleres Gráficos "Colón," 1929.
"Dos poemas: Cangrejal, Fabián Tolosa," *Argentina*, No. 1, Nov., 1930, p. 5.
"Carta a Victoria Ocampo," *Sur*, año I, 1931, pp. 101-104.
"A Valery Larbaud," *ibid.*, pp. 105-108, 113-117.
"A su madre," *ibid.*, pp. 108-112.
"Carta a Valery Larbaud," *ibid.*, pp. 181-186.
"A Jules Supervielle," *ibid.*, pp. 187-191.
Pedro Fígari. San Antonio de Areco, Imprenta Monserrat, 1939.
"Tango," in *El compadrito. Su destino, sus barrios, su música* [a collection of poems and essays assembled by Jorge Luis Borges]. Buenos Aires, Emecé, 1945, pp. 84-85.
Mi hospitalidad. San Antonio de Areco, Homenaje de Talleres Gráficos de F. A. Colombo, 1949.
"Una carta de Ricardo Güiraldes [a Victoria Ocampo], *Sur*, Nos. 217-218, 1952, pp. 6-9.
"La estancia vieja," in *Cuentos de nuestra tierra* (Antonio Pagés Larraya, ed.). Buenos Aires, Editorial Raigal, 1952, pp. 181-185.
El pájaro blanco. San Antonio de Areco, Casa Impresora Francisco A. Colombo, 1952.
"Pampa," *Buenos Aires Literaria*, año I, No. 2, 1952, p. 2.
"Carta a Valery Larbaud, en la isla de Elba," *Sur*, No. 233, 1955, pp. 110-117.

II. Translations

1. Translations of *Don Segundo Sombra*

Don Segundo Sombra. Translated into French by Marcelle Auclaire. Paris, Librairie Gallimard, 1932.
Don Segundo Sombra. Translated into German by H. Ollerich. Berlin, Bruno Cassirer Verlag, 1934.
Don Segundo Sombra: Shadows on the Pampas. Translated into English by Harriet de Onís. London, Oxford University Press, 1935.
Idem. Translated into English by Harriet de Onís. New York, Farrar and Rinehart, Inc., 1935.
Idem. Translated into English by Harriet de Onís. West Drayton, Middlesex, England, Penguin Books [date not known].
Zhavá Zemé. Translated into Czech by Zdenek Smid. Prague, Symposium, 1936.
Don Segundo Sombra; Shadows on the Pampas. A summary of the translation into English by Harriet de Onís. *Reader's Digest*, IX, No. 54, 1945.
Don Segundo Sombra. Translated into Ukranian by Olexij Saciuk. Buenos Aires, Mykola Denysiuk, ed., 1946.
Idem. Translated into Yiddish by Pini Katz. Buenos Aires, published in the magazine section of the Argentine newspaper *Die Presse* [date not known. See editorial "*Don Segundo Sombra* en lengua ukraina," *La Nación* (Buenos Aires), 15 abril de 1956].

Idem. Translated into Danish. Copenhagen, Glydensdalske Forlag [date not known].
Idem. Translated into Dutch by J. Slaverhoff and R. Schreuder. Maestricht, Master Printer A. A. M. Stols [date not known].
Don Segundo Sombra. Roman van een Gaucho. Translated into Dutch. Antwerp, De Boekengilde "Die Poorte," [date not known].
Don Segundo Sombra. Translated into Italian. Modena, Edit. Ugo Guanda [date not known].
Idem. Translated into Japanese. See note by Harriet de Onís, without further information, in *Spanish Stories and Tales,* p. 165. New York, Alfred A. Knopf, 1954, p. 165.
Idem. Translated into Portuguese. Lisbon, published by the newspaper *O Seculo,* Soc. Nac. de Tipografia [date not known].
Idem. Translated into Swedish. Stockholm, P. A. Norstedt & Soener [date not known].

2. Translations from Other Books

"The Old Ranch," translated into English by Harriet de Onís in *Spanish Stories and Tales.* New York, Alfred A. Knopf, 1924, pp. 165-170.
"Xaimaca," a fragment of *Xaimaca* translated into French by Francis de Miomandre, in *La Revue Européenne,* V. No. 27, 1925, pp. 1-12.
"Poèmes Mystiques," a translation of *Poemas místicos* into French by Valery Larbaud, in *Le Roseau d'Or. Oeuvres et Chroniques* (Paris), No. 6, 1928, pp. 67-72.
"Poemas Solitarios. *Poèmes Solitaires,*" translated into French by Valery Larbaud, in *Commerce* (Paris), XV, 1928, pp. 89-107.
"Rosaura," translated into English by Anita Brenner, in *Tales from the Argentine.* New York, Farrar and Rinehart, 1930.

III. Critical and Biographical Material

ABALOS, JORGE W., "La fauna en *Don Segundo Sombra,*" *La Nación,* Jun. 29, 1947.
ACEVEDO, EDUARDO, *"Don Segundo Sombra, Reminiscencia Infantil,"* *El Hogar,* May 25, 1956.
ACUÑA, ANGEL, "Conferencia pronunciada en el Jockey Club sobre *Don Segundo Sombra* de Carlos [sic] Güiraldes," *La Literatura Argentina,* Año VII, No. 74, 1934, pp. 35-37.
ACUÑA, JUAN E., "La nueva poesía Argentina," *Humanidades* (La Plata), XXIX, 1944, pp. 179-190.
——, "Adrienne Monnier y los argentinos," *La Nación,* Oct. 23, 1955.
AITA, ANTONIO, *Algunos aspectos de la literatura argentina.* Buenos Aires, Edición de *Nosotros,* 1930, pp. 38-40.
——, *La literatura argentina contemporánea, 1900-1903.* Buenos Aires, L. J. Rosso, 1931, pp. 127-156.
——, "Personalidad literaria de Ricardo Güiraldes," *La Gaceta* (Buenos Aires), Oct. 16, 1938.
——, "Ricardo Güiraldes" in *Cuatro ensayos.* Buenos Aires, Talleres Gráficos Pesce y Cía, 1939, p. 97.
——, "Ricardo Güiraldes," in *Expresiones.* Buenos Aires, "La Bonaerense," 1933, pp. 45-64.
——, "Scrittori argentini: Riccardo Güiraldes," *Espero* (Genova), 1933.
ALBUQUERQUE, TENORIO D., "Brasileirismos em *Don Segundo Sombra,*"

Questões Linguisticas Americans, Rio de Janeiro, Editorial Aurora, 1949, pp. 49-66.
ALDAO, MARTÍN, "Releyendo *Don Segundo Sombra*," *Notas y recuerdos* and *Las flechas de Ulises*. Buenos Aires, Talleres Gráficos Taladriz, 1948, pp. 50-54.
ALEGRÍA, FERNANDO, "Ricardo Güiraldes," *Breve historia de la novela hispanoamericana*. Mexico, 1959, pp. 181-190.
ALEGRÍA, CIRO, "Notas sobre el personaje en la novela hispanoamericana," in *La novela iberoamericana*. Albuquerque, University of New Mexico Press, 1952, pp. 49-58.
ALMEIDA PINTOS, R., "El sueño de *Don Segundo Sombra*," *Nacional* (Montevideo), No. 69, Sept. 1943, pp. 363-374.
ALONE (HERNÁN DÍAZ ARRIETA), "*Seis Relatos* de Ricardo Güiraldes," *La Nación* (Santiago), 1930.
ALONSO, AMADO, "Un problema estilístico de *Don Segundo Sombra*," *La Nación*, July 27, 1930; also in *Materia y forma en poesía*. Madrid, Editorial Gredos, 1955, pp. 418-428.
———, "Ricardo Güiraldes: *Das buch von Gaucho Sombra*. Traducción autorizada de H. Ollerich. Berlin, B. Cassirer, 1934, 342 páginas," *Sur*, V. 1935, pp. 101-104.
ANDERSON IMBERT, ENRIQUE, "Güiraldes y lo sobrenatural," *Sur*, No. 224, 1953, 121-122, and in *Los grandes libros de Occidente*, Mexico, Ediciones de Andrea, 1957.
———, *Historia de la literatura argentina*. México-Buenos Aires, Fondo de Cultura Económica, 1954, pp. 283-285.
ANONYMOUS, "Banquete literario," *Nosotros*, LI, 1925, p. 417.
———, "*El cencerro de cristal*," *La Nación*, Oct. 10, 1952.
———, "*El cencerro de cristal*," *La Nación*, Jun. 7, 1953.
———, "Comenzó un curso en homenaje a Ricardo Güiraldes," *La Prensa* (Buenos Aires), June 26, 1956.
———, "*Don Segundo Sombra* en idioma checo," *Clarín* (Buenos Aires), Feb. 22, 1956.
———, "*Don Segundo Sombra* en lengua ucrania," *La Nación*, Apr. 15, 1956.
———, "*Don Segundo Sombra*. (Traducción al ucraniano, por Olexij Saciux)," *La Prensa* (Buenos Aires), Apr. 22, 1956.
———, "Dos actos positivos de la generación de 1925 (Macedonio Fernández y Ricardo Güiraldes)." *La Nación*, Feb. 15, 1952.
———, "La figura espiritual de Ricardo Güiraldes," *La Nación*, Dec. 27, 1953.
———, "Homenaje a Ricardo Güiraldes," *El Mundo* (Buenos Aires), Oct. 9, 1947.
———, "Homenaje a Ricardo Güiraldes y Don Segundo Sombra", *El Pago* (San Antonio de Areco), Año III, No. 70, Oct. 18, 1936.
———, "Honras a Ricardo Güiraldes en su pago de Areco," *La Nación*, Oct. 7, 1957.
———, "Manuel J. Güiraldes," *La Nación*, January 18, 1957.
———, "*Proa*," *Nosotros*, LI, 1926, pp. 416-417.
———, "El puente viejo," *El Hogar* (Buenos Aires), Oct. 18, 1957, p. 3.
———, *Ricardo Güiraldes* (Archivo Letra G, No. 1567). Buenos Aires, Ed. Asociación Prometeo [no date].
———, "Ricardo Güiraldes," [includes sketch by Pedro Deluchi], *Fiesta* (Buenos Aires), Año I, Nos. VI-VII, Oct. 15, 1927, pp. 11-15.

——, "Ricardo Güiraldes (1886-1927)," *Guía*, Ed. Comisión Nacional de Cultura, Año III, No. 51, Sept. 1949.
——, "Ricardo Güiraldes," *Nosotros*, LVIII, 1927, 142-143.
——, "Ricardo Güiraldes," *Síntesis* (Buenos Aires), II, 1927, pp 383-384.
——, "Ricardo Güiraldes," *El Tiempo* (Bogotá), Oct. 8, 1952.
——, "Ricardo Güiraldes a través de varios de nuestros escritores," *Crítica* (Buenos Aires), Oct. 10, 1927.
——, "Ricardo Güiraldes. *Don Segundo Sombra*," [a review of the French translation by Marcelle Auclair]. *Síntesis*, X, 1929, pp. 171-180.
——, "Ricardo Güiraldes, recio símbolo de argentinismo," *Clarín* (Buenos Aires), Oct. 6, 1957.
——, "Se cumplen 25 años del creador de *Don Segundo Sombra*," *Clarín* (Buenos Aires), Oct. 7, 1952.
——, "El sentido de un homenaje," *La Nación*, Oct. 10, 1952.
——, "Una tradición alemana de *Don Segundo Sombra*," *Caras y Caretas* (Buenos Aires), No. 1940, Dec. 1935.
——, "*Xaimaca*," *La Nación*, Dec. 30, 1923.
ANZOATEGUI, IGNACIO B., "Ricardo Güiraldes," *Criterio* (Buenos Aires), No. 21, July 26, 1928, and No. 84, Oct. 10, 1929.
APRILE, BARTOLOMÉ RODOLFO, *El Ahijado de Don Segundo o Fabio Cáceres. Poema Gaucho, inspirado en las páginas de "Don Segundo Sombra" y en los campos del sud y sudoeste argentinos*. Buenos Aires, Editorial Plus Ultra, 1935.
ARA, GUILLERMO, *Ricardo Güiraldes*. Buenos Aires, Editorial "La Mandrágora," 1961.
ARDISSONE, ENRIQUE, "Poemas inéditos de Güiraldes," *Noticias Gráficas* (Buenos Aires), May 24, 1955.
ARLT, ROBERTO, "Ricardo Güiraldes en la intimidad," *Crítica* (Buenos Aires), Oct. 10, 1927.
AUCLAIR, MARCELLE, "La traducción francesa de *Don Segundo Sombra*," *Síntesis*, X, 1929, pp. 171-180.
AYALA, FRANCISCO, "Notas sobre *Don Segundo Sombra*," *Asomante*, VI, 1950, pp. 28-33.
BARBAGELATA, HUGO B., *La novela y el cuento en Hispanoamérica*. Montevideo, Enrique Miguez y Cía., 1947, pp. 85-89.
BARGA, CORPUS, "Güiraldes y su sombra," *El Sol* (Madrid), 16 October 1927.
BARLETTA, LEONIDAS, "*Don Segundo Sombra*," *El Telégrafo* (Buenos Aires), July 2, 1928.
BARRENECHEA, MARIANO A., "¿A dónde vamos?," *Nosotros*, LXII, Oct. 1928, pp. 5-22.
BARROS, ALFONSO, "La ascensión de Ricardo Güiraldes (Buenos Aires)," *Vea y Lea*, Jun. 1933, pp. 8-13.
BATTISTESSA, ANGEL J., "Advertencia," *Seis Relatos* (by Ricardo Güiraldes). Buenos Aires, Editorial Perrot, 1957, pp. 7-11.
——, "Breve historia de una revista de vanguardia," *Verbum* (Buenos Aires), Nos. 2-3, Dec. 1942, pp. 25-37.
——, "Breve noticia bibliográfica de Ricardo Güiraldes," *Literatura Argentina*, VII, No. 75, Nov. 1934, pp. 67.
——, "Don Segundo Sombra en París," *La Nación*, Sept. 19, 1950.
——, "Güiraldes y Laforgue," *Nosotros*, No. 71, Feb. 1942, pp. 149-170.

BAZIN, R. *Histoire de la littérature américaine de la langue espagnole.* Paris, Hachette, 1935, pp. 323-324.

BECCO, HORACIO JORGE, "Al margen de *Don Segundo Sombra,*" *Asomante,* No. 1, Jan.-Mar., 1954, pp. 39-40.

——, "Aspectos temáticos en *Don Segundo Sombra,*" *La Gaceta* (Buenos Aires), XVI, Oct. 7, 1952.

——, "*Don Segundo Sombra,* libro de evocación y nostalgia pampeana," *La Gaceta* (Buenos Aires), No. 859, Nov. 14, 1953.

——, "*Don Segundo sombra y su vocabulario. (Nueva ed. aumentada.)*" Buenos Aires, Ollantay, 1952.

——, "Güiraldes y la poesía," *Saber Vivir* (Buenos Aires), No. 86, May 1954.

——, "Güiraldes y Raucho," *La Gaceta* (Buenos Aires), XVIII, No. 896, Aug. 14, 1954.

——, "Güiraldes y su ficción de la pampa," *Capricornio* (Buenos Aires), Año I, No. 1, July 1953, pp. 58-59.

——, "Hacia una definición del gaucho (textos inéditos de Ricardo Güiraldes)," *Norte* (Tucumán), No. 8, 1955, pp. 31-34.

——, et al., "Homenaje a Ricardo Güiraldes," *Buenos Aires Literaria,* Año I, No. 2, Nov. 1952.

——, "Homenaje a Ricardo Güiraldes," *La Gaceta* (San Antonio de Areco), Oct. 7, 1952.

——, and Alberto G. Lecot, "Homenaje a Ricardo Güiraldes," *La Gaceta* (San Antonio de Areco), Oct. 5, 1957.

——, "Introducción," in *Pampa* (by Ricardo Güiraldes). Buenos Aires, Editorial Ollantay, 1954.

——, "El misterio y *Don Segundo Sombra,*" *Saber Vivir* (Buenos Aires), Año IX, No. 107, Jan.-Mar., 1954, pp. 36-37.

——, "La Noche en *Don Segundo Sombra,*" *Filarmonía* (Buenos Aires), Año I, No. 1, June 1951.

——, "Nota sobre *Don Segundo Sombra* y lo fantástico," *La Gaceta* (Buenos Aires), XX, No. 991, July 7, 1956.

——, "Noticia," in "Carta a Valery Larbaud en la Isla de Elba," *Sur,* No. 233, Mar.-Apr., 1955, pp. 31-34.

——, "La obra de Ricardo Güiraldes y sus traducciones," *Alada* (Buenos Aires), Año II, No. 4, May 1953.

——, *Paisano en el tiempo.* Buenos Aires, Editorial Sed, 1957, pp. 9, 42.

——, "*Pampa.* (Poemas inéditos de Ricardo Güiraldes)," *La Gaceta* (Buenos Aires), XVIII, No. 915, Dec. 18, 1954.

——, "Un poema al río de Areco," *La Gaceta* (Buenos Aires), XVIII, No. 89, July 1954.

——, "Ricardo Güiraldes. *Rosaura (novela corta) y siete cuentos* (etc.)," *Revista Hispánica Moderna,* XX, 1954, p. 84.

——, "Ricardo Güiraldes, *Rosaura y siete cuentos,*" *Sur,* No. 223, July-Aug. 1953, pp. 142-143.

——, "Ricardo Güiraldes y Juan Carlos Dávalos en Salta," *Ficción* (Buenos Aires), No. 10, Nov.-Dec., 1957, pp. 83-88.

——, "Ricardo Güiraldes y su novela de la pampa," *Cultura* (San Juan, Argentina), Año II, No. 12, Aug., 1954, pp. 45-47.

——, "El silencio en *Don Segundo Sombra,*" *Buenos Aires Literaria,* Año I, No. 2, 1952, pp. 37-41.

——, "Sobre Güiraldes, *Rosaura, y siete cuentos,*" *Sur,* No. 223, 1953.

——, "Un sueño que Ricardo Güiraldes recupera," *La Gaceta* (Buenos Aires), XXI, No. 1054, Oct. 5, 1957.

BENEDETTI, MARIO, "Los temas del novelista hispanoamericano," *Número* (Montevideo), II, Nos. 10-11, Sept.-Dec., 1950, pp. 491-502.

BERDIALES, GERMÁN, "El gaucho en las letras, *Don Segundo Sombra* y su creador: Ricardo Güiraldes," *Pampa Argentina*, XXI, October, 1947, pp. 28-29.

——, "Ramón Subiratz, el pintor que retrató a don Segundo Sombra," *Pampa Argentina*, XXIII, 1949, pp. 20, 30.

BERNÁRDEZ, FRANCISCO LUIS, "Mis recuerdos de Ricardo Güiraldes," *El Nacional* (Caracas), Jan. 15, 1953.

——, "La poesía de Güiraldes," *Buenos Aires Literaria*, Año I, No. 2, 1952, pp. 33-36.

——, "Ricardo Güiraldes," *Boletín de la Sociedad Argentina de Escritores*, XV, No. 30, 1947.

——, "Ricardo Güiraldes como poeta," *El Nacional* (Caracas), June 18, 1953.

——, "Ricardo Güiraldes en mi recuerdo," *Criterio* (Buenos Aires), XXVI, 1953, pp. 874-875.

BIANCHI, ALFREDO A., "Carta Abierta," *Claridad* (Buenos Aires), No. 196, Dec. 14, 1929, p. 30.

BLASI, ALBERTO OSCAR, "En torno a una estética," *Estudios* (Buenos Aires, No. 466, Jan.-Mar., 1955, pp. 20-33.

——, "Güiraldes en el ultraísmo," *Estudios* (Buenos Aires), LXXXVI, 1953, pp. 330-335.

——, "Güiraldes: su poesía," *Democracia* (Buenos Aires), Nov. 6, 1952.

——, "La poesía de Ricardo Güiraldes," *Estudios* (Buenos Aires), No. 463, July-Aug. 1954, pp. 319-324.

BOJ, SILVERIO (W. G. WÉYLAND), *Ubicación de Don Segundo Sombra y otros ensayos*. Tucumán, B. S. Paraván 1940, pp. 7-88.

BONESATTI, TOBÍAS, "Ricardo Güiraldes," *Indice* (Bahía Blanca), Año I, No. 4, Oct. 22, 1927.

BONET, CARMELO M., "Aproximación a Carlos Reyles," *Cursos y Conferencias* (Buenos Aires), No. 269, Jun. 1955, pp. 110-147.

——, et. al., "Homenaje a Ricardo Güiraldes," *Surestada* (La Plata), Año I, No. 2, Oct. 10, 1952.

——, "La novela argentina en el siglo XX," *Cursos y conferencias* (Buenos Aires), April-June, 1951, pp. 57-81.

——, "Ricardo Güiraldes," in *Gente de Novela*. Buenos Aires, pp. 77-101.

——, "Ricardo Güiraldes, novelista de la pampa," *La Nación*, April 16, 1950.

BORGES, JORGE LUIS, "Carta en la defunción de *Proa*," in *El tamaño de mi esperanza*. Buenos Aires, Editorial Proa, pp. 85-87.

——, "El escritor argentino y la tradición," *Cursos y Conferencias* (Buenos Aires), XLII, Nos. 250-252, pp. 57-64.

——, "El lado de la muerte en Güiraldes," *Síntesis*, V, 1928, pp. 63-66.

——, "El *Martín Fierro*," *Sur*, I, 1931, pp. 134-145.

——, "Sobre *Don Segundo Sombra*," *Sur*, Nos. 217-218, Nov.-Dec., 1952, pp. 9-11.

——, "Tareas y destino de Buenos Aires," in *Homenaje a Buenos Aires en el Cuarto Centenario de su Fundación*. Buenos Aires. Edición de la Municipalidad de la Ciudad de Buenos Aires, 1936.

Bosco, Eduardo Jorge, "Un viaje a San Antonio de Areco," *Buenos Aires Literaria*, Año I, No. 2, 1952, pp. 20-22.
Brandán Caraffa, Alfredo, "Güiraldes inédito," *Síntesis*, V, 1928, pp. 272-274.
Brenner, Anita, "Man's Fate on the Pampas. *Don Segundo Sombra: Shadows on the Pampas*," *The Nation* (New York), CXL, 1935, pp. 133-134.
Broca, Brito, "Literatura Latino-americana VIII. (Ricardo Güiraldes)," *Cultura Política* (Rio de Janeiro), XV, 1942, pp. 299-302.
——, "Ricardo Güiraldes," *Americanas (Coleção Caderno Azul)*, Curitiba-São Paulo-Rio de Janeiro, Editora Guaira Limitada, 1944, pp. 18-25.
Brickell, H., "Ricardo Güiraldes: *Don Segundo Sombra: Shadows in the Pampas*," *New York Evening Post*, Jan. 19, 1935.
Brumana, Anita, "*Don Segundo Sombra*, padrino," *La Nación*, Feb. 27, 1944.
——, "El final de dos novelas argentinas," *La Nación*, Feb. 4, 1951.
——, "¡Hacete duro, muchacho!," *La Nación*, Dec. 9, 1945.
——, *Obras Completas*. Buenos Aires, Edición Amigos de Herminia Brumana, 1958.
——, "Pasión de *Don Segundo Sombra*," *La Nación*, Feb. 6, 1949.
——, "Sentido social de *Don Segundo Sombra*," *La Nación*, July 18, 1944.
——, "Si es que te has caído..." *Pan (Arte y Letras)*, (Azul, Buenos Aires), Año I, No. 6, Dec. 1954.
Brumana, Herminia, "El amor en *Don Segundo Sombra*," *La Nación*, December 29, 1947.
Caldiz, Juan Francisco, *Lo que no se ha dicho de Don Segundo Sombra*. La Plata, A. Domínguez, 1952.
Cambours Ocampo, Arturo, "*Don Segundo Sombra*," *Indagaciones sobre Literatura Argentina*. Buenos Aires. Editorial Albatros, 1952, pp. 16-19.
——, "*Don Segundo Sombra*," *Lugones. El escritor y su lenguaje*. Buenos Aires, Ediciones Theoría, 1957, pp. 38-45.
Carilla, Emilio, "Ricardo Güiraldes: *Pampa (Poemas Inéditos)*", *Humanitas* (Tucumán), Año III, No. 8, 1957, p. 202.
——, "Trayectoria de Ricardo Güiraldes," *Mar del Sur* (Lima), VIII, 1952, pp. 38-43; also in *Norte* (Tucumán), III, 1952, pp. 53-61.
Cascella, Armando, "Lección de pampa," *La Gaceta del Sur* (Rosario), Nos. 4-5, June-July, 1928.
Castagnino, Raúl H., *El análisis literario*. Buenos Aires, Editorial Nova, 1953, pp. 130-254.
Cavazzana, Rosanna, "Lo autóctono y lo tradicional ibérico en los cuentos de *Don Segundo Sombra*," *El Mundo* (Buenos Aires), Oct. 22, 1958.
Chapman, Arnold, "Pampas and Big Woods: Heroic Initiation in Güiraldes and Faulkner," *Comparative Literature*, XI, 1959, pp. 61-77.
Cocaro, Nicolás, "Poesía, pasión y búsqueda en Ricardo Güiraldes," *Clarín* (Buenos Aires), Mar. 10, 1957.
Collantes de Terán, Juan, "En torno al simbolismo e impresionismo en *Don Segundo Sombra*," *Revista de Estudios Americanos* (Valencia), XIII, 1957, pp. 17-39.
——, *Las novelas de Ricardo Güiraldes*. Sevilla, C.S.I.C., 1959.

COLOMBO, ISMAEL B., *Ricardo Güiraldes, el poeta de la pampa.* San Antonio de Areco, Edición Francisco A. Colombo, 1952.

CONTRERAS, F., "La Litterature d'Avant-Garde: *Don Segundo Sombra,* Proa, Buenos Aires," *Le Mercure de France,* 15 April, 1927, pp. 489-495.

———, "Ricardo Güiraldes," *L'Esprit de L'Amérique Espagnole.* Paris, 1931.

CORTÁZAR, AUGUSTO RAÚL, *"Cuentos de muerte y de sangre,"* *La Nación,* Nov. 19, 1933.

———, *"Cuentos de muerte y de Sangre,"* Edición Losada, *La Nación* (Buenos Aires), June 20, 1952.

———, *Valoración de la naturaleza en el habla del gaucho (a través de "Don Segundo Sombra").* Buenos Aires, Instituto de la Literatura, 1941.

CROW, JOHN A., "A Critical Appraisal of the Spanish American Novel," *Hispania,* XXIV, 1951, p. 155.

CUNEO, SANTIAGO, A., "Don Segundo Sombra en los Estados Unidos," *La Nación* (Buenos Aires), Dec. 8, 1957.

DA CAL, ERNESTO G., *"Don Segundo Sombra,* teoría y símbolo del gaucho," *Cuadernos Americanos,* XLI, 1948, pp. 245-259.

DELFINO, AUGUSTO MARIO, "A los diez años de *Don Segundo Sombra,"* *La Nación,* July 5, 1936.

———, "El argentino Ricardo Güiraldes," *París en América* (Buenos Aires), Año VI, No. 23, Sep. 1952, pp. 48-49.

———, "Cómo apareció *Don Segundo Sombra,"* *Arte y Plata* (Mexico), III, Feb., 1947, pp. 34-36.

———, "En el amanecer de la gloria de *Don Segundo Sombra,"* *Saber Vivir* (Buenos Aires), Año VI, No. 64, 1946, pp. 48-51.

———, "Don Roberto y Don Segundo," *Saber Vivir,* No. 100, Apr.-Jun. 1952, pp. 44-46.

———, "Fabio Cáceres y muchos," *El Hogar,* Oct. 4, 1957, pp. 14-15.

———, "La guardia vieja: Ricardo Güiraldes," *Continente* (Buenos Aires), No. 4, Jul., 1947.

———, "El hombre," *Buenos Aires Literaria,* Año I, No. 2, 1952, pp. 17-19.

———, "El Pago de Areco: (1) El Pago de Areco; (2) Un pozo de recuerdos; (3) El pial; (4) Los reseros; (5) En el fogón; (6) Don Segundo Sombra; (7) Ricardo Güiraldes," *El Suplemento* (Buenos Aires), Mar. 27 - May 8, 1935.

———, "La primavera de Ricardo Güiraldes. Veinticinco años después de *El cencerro de cristal,"* *El Hogar* (Buenos Aires), 1940.

———, "Ricardo Güiraldes publicó hace veinticinco años su primer libro," *Argentina Libre,* Sep. 26, 1940.

———, "Ricardo Güiraldes," *Argentina Libre,* January 29, 1942.

———, "Una semblanza de Ricardo Güiraldes," *Boletín de la Sociedad Argentina de Escritores,* XV, No. 30, 1947.

———, "Un valioso antecedente de 'El Pago de Areco'," *El Suplemento* (Buenos Aires). Mar. 20, 1935.

DELFINO, ESTHER, "Literatura y diplomacia en el 'Pago de Areco'," *La Nación,* Oct. 20, 1962, p. 7.

DEL RÍO, ANGEL, "Sobre *Don Segundo Sombra,"* *Revista de Estudios Hispánicos* (New York), I, 1928, pp. 72-74.

———, *"Don Segundo Sombra,"* *El Diario* (Buenos Aires), Sep. 20, 1926.

DE MAEZTU, RAMIRO, "Don Segundo Sombra," *El Sol* (Madrid), December 12, 1926.
——, "Los mitos literarios sobre *Don Segundo Sombra* y algo sobre 'Don Juan'," *La Prensa* (Buenos Aires), June 26, 1927.
DE ONÍS, FEDERICO, "Ricardo Güiraldes (1886-1927)," in *Antología de la poesía española (1882-1932)*. Madrid, Casa Editora Hernando (S.A.), 1934, p. 964.
DE TORRE, GUILLERMO, "Una carta-autobiografía de Ricardo Güiraldes," *Buenos Aires Literaria*, Año I, No. 2, 1952, pp. 3-16.
——, "*Don Segundo Sombra* en edición de lujo," *La Nación*, December 29, 1929.
——, *Literaturas europeas de vanguardia*. Madrid, R, Caro Raggio, 1925, pp. 80 (Note 1), p. 317.
DEVOTO, DANIEL, "Sobre paremiología musical porteña. Bailes e instrumentos en el habla bonaerense," *Filología* (Buenos Aires), Año III, Nos. 1-2, Jan.-Aug. 1951, pp. 6-83.
DIEGO, CECILIA DE, "Alrededor de *Don Segundo Sombra*," *Ficción* (Buenos Aires), No. 6, Mar.-Apr. 1957, pp. 66-81.
——, "La torcaza encandilada," *Atlántida* (Buenos Aires), No. 1080, Feb. 1957.
DÍEZ-CANEDO, ENRIQUE, "Al margen de Ricardo Güiraldes," *Argentina Libre*, January 29, 1942; also under title of "Entre pampa y París," in *El Sol* (Madrid), April 17, 1932; and as "Al margen de Ricardo Güiraldes," in *Letras de América*. Mexico, Fondo de Cultura Económica, 1949, pp. 332-340.
——, "*Xaimaca*," *Revista de Occidente* (Madrid), XII, Jun. 1924, pp. 389-392.
DOLL, RAMÓN, "Segundo Sombra y el gaucho que ve el hijo del patrón," *Nosotros*, LVIII, Nos. 222 and 223, 1927, pp. 270-281.
DOTOR, ANGEL, "Güiraldes y su Don Segundo," *El Diario Español* (Buenos Aires), Feb. 25, 1931.
E. J. M., "Año 1927: Martín Fierro y Güiraldes mueren juntos," *La Nación*, Oct. 27, 1957.
——, "Obras Completas de Ricardo Güiraldes," *La Nación*, June 23, 1957.
——, "Reedición de uno de los *Cuadernos del Plata*," *La Nación*, Feb. 2, 1958.
E. N. S., "El terruño de *Don Segundo Sombra*: El pago de Areco," *Clarín* Buenos Aires), Jul. 28, 1957.
ECHEGARAY, ARISTÓBULO, "Daniel Belmar y *Don Segundo Sombra*," *La Gaceta* (Tucumán), June 13, 1958.
——, *Don Segundo Sombra, reminiscencia infantil de Ricardo Güiraldes*. Buenos Aires, Ediciones Doble P., 1955.
ERNST, FEDERICO, "Recuerdo de don Segundo," *El Hogar* (Buenos Aires), October 18, 1957.
——, "San Antonio en su historia y su realidad presente," *El Hogar* (Buenos Aires), Oct. 25, 1957.
ERRO, CARLOS ALBERTO, "Al margen de *Don Segundo Sombra*," in *Medida de criollismo*. Buenos Aires, 1929, pp. 165-183.
ESCOPE, ENRIQUE MARIO, "Los motivos de *Don Segundo Sombra*," *La Prensa* (Buenos Aires), May 11, 1958.
ESPINOSA, C. A., "*Don Segundo Sombra* en esta lejanía de sierra," *Euterpe* (Buenos Aires), Año V, No. 14, Sept. 1953.
ESPINOSA, J. E., "Notes on the Role of Gaucho Literature in the Evolu-

tion of Americanism in Argentina," *Hispania*, XIX, 1936, pp. 85-92.

ESPINOSA BRAVO, CLODOALDO ALBERTO, *"Don Segundo Sombra* en lejana serranía," *La Nueva Democracia* (New York), XXXIII, No. 2, 1953, pp. 108-111.

ETCHEBARNE, DORA PASTORIZA DE, *Elementos románticos en las novelas de Ricardo Güiraldes.* Buenos Aires, Editorial Perrot, 1957.

ETCHEBARNE, MIGUEL D., *La influencia del arrabal en la poesía argentina culta.* Buenos Aires, Editorial Kraft, 1955.

FABIÁN, DONALD, "La acción novelesca de *Don Segundo Sombra,*" *Revista Iberoamericana* (Mexico), XXIII, No. 45, Jan. June, 1958, pp. 147-153.

FASSINA, MARÍA, "Don Segundo Sombra, Quijote y Sancho argentinos," in *De La Poesía Gauchesca.* Buenos Aires, 1950.

FERNÁNDEZ, MACEDONIO, "Brindis en el banquete a Ricardo Güiraldes," *Martín Fierro*, Segunda época, Año III, No. 36, 1926, p. 2.

——, "Carta a Ricardo Güiraldes," *Proa* (Buenos Aires), Jun. 1925, p. 48.

——, "Hechizada memoria de *Don Segundo Sombra,*" *Boletín de la Sociedad Argentina de Escritores*, XV, No. 30, 1947.

FERNÁNDEZ HUTTER, JULIÁN, *El alma errante de "Don Segundo Sombra,"* Santa Fe, Argentina, 1952.

FERNÁNDEZ MORENO, CÉSAR, "Güiraldes y el ultraísmo," *Clarín* (Buenos Aires), Dec. 14, 1952.

——, *Introducción a Fernández Moreno,* Buenos Aires, Emecé Editores, 1956.

FIGUEROA BALCARCE, J. G., "Ricardo Güiraldes: *Don Segundo Sombra,*" *Sagitario* (La Plata), II, 1926, pp. 421-423.

FISHEROVA BECH, VERA, " Las heroínas en la novelística argentina," *Revista Hispánica Moderna* (New York), Nos. 3 and 4, June 1944, pp. 231-250.

FONDANE, B., "Visage de la pampa. (A propos de *Don Segundo Sombra*)," *Revue Argentine* (Paris), Año I, No. 3, 1934.

FOURNIER, CHRISTIANE, *"Don Segundo Sombra,"* *Revue de l'Amérique Latine* (Paris), XIV, 1927, p. 365.

FRANK, WALDO, "Introduction" in *Don Segundo Sombra; Shadows on the Pampas.* Translated into English by Harriet de Onís. New York, Farrar and Rinehart, 1935, pp. vii-xii.

GÁLVEZ, MANUEL, "Acotaciones a una crítica de *Don Segundo Sombra,*" *Noticias Gráficas* (Buenos Aires), Nov. 1, 1955.

GARCÍA, GERMÁN, "El perfume del pasado," in *La novela argentina.* Buenos Aires, Editorial Sudamericana, 1952, p. 137.

GARCÍA PINTO, ROBERTO, "Cruz Guíez y Segundo Sombra," *Círculo* (Salta), No. 2, Jan. 1954, pp. 1-2.

GATES, EUNICE JOINER, "The Imagery of *Don Segundo Sombra,*" *Hispanic Review*, XVI, 1948, pp. 33-49.

——, "A note on the Resemblance between Don Segundo Sombra and Don Quijote," *ibid*, XIV, 1946, pp. 342-343.

GENE, JUAN CARLOS, *El herrero y el diablo.* Buenos Aires, Editorial Talía, 1957.

GHIANO, JUAN CARLOS, "El asunto de *Don Segundo Sombra,*" in *Temas y Aptitudes.* Buenos Aires, Editorial Ollantay, 1949, pp. 19-37.

214   GIOVANNI PREVITALI

——, "La composición en *Don Segundo Sombra*," *Humanidades* (La Plata), XXXIII, 1950, pp. 337-361.
——, "De la literatura argentina; siglo XX," *Revista de Guatemala*, II, January-March, 1952, pp. 51-69.
——, "Güiraldes novelista," in *Constantes de la Literatura Argentina*. Buenos Aires, Editorial Raigal, 1953, pp. 81-107.
——, "Güiraldes y la poesía," *Saber Vivir* (Buenos Aires), No. 111, Jan.-Mar. 1955, p. 43.
——, *Introducción a Ricardo Güiraldes*. Buenos Aires, Ediciones Culturales Argentinas, Ministerio de Educación y Justicia, Dirección General de Cultura, 1961.
——, "Itinerario de Güiraldes," *Davar* (Buenos Aires), No. 4, July-Aug. 1952, pp. 26-55.
——, "El protagonista de la novela argentina," *Cursos y Conferencias* (Buenos Aires), XLV, 1954, pp. 150-169.
——, "Ricardo Güiraldes," in *Poesía Argentina del Siglo XX*. Buenos Aires-México, Edición Fondo de Cultura Económica, LVX, 1957, pp. 89-95.
——, *Testimonio de la novela argentina*. Buenos Aires, Editorial Leviatán, 1956.
GICOVATE, BERNARDO, "Notes on *Don Segundo Sombra*, The Education of Fabio Cáceres," *Hispania*, XXXIV, 1951, pp. 366-368.
GIMÉNEZ VEGA, E. S., "Pamfletos y pamfletistas," *Histonium* (Buenos Aires), Año XVII, No. 195, 1955, pp. 15-16.
GIORGI, MANUEL L., *Curso de historia de la literatura hispano-americana*. Buenos Aires, "El Misionero," 1937, pp. 359-360.
GIRONDO, OLIVERIO (with co-authors Eduardo J. Bullrich, Evar Méndez, and Alberto Prebisch), *El periódico Martín Fierro, 1924-1949*. Buenos Aires, Francisco A. Colombo, 1949, pp. 13, 19-20, 26, 33, 41, 44.
GIUSTI, ROBERTO F., "Dos novelas del campo argentino (Ricardo Güiraldes, *Don Segundo Sombra*. Enrique Larreta, *Zogoibi*)," *Nosotros*, LIV, 1926, pp. 125-133; also in *Crítica y polémica*. Buenos Aires, Cooperativa Editorial Limitada, 1927, pp. 147-160.
——, "La novela y el cuento argentinos," *Nosotros*, LVII, 1927, pp. 93-94.
——, "Nuestros novelistas," in *Crítica y polémica*. Buenos Aires, Cooperative Editorial Limitada, 1927, pp. 139-140.
——, "Panorama de la literatura argentina contemporánea," *Nosotros*, XIV, 1941, p. 129.
——, "*Raucho. Momentos de una juventud contemporánea*, por Ricardo Güiraldes. Buenos Aires, 1917," *Nosotros*, XXVII, 1917, pp. 391-394.
——, "Ricardo Güiraldes," in *Lecciones de literatura argentina e hispano-americana*. Buenos Aires, Editorial Angel Estrada, 1947, pp. 434-436.
——, "Ricardo Güiraldes," in *Lecciones de Literatura Española, Argentina e Hispanoamericana*. Buenos Aires, Editorial Angel Estrada, 1953, pp. 492-494.
GLANZER, NATALIO, "A treinta años de la desaparición del autor de *Don Segundo Sombra*, "El Día" (La Plata), Oct. 6, 1957.
GÓMEZ DE LA SERNA, R., "Requiem por Güiraldes, *Revista de Occidente* (Madrid), XVIII, 1927, pp. 103-105.

GONZÁLEZ, JUAN B., "Un libro significativo, *Don Segundo Sombra*, "Nosotros", LIV, 1926, pp. 377-385.
GONZÁLEZ LANUZA, EDUARDO, *Los martinfierristas.* Buenos Aires, Ediciones Culturales Argentinas, 1961.
GONZÁLEZ TUÑÓN, ENRIQUE, *Apología del hombre santo.* Buenos Aires, Francisco A. Colombo, 1930.
GOTI AGUILAR, J. C., "Don Segundo Sombra," in *Crítica Nuestra.* Buenos Aires, Editorial Viau y Zona, 1935, pp. 12-88.
GRIMOLDI, DIEGO, *"Pampa.* Un libro inédito de Ricardo Güiraldes," *Esto Es* (Buenos Aires), Año II, No. 26, May 25, 1954, pp. 30-31.
GÜEMES, J. A., "Don Segundo Sombra fué muerto a traición," *Histonium* (Buenos Aires), VII, No. 84, May 1946, p. 268.
Guía de Museos. La Plata, Ministerio de Educación, 1958, pp. 71-80.
GUILLOT MUÑOZ, A., "El solitario de San Antonio de Areco," *La Gaceta Literaria* (Madrid), April 15, 1931.
GÜIRALDES, ADELINA DEL CARRIL DE, "Carta a Nicolás Olivari, evocando a Ricardo Güiraldes," *El Hogar* (Buenos Aires), Sept. 26, 1947.
———, Enrique Udaondo; Valery Larbaud, et al., *Donación Güiraldes y Homenaje a su Memoria.* Luján (Buenos Aires), Publicación del Museo Colonial e Histórico de la Provincia de Buenos Aires, 1929.
———, "La gestación de *Don Segundo Sombra*," *Ilustración,* 1937.
———, "Nota preliminar," in *El cencerro de cristal.* Buenos Aires, Editorial Losada, 1952, pp. 7-8.
———, "Nota preliminar," in *Don Segundo Sombra,* Buenos Aires, Editorial Kraft, 1952.
———, "Nota preliminar," in *Rosaura (novela corta) y siete cuentos.* Buenos Aires, Editorial Losada, 1952, pp. 7-9.
———, "Prólogo," *Buenos Aires Literaria,* Año I, No. 2, 1952, p. 1.
———, Ricardo Güiraldes. Su vida, su obra," *Revista del Consejo de Mujeres de la República Argentina,* XXXV, No. 125, Jan.-May 1935, pp. 28-52.
———, "Valery Larbaud y Ricardo Güiraldes," *La Nación,* March 24, 1957.
———, *"Vida y obra de Ricardo Güiraldes,"* *La Prensa* (Buenos Aires), Jun. 26, 1956.
HENRÍQUEZ UREÑA, MAX, "El momento literario argentino," *Revista Cubana,* XXV, 1949, pp. 43-60.
HENRÍQUEZ UREÑA, PEDRO, Las corrientes literarias en la América hispánica. México-Buenos Aires, Fondo de Cultura Económica, 1949, pp. 203, 254, 265, 269, 273.
HERNÁNDEZ DE ROSARIO, *"Don Segundo Sombra* y el soliloquio," *Ahora* (Rosario), No. 1, Feb. 4, 1928.
HIPWELL, H. H., *"Don Segundo Sombra* by Ricardo Güiraldes," *Saturday Review of Literature,* V, 1928, p. 432.
HUERTAS, JOSÉ GUILLERMO, "Los cuentos de *Don Segundo Sombra,"* *Histonium* (Buenos Aires), XVI, No. 182, July 1954, pp. 11-12.
HURTADO, LEOPOLDO, *"Don Segundo Sombra* de Ricardo Güiraldes," *Verbum* (Buenos Aires), Año XX, No. 69, 1927.
I. B. A., "Ricardo Güiraldes," *Criterio* (Buenos Aires), 11, 1929, p. 172.
IGLESIAS, EUGENIO JULIO, *"Don Segundo Sombra,"* *Caras y Caretas* (Buenos Aires), Dec. 17, 1927.
———, et al., "Ricardo Güiraldes en el primer aniversario de su desaparición," *El Mentor* (San Antonio de Areco), Año VI, No. 274, Oct. 14, 1928.

——, "El rincón del poeta," *Plus Ultra* (Buenos Aires), April 30, 1928.

IRASTUZA, JULIO, "Releyendo la obra maestra de Güiraldes," *Clarín* (Buenos Aires), Dec. 5, 1954.

IRVING, T. B., "Myth and Reality in *Don Segundo Sombra*," *Hispania*, XL, 1957, pp. 44-48.

ISUSI, ALEJANDRO DE, "Aniversario de *Don Segundo Sombra*," *Democracia* (Buenos Aires), Nov. 5, 1951.

——, "Supervivencia de *Don Segundo Sombra*," *Atlántida* (Buenos Aires), No. 1081, Mar. 1957, p. 73.

J. A. F., "Se fue como quien se desangra," *Mundo Argentino*, Aug. 26, 1936.

JOHNSON JR., ERNEST A., "*Don Segundo Sombra*, Ciertos Valores Poéticos," *Hispanófila*, IV, No. 1, Sept. 1960, pp. 57-70.

JONES, WILLIS KNAPP, "River Plate Reading: Past and Present Literature in the Argentine and Uruguay," *The Pan American* (New York), VII, pp. 51-54.

JOSEF, BELLA, "Dualidade em *Don Segundo Sombra*," [Thesis]. Rio de Janeiro, 1957.

KIRKWOOD, KENNETH PORTER, "Ricardo Güiraldes and *Don Segundo Sombra*," in *Excursion among Books*. Buenos Aires, Mitchell's Bookstore, 1949, pp. 315-329.

KORN, ALEJANDRO, "La figura espiritual de Ricardo Güiraldes," *La Nación*, Dec. 27, 1953.

——, "La otra vertiente de Ricardo Güiraldes," *La Nación*, Apr., 20, 1952.

——, "Ricardo Güiraldes: *Don Segundo Sombra*," *Valorizaciones* (La Plata), No. 10, Aug. 1926.

KOVACCI, OFELIA, *La pampa a través de Ricardo Güiraldes*. Buenos Aires, Universidad de Buenos Aires, Facultad de Filosofía y Letras, 1961.

LAFINUR, MELIÁN ALVARO, "Discurso en memoria de Ricardo Güiraldes," *Repertorio Americano* (San José, Costa Rica), XIX, 1929, pp. 321-322.

LARBAUD, VALERY, *Lettre à deux amis*. Buenos Aires, Francisco A. Colombo, 1962.

——, "Lettres argentines et uruguayennes," *La Revue Européenne*, VI 1925, p. 60.

——, "L'Oeuvre et la Situation de Ricardo Güiraldes (1925)," *ibid*, V, 1925, pp. 22-27; also as "La obra y la posición de Ricardo Güiraldes (1925)," in *Nosotros*, L, 1925, pp. 543-546.

——, "Poètes Espagnols et Hispano-Americains Contemporains," *La Nouvelle Revue Française*, XV, 1920, pp. 143-146.

——, "Ricardo Güiraldes (1886-1927)," *Oeuvres et Chroniques* (Paris), No. 6, 1928, 63-66; also in *La Nación* January 1, 1928, and in *La Nouvelle Revue Française*, XXX, 1928, pp. 132-137.

LATCHMAN, RICARDO A., "Latin American Writers. Ricardo Güiraldes," *Panorama*, No. 16, 1940, pp. 11-14.

LATORRE, MARIANO, "Sobre *Don Segundo Sombra*," *La Información* (Santiago de Chile), XII, January 1927, pp. 42-43.

LECOT, ALBERTO GREGORIO, "La idea de libertad en *Don Segundo Sombra*," *La Gaceta* (San Antonio de Areco), XXI, No. 1054, Oct. 5, 1957.

——, "El retrato de Güiraldes pintado por Centurión," *La Prensa*, Sección Tercera (Buenos Aires), 8 July, 1962.

LEGUIZAMÓN, JULIO A., "Ricardo Güiraldes," *Historia de la literatura hispanoamericana.* Buenos Aires, Editoriales Reunidas, II, 1954, pp. 412-413, 500, 504.

LEGUIZAMÓN, MARÍA LUISA C. DE, "Ricardo Güiraldes y algunos aspectos de su obra," *Cuadernos Americanos,* No. 12, XIX, Apr.-May 1953, pp. 278-290.

LEONARD, IRVING; JOHN T. REID; JOHN ENGELKIRK and JOHN A. CROW, *An Outline History of Spanish American Literature* (2nd. edition). New York, F. C. Croft's 1944.

LERNER, ISAÍAS, "El paisaje en *Don Segundo Sombra,*" *Davar* (Buenos Aires), No. 73, Nov.-Dec. 1957, pp. 79-89.

LIBERAL, JOSÉ R., "*Don Segundo Sombra: de Ricardo Güiraldes. Comentado y anotado estudio del vocabulario y fraseología.* Buenos Aires, Francisco A. Colombo, 1946.

LIZASO, F., "La lección de Güiraldes," *Revista de Avance* (La Habana), III, 1928, pp. 118-120, 135; also in *Repertorio Americano* (San José, Costa Rica), July, 1928, pp. 40, 47-48.

LONCÁN, ENRIQUE, "Raucho," in *Las charlas de mi amigo.* Buenos Aires, 1922, pp. 169-176.

LOPE, J. M., "*Don Segundo Sombra* y su vocabulario," [a review of H. J. Becco's book], *Nueva Revista de Filología Hispánica,* IX, 1955, pp. 170-171.

LUGAND, JORGE R., "Lo descriptivo en el verso de Güiraldes," *La Prensa,* Nov. 16, 1952.

LUGONES, LEOPOLDO, "Don Segundo Sombra," *La Nación,* Sept. 12, 1926; also in *Atenea* (Concepción), XXIII, 1933, pp. 319-325.

———, "El lenguaje torpe", *La Nación,* Dec., 29, 1929.

———, *Palabras en la tumba de Ricardo Güiraldes.* San Antonio de Areco, Imprenta Monserrat, 1938.

MACÍAS, HUGO, *Crónica del corazón gaucho de Ricardo Güiraldes.* San Antonio de Areco, 1939.

MANDOLINI, HERNANI, "Plástica y psicología de la novela argentina," *Nosotros,* LXXXI, 1934, pp. 64-70.

MANGUDO, CARLOS E., "Ricardo Güiraldes, novelista criollo," *Caras y Caretas* (Buenos Aires), 1926.

MARCONATO, PEDRO L., "Síntesis histórica del viejo pago de Areco," *Farol* (Buenos Aires), September 1953, pp. 20-24.

MARECHAL, LEOPOLDO, "Don Segundo Sombra y el ejercicio ilegal de la crítica," *Sur,* V, pp. 76-80.

———, "El gaucho y la nueva literatura rioplatense," *Martín Fierro,* III, No. 34, Oct. 5, 1926.

MARECHAL, LEOPOLDO and ELBIA R. MARECHAL, "Ricardo Güiraldes (1886-1927)," in *Antología didáctica de la prosa argentina.* Buenos Aires, Kapelusz, 1954, pp. 646-651.

MARINELLO, JUAN, "Tres novelas ejemplares," *Sur,* VI, 1936, pp. 59-75; also in *Literatura hispanoamericana.* México, Colecciones de la Universidad Nacional de México, 1939, pp. 143-163.

MARSH, F. T., "A Tale of the Spanish-American Wild West. *Don Segundo Sombra: Shadows on the Pampas,*" New York Times (Magazine Section), January 6, 1935.

MARTÍNEZ ESTRADA, E., *Muerte y transfiguración de Martín Fierro.* México, Fondo de Cultura Económica, V, 1948, p. 60.

MATA, RAMIRO W., "Estructura y significación de *Don Segundo Sombra* de Ricardo Güiraldes," *Revista Nacional* (Montevideo), LII, 1951, pp. 109-134.

MATEO, ABEL, "Los escritores y la literatura. *Don Segundo Sombra:* nuestra novela representativa," *El Hogar* (Buenos Aires), Oct. 26, 1956, pp. 31-118.

MELÉNDEZ, CONCHA, "Retorno a Alfonso Reyes (1889). Onda pampera," in *Figuración de Puerto Rico y otros estudios*. San Juan de Puerto Rico, Instituto de Cultura Puertorriqueña, 1958, pp. 181-183.

———, "Tres novelas de la naturaleza americana: *Don Segundo Sombra, La vorágine, Doña Bárbara,*" *Revista Bimestre Cubana*, XXVIII, 1931, pp. 82-93.

MÉNDEZ, EVAR, "La generación de poetas del periódico *Martín Fierro,*" *Contrapunto* (Buenos Aires), Año 1, No. 5, Aug. 1945, pp. 8-9, 13-14.

———, "La nueva revista *Proa,*" *Martín Fierro*, Segunda época, Año I, Nos. 8-9, 1924, p. 9.

MERTI, CARLOS A., "Un ave en *Don Segundo Sombra*: Halcón," *La Gaceta* (San Antonio de Areco), XVI, No. 803, Oct. 7, 1952.

MILLER, BARBARA LEE, Ricardo Güiraldes, *¿hombre de la pampa o escritor culto?* [Unpublished thesis], México, D. F., Mexico City College, 1953.

MIOMANDRE, FRANCIS DE, "Recuerdo de Ricardo," *La Nación*, January 7, 1940.

MOGLIA, RAÚL, "Un cuento de *Don Segundo Sombra* y un cuento popular ruso," *Nosotros*, LXIII, No. 233, Oct. 1928, pp. 113-114.

MOLINA AGUIRRE, JULIO, "Ricardo Güiraldes (1886-1927), *Don Segundo Sombra*. Madrid, Editorial Aguilar, 1948, pp. 11-24.

MONSERRAT, RICARDO, *Ricardo Güiraldes en La Porteña*. San Antonio de Areco, Imprenta Monserrat, 1952.

MONTARCE LASTRA, A., "El fondo español de lo gauchesco," *Cuadernos Hispánicos* (Madrid), July-Aug. 1948, pp. 43-71.

MORBY, EDWIN S., "¿Es *Don Segundo Sombra* novela picaresca?" *Revista Iberoamericana*, I, 1939, pp. 375-380.

MORENO, IVÁN G., *Linaje troncal de los Ruíz de Arellano en el Río de la Plata*. Buenos Aires. Imprenta López, 1937.

MORLEY, SYLVANUS G., "La novelística del *cowboy* y la del gaucho," *Revista Iberoamericana* (México), Año VII, No. 14, Feb. 1944, pp. 255-270.

MURGUÍA, THEODORE, "The Timeless Aspect of *Don Segundo Sombra,*" *Hispania*, XLVI, No. 1, March 1963, pp. 88-92.

NEYRA, JUAN CARLOS, *El mito gaucho en "Don Segundo Sombra."* Bahía Blanca, Editorial Pampa-Mar, 1952.

NEYRA, JOAQUÍN, "Aristóbulo Echegaray: '*Don Segundo Sombra,*' reminiscencia infantil de Ricardo Güiraldes," *Vea y Lea* (Buenos Aires), No. 224, Dec. 1, 1955.

———, "Mito y realidad de *Don Segundo Sombra,*" *Vea y Lea* (Buenos Aires), No. 147, Sept. 18, 1952, p. 14.

———, "El sentido de la tierra en la literatura argentina," *Histonium*, March, 1949, pp. 21-24.

NICHOLS, MADALINE W., "The Gaucho in Literature," *The Maraga Quarterly*, Winter, 1936, pp. 73-82.

———, "The Gaucho Motif in Río de La Plata Life," *Spanish Review*, II, 1935, pp. 87-89.

NIGOUL, V. A., "Carta póstuma a Güiraldes," *El Argentino* (Suplemento), Jan. 5, 1929.

NOÉ, JULIO, "La obra de Ricardo Güiraldes," *La Nación*, Nov. 13 1927.

——, "Ricardo Güiraldes," *Antología de la Poesía Argentina Moderna*. Buenos Aires, Editorial "El Ateneo," 1931.

NOEL, MARTÍN S., "Las últimas páginas de Güiraldes," *Síntesis* (Buenos Aires), II, 1927, pp. 301-304.

NUCLEO, DIÓGENES, "Ricardo Güiraldes," *Ideario Nuclear*. Buenos Aires. Editorial "El Ateneo," 1928, pp. 196-198.

OBERTI, FEDERICO, "Cumplió ochenta y cinco años Don Segundo Sombra," *Caras y Caretas* (Buenos Aires), XXXIX, No. 1971, Jun. 11, 1936, pp. 26-27.

——, "Don Segundo Sombra," *El Sol* (San Antonio de Areco), Dec. 6, 1936.

——, *Don Segundo Sombra, El mejor recuerdo gráfico.* [28 photographs]. Colón (Prov. of Buenos Aires), Impresores Blanco Hermanos [no date].

——, "Don Segundo Sombra, morrudo de hombría, se extinguió serenamente," *La Tribuna* (Arrecifes, Prov. of. Buenos Aires), Sept. 3, 1936.

——, "Don Segundo Sombra, símbolo pampeano y hombre verdadero," *Caras y Caretas* (Buenos Aires), 1936.

——, *Don Segundo Sombra. Su realidad. De la leyenda a la vida.* [Includes 26 photographs]. San Antonio de Areco, 1936.

——, "Don Segundo Sombra, el último gaucho murió en el pago de Areco," *Crítica* (Buenos Aires), Aug. 20, 1936.

——, "El gaucho tiene su museo viviente en el pago de Don Segundo Sombra," *Mundo Argentino*, 1939.

——, "Ideario de Don Segundo Sombra," *Crítica* (Buenos Aires), Aug. 18, 1949.

——, "Murió Don Segundo Sombra, el viejo gaucho que inmortalizo en su novela Ricardo Güiraldes," *Mundo Argentino*, 1936.

——, "La sombra de Don Segundo," *La Gaceta* (San Antonio de Areco), XVI, No. 803, Oct. 7, 1952.

OBERTI, TOMÁS, "Algunas anécdotas de Don Segundo Sombra," *Atlántida* (Buenos Aires), Nov. 9, 1933.

——, "Don Segundo Sombra en anécdotas," *La Gaceta* (San Antonio de Areco), Oct. 16, 1938.

OBLIGADO, JORGE, *Influencia del gaucho y su literatura en el argentino contemporáneo*. Los Angeles (Cal.), Memoria del 2do. Congreso de Literatura Iberoamericana, Aug. 1940, pp. 219-226.

OCAMPO, VICTORIA, "Carta a Ricardo Güiraldes," *Sur*, Nos. 217-218, 1952.

——, "Ricardo Güiraldes," *Revista Hispánica Moderna* (New York), XII, No. 1-2, Jan.,-Apr. 1946, p. 50.

——, "Supremacía del alma y de la sangre," in *Testimonios*. Buenos Aires, 1941, pp. 289-326.

OLIVERA, EDUARDO A., "A Ricardo Güiraldes," *La Nación*, Jan. 1, 1938.

ONÍS, FEDERICO DE, "La literatura hispano-americana," *La Nación*, May 19, 1949.

——, "La originalidad de la literatura hispano-americana," *La Prensa* (Buenos Aires), May 15, 1949.

220   GIOVANNI PREVITALI

ONÍS, HARRIET DE, "Don Segundo Sombra es mi hijo predilecto," El
    Hogar (Buenos Aires), June 10, 1949.
——, "Ricardo Güiraldes," The Golden Land. An Anthology of Latin
    American Folklore. New York, Alfred A. Knopf, 1948, pp. 213-
    214.
ORTIZ, ECHAGÜE, F., "La atribulante noticia," El Mentor (San Antonio
    de Areco), October 14, 1928.
——, "El homenaje a Ricardo Güiraldes," Síntesis (Buenos Aires), II,
    1927, pp. 383-384.
——, "Ricardo Güiraldes," Revue de l'Amérique Latine (Paris), XIV,
    1927, pp. 504-505.
OVIEDO, JESÚS J., La literatura gauchesca dentro de la literatura argentina.
    [Unpublished thesis]. Mexico, D. F., National University of Me-
    xico, 1934.
PAGÉS LARRAYA, ANTONIO, "Ricardo Güiraldes," in Cuentos de nuestra
    tierra. Buenos Aires, Editorial Raigal, 1952.
——, "Don Segundo Sombra y el retorno," Buenos Aires Literaria, Año I,
    No. 2, 1952, pp. 21-23.
PALACIO, ERNESTO, " La poesía cristiana de Ricardo Güiraldes," La Na-
    ción, May 27, 1928.
——, "Ricardo Güiraldes," Nosotros, LVIII, No. 221, Oct. 1927.
PALOMAR, FRANCISCO A., "Cómo conocí D. Segundo Sombra," O Jornal
    (Río de Janeiro), Jul. 1, 1928.
PELLEGRINI, JUAN CARLOS, "El sendero olvidado," Buenos Aires Litera-
    ria, Año I, 1952, pp. 45-47.
PEREIRA, CUTI, "Don Segundo," Boletín de la Sociedad Argentina de
    Escritores, XV, No. 30, 1947.
PÉREZ FERRERO, MIGUEL, "Marcelle Auclair, la traductora de Don Se-
    gundo Sombra al francés," El Hogar (Buenos Aires), Aug. 26,
    1938.
PETIT DE MURAT, ULISES, "Ricardo Güiraldes y la revolución literaria
    de Martín Fierro," Correo Literario (Buenos Aires), Año II,
    No. 4-5, Jan. 1-15, 1944.
——, "Ricardo Güiraldes," La Mañana (Montevideo), Apr. 20, 1950.
PETIT DE MURAT, V., "Ricardo Güiraldes," Aurea (Buenos Aires), No.
    10, Feb. 1928, pp. 29-30.
PETRICONI, HELMUTH, Spanisch-Amerikanische Romane der Gegenwart.
    Hamburg, Verlag Conrad Behre, 1938, pp. 23-27, p. 28.
PILLEPICH, PIERO, "Ricardo Güiraldes e il suo Don Segundo Sombra,"
    L'Eroica (Milano), No. 155, 1937, pp. 35-37.
PINETA, ALBERTO, "La promesa de la nueva generación literaria," Síntesis
    (Buenos Aires), Año III, No. 29, Oct. 1929, pp. 207-218.
PINTO, JUAN, Breviario de la literatura argentina contemporánea. Buenos
    Aires, Editorial Mandrágora, 1958.
——, Literatura argentina del siglo XX. Buenos Aires, Ediciones Argen-
    tinas, 1943, pp. 104-105.
PINTO, LUIS C., "Don Segundo Sombra,,' y sus críticos. Avellaneda,
    Editorial Vida, 1956.
PIÑEIRO, SERGIO, "Don Segundo Sombra, Relato de Güiraldes," Martín
    Fierro, May 18, 1956.
PLA, ROGER, "La novela argentina contemporánea," El Hogar (Buenos
    Aires), May 18, 1956.
PREDMORE, MICHAEL P., "The Function of Symbolism of Water Imagery

in *Don Segundo Sombra*," *Hispania*, XLIV, No. 3, Sep. 1961, pp. 428-431.

PREVITALI, GIOVANNI, *Ricardo Güiraldes and "Don Segundo Sombra,"* [Unpublished dissertation], New Haven, Yale University, 1958.

——, *Vida de Ricardo Güiraldes. Revisada por Adelina del Carril de Güiraldes. Traducción española de Pablo Max Ynsfran.* Mayagüez, Puerto Rico, 1960.

QUIROGA, CARLOS B., *"Don Segundo Sombra y Zogoibi,"* in *El paisaje en función de arte.* Buenos Aires, 1933, pp. 41-50.

REGA MOLINA, HORACIO, "Xaimaca por Ricardo Güiraldes," *Martín Fierro*, Año I, No. 7, July 25, 1924.

REID, JOHN T., *El americanismo en la literatura americana.* Quito, Imp. de la Universidad, 1943, pp. 20-21.

REILLY, WALTER HUGO, "¿Por qué denostar a los novelistas criollos?", *La Prensa* (Buenos Aires), Nov. 27, 1955.

REYES, ALFONSO, "A la memoria de Ricardo Güiraldes," in *Obra Poética.* México, Fondo de Cultura, 1952, pp. 102-105.

RODRÍGUEZ, ERNESTO B., "Las ilustraciones de *Don Segundo Sombra,"* *Boletín del Museo Nacional de Arte Decorativo,"* Buenos Aires, Año V, Nos. 14-15, 1950.

RODRÍGUEZ, HERMAN, "Por la huella de Don Segundo," *Nueva Expresión* (Buenos Aires), Año I, No. 1, Jan. 1958, p. 6.

RODRÍGUEZ, MARÍA DEL CARMEN, *El paisaje en Don Segundo Sombra y otros ensayos.* Paraná, Editora Nueva Impresora, 1950.

RODRÍGUEZ-ALCALÁ, HUGO, *Korn, Romero, Güiraldes, Unamuno, Ortega...* México, Ediciones de Andrea, 1958, pp. 129-139.

——, "Sentido y alcance de las comparaciones en *Don Segundo Sombra,"* in *La Cultura y la Literatura Iberoamericanas.* Berkeley, University of California Press (Ediciones de Andrea, México, D. F.), 1957, pp. 155-163.

ROJAS, RICARDO, *Historia de la literatura argentina. Los Modernos. Tomo II.* Buenos Aires, Editorial Losada, 1949, pp. 639-640.

ROJAS PAZ, PABLO, "Caudal lexigráfico de Ricardo Güiraldes," in *Don Segundo Sombra.* Buenos Aires, Editorial Pleamar, 1943, pp. 286-291.

——, "Del ser y el nombre," *La Prensa* (Buenos Aires), Jun. 17, 1956.

——, "Descubrimiento y conquista de la pampa," in *El perfil de nuestra expresión.* Buenos Aires, El Inca, 1929, pp. 38-47.

——, "Un homenaje a Güiraldes," *Síntesis* (Buenos Aires), No. 20, Jan. 1929, pp. 248-249.

——, "El resero de la soledad," in *El canto de la llanura.* Buenos Aires, Editorial Nova, 1955, pp. 168-185.

——, "Ricardo Güiraldes," *Crítica* (Buenos Aires), Oct. 10, 1927.

——, "Ricardo Güiraldes," *La Nación*, November 13, 1927; also in *Síntesis*, II, 1927, pp. 369-381.

ROMERO, FRANCISCO, "Indice de problemas," *Humanidades* (La Plata), XIX, 1929, pp. 181-194.

ROVNER, ANA, "Una entrevista con Adelina del Carril de Güiraldes," *El Hogar* (Buenos Aires), Año LIII, February 24, 1956, pp. 4-5.

S. P., "*Don Segundo Sombra*, relato de Ricardo Güiraldes," *Martín Fierro*, Segunda época, Año III, 1926, p. 6.

SABELLA, ANDRÉS, "Don Segundo Pampa y su sombra," *La Prensa* (Buenos Aires), May 24, 1953.

222   GIOVANNI PREVITALI

SACIUK, OLEXIJ, *"Don Segundo Sombra* en lengua ucraniana," *Horizonte* (Buenos Aires), Año VII, No. 10, 1955.

SAINZ DE ROBLES, F. C., *Diccionario de la literatura, Tomo II. Escritores españoles e hispanoamericanos.* Madrid, Editorial Aguilar, 1949, pp. 724-725.

SALAMA, ROBERTO, "Ricardo Güiraldes," *Cuadernos de Cultura* (Buenos Aires), Aug. 1955, pp. 26-48.

SÁNCHEZ, LUIS ALBERTO, *América: Novela sin novelistas.* Santiago, Chile, Ediciones Ercilla, 1940, pp. 186-194.

——, *Escritores representativos de América.* Madrid, Editorial Gredos, 1954.

——, *Proceso y contenido de la novela hispano-americana.* Madrid, Editorial Gredos, 1953.

——, "Ricardo Sombra," in *Don Segundo Sombra.* Santiago de Chile, Editorial Ercilla, 1935, pp. 9-19.

SÁNCHEZ-PAEZ, BRAULIO, "A novela rural argentina," *Revista da Universidade de São Paulo,* June, 1953, pp. 16-21.

SANSONE, ENEIDA, *Ricardo Güiraldes y Don Segundo Sombra* [Cuadernos de Estudiantes]. Montevideo, Facultad de Humanidades y Ciencias, 1951.

SANZ, DÍAZ, J., "Ricardo Güiraldes," *Antología de Cuentistas Hispanoamericanos.* Madrid, Editorial Aguilar, 1948, pp. 44-56.

SARFATTI, MARGHERITA G., "Retoños criollos," *Pan American Union Bulletin,* CXXVI, 1942, p. 690.

SAURAT, DENIS, *"Don Segundo Sombra* par Ricardo Güiraldes," *La Nouvelle Revue Française,* 1934, XLII, pp. 869-871.

SAZ, AGUSTÍN DEL, "La novela criolla de la tierra," in *Resumen de Historia de la Novela Hispanoamericana.* Madrid, Editorial Atlántida, 1949, pp. 127-130.

SILBERSTEIN, ENRIQUE, "De Martín Fierro y Don Segundo Sombra," *Noticias Gráficas* (Buenos Aires), Nov. 18, 1939.

SISTO, DAVID, "A possible fictional source for *Don Segundo Sombra,*" *Hispania,* XLII, No. 1, Mar. 1959, pp. 75-78.

SMITH, HEBERT G., *El amor y la mujer a través de "Don Segundo Sombra,"* La Plata, Cuadernos Rioplatenses, No. 1, 1949.

——, "Los árboles en Don Segundo Sombra," *Aberdeen Angus* (Buenos Aires), No. 35, 1947, pp. 36-42.

——, *"Don Segundo Sombra," Su influencia en la argentinidad.* La Plata, 1946.

——, "La figura de Don Segundo Sombra," *Revista de Educación* (La Plata), Feb. 1949, 132-138, and corrected in *Surestada* (La Plata), Año I, No. 2, Oct. 10, 1952.

——, *"El Libro Bravo* de Ricardo Güiraldes," *La Nueva Provincia* (Bahía Blanca), Jan. 25, 1948.

——, "Lingüística y Temática de *Don Segundo Sombra,*" *Surestada* (La Plata), Año I, No. 1, Sept. 25; No. 2, Oct. 10; No. 3, Oct. 25; No. 4, Nov. 10, 1952.

——, *La tradición y "Don Segundo Sombra."* La Plata, 1944.

SOLER CAÑAS, LUIS, "¿Es *Don Segundo Sombra una novela?" Histonium* (Buenos Aires), No. 161, 1952, pp. 9-10.

——, "La estética de Güiraldes," *Democracia* (Buenos Aires), Oct. 23, 1952.

——, "Güiraldes, escritor de la patria," *Democracia* (Buenos Aires), Oct. 23, 1952.

——, "Rememoración de Güiraldes," *Lyra* (Buenos Aires), Nos. 49-50, Sept. 1949.

SOLER-DARAS, "Ricardo Güiraldes',, *La Gaceta del Sur* (Rosario), Nos. 4, 5, Jun.-Jul. 1928.

SORRENTINO, L., "Riccardo Güiraldes," *Il Mattino d'Italia* (Buenos Aires), Oct. 9, 1930, p. 3.

SOTO, LUIS EMILIO, "Literatura argentina de tierra adentro," *Letras del Ecuador* (Quito), January-February, 1950, pp. 9-11.

——, "Ricardo Güiraldes," *Davar* (Buenos Aires), No. 14, Nov. 1947, pp. 48-54.

——, "Ricardo Güiraldes a los 25 años de su muerte," *Cultura Argentina,* Año I, No. 1, Nov. 1952, pp. 43-45.

SPELL, JEFFERSON REA, "Ricardo Güiraldes, Stylistic Depicter of the Gaucho," in *Contemporary Spanish American Fiction.* Chapel Hill, University of North Carolina Press, 1944, pp. 191-204.

SPERATTI, PIÑERO, EMMA SUSANA, "Un relato de Ricardo Güiraldes," *Universidad de México,* XI, 1955, p. 4.

——, "Realidad, mito y creación artística en un relato de Güiraldes," *Buenos Aires Literaria,* Año I, No. 2, 1952, pp. 41-45.

STANFORD, G. A., "A Study of the Vocabulary of Ricardo Güiraldes' *Don Segundo Sombra," Hispania,* XXV, 1942, 181-188.

SUÁREZ CALIMANO, E., "Directrices de la novela y el cuento argentinos (1920-1932), *Nosotros,* LXXX, 1933, pp. 337-370.

SUPERVIELLE, JULES, "Préface," in *Don Segundo Sombra,* Paris, Librairie Gallimard, 1932, pp. 9-10.

TAGLE, ARMANDO, "Ricardo Güiraldes" in *Nuevos estudios psicológicos, Segunda serie.* Buenos Aires, M. Gleizer, 1934, pp. 99-122.

TINKER, EDWARD LAROCQUE, *The Cult of the Gaucho and the Creation of a Literature.* (Reprinted from the Proceedings of the American Antiquarian Society for October 1947.) Worcester, Massachusetts, 1947.

——, *The Horsemen of the Americas and the Literature They Inspired.* New York, Hastings House, 1953.

——, *Los jinetes de las Américas y la literatura por ellos inspirada.* Buenos Aires, Editorial Kraft, 1952.

TORRES-RIOSECO, ARTURO, "Definición de *Don Segundo Sombra,"* in *La novela iberoamericana. Memoria del quinto congreso del Instituto Internacional de Literatura Iberoamericana.* Albuquerque, University of New Mexico Press, V, 1952, pp. 123-132.

——, *"Don Segundo Sombra,"* in *Ensayos sobre la literatura latino-americana.* México, D. F., Fondo de Cultura Económica, 1953, pp. 113-120.

——, *The Epic of Latin Amerian Literature.* New York, Oxford University Press, 1942, pp. 164-165.

——, "La literatura gauchesca," in *La gran literatura iberoamericana.* Buenos Aires, Emecé Editores, S. A., 1945, pp. 157-193.

——, *New World Literature.* Berkeley and Los Ángeles, University of California Press, 1949, pp. 16, 115.

——, "La novela en la América hispana," *University of California Publication in Modern Philology,* Vol. XXI, No. 2, pp. 59-256.

——, "Ricardo Güiraldes," *Atenea* (Concepción), LVII, 1939, pp. 464-490.

——, "Ricardo Güiraldes," *Grandes novelistas de la América hispana 1* (*Novelistas de la tierra*). Berkeley and Los Angeles, University of California Press, 1941, pp. 79-107.

——, "Ricardo Güiraldes," in *Novelistas contemporáneos de América.* Santiago, Chile, Editorial Nacimiento, 1939, pp. 123-149.

——, "The Twenty-fifth Anniversary of *Don Segundo Sombra*," *New Mexico Quarterly* (Albuquerque), XXI, 1951, pp. 274-280.

TYS, JORGE, "El autor de *Don Segundo Sombra*," *Horizonte* (Buenos Aires), VII, No. 12, 1955.

UDAONDO, ENRIQUE, "El parque criollo 'Ricardo Güiraldes' y el Museo Gauchesco de San Antonio de Areco," *La Nación*, Jan. 1, 1938.

URRUTIA, VÍCTOR, "Un libro inédito de Ricardo Güiraldes," *Continente* (Buenos Aires), No. 80, May 1954, pp. 123-125.

USLAR PIETRI, ARTURO, "Lo criollo en la literatura," *Cuadernos Americanos* (México), Año IX, No. 1, Jan.-Feb. 1950, pp. 266-270.

VERBITSKY, BERNARDO, "Don Segundo Sombra, señor de la pampa," *Mundo Argentino*, Feb. 15, 1956, pp. 10-14.

VICTORIA, MARCOS, "El humorismo en la literatura argentina actual. *Don Segundo Sombra*," *Cuadernos Americanos* (México), Sep.-Oct. 1943.

VILLANUEVA, AMARO, "Un parecer . . . ," *Cuadernos de Cultura* (Buenos Aires), No. 24, Mar. 1956, pp. 149-151.

VILLASEÑOR, EDUARDO, "*Xaimaca, Don Segundo Sombra*; ¿De qué se trata?," in *De la curiosidad y otros papeles*. Mexico, Letras de México, 1925, pp. 101-105.

VIÑAS, ISMAEL, "Güiraldes," *Contorno* (Buenos Aires), Nos. 5-6, Sep. 1955, pp. 22-25.

VOSSLER, KARL, *La vida espiritual en Sud América*. Buenos Aires, Imprenta de la Universidad, 1935, pp. 40-42.

WEISS, G. H., "Argentina, the Ideal of Ricardo Güiraldes," *Hispania*, XLI, 1958, pp. 149-153.

——, *Ricardo Güiraldes, argentino 1886-1927*. [Unpublished dissertation]. Syracuse, New York, Syracuse University, 1955.

——, "The Spirituality of Ricardo Güiraldes," *Symposium*, X, 1956, pp. 231-242.

——, "Technique in the works of Ricardo Güiraldes," *Hispania*, XLIII, No. 3, Sept. 1960, pp. 353-358.

WERSHOW, ROBERT IRVING, *Aspects of Gaucho Literature*. [Unpublished dissertation]. New Haven, Connecticut, Yale University, 1942.

WILLIAMS ALZAGA, ENRIQUE, *La pampa en la novela argentina*. Buenos Aires, Estrada Editores, 1955, pp. 235-253, 365-366.

WOGAN, DANIEL, "A literatura argentina no Brasil," *Revista Iberoamericana*, XII, 1947, pp. 135-141.

ZAS, L., "Recuerdo de Ricardo Güiraldes," *Clarín* (Buenos Aires), Apr. 26, 1959.

IV. Other Bibliographies

AMIGOS DEL LIBRO, *Catálogo de la Exposición Ricardo Güiraldes (1886-1927). Homenaje de la Asociación del libro en el XXV aniversario de la muerte del poeta.* Buenos Aires, Salón Kraft, Oct. 1952.

BECCO, HORACIO JORGE, "Algunas ediciones de *Don Segundo Sombra,*" in *Don Segundo Sombra y su vocabulario.* Buenos Aires, Editorial Ollantay, 1952.

——, Apéndice bibliográfico" in Ricardo Güiraldes' *Don Segundo Sombra,* with illustrations by Alberto Güiraldes. Buenos Aires, Compañía General Fabril Editora, 1961.

——, "Contribución a la Bibliografía Argentina Contemporánea: Ricardo Güiraldes (1886-1927)," *Alada* (Buenos Aires), Año II, No. 8, Oct. 1954, pp. 1-8.

——, "Obra de Ricardo Güiraldes," in *Don Segundo Sombra y su vocabulario.* Buenos Aires, Editorial Ollantay, 1952.

——, *Ricardo Güiraldes. Guías Bibliográficas 1.* Buenos Aires, Universidad de Buenos Aires, 1959.

BELÁUSTEGUI, MARÍA TERESA, "Contribución para el conocimiento de la bibliografía de Ricardo Güiraldes," *Buenos Aires Literaria,* Año I, No. 2, 1952, pp. 48-55.

The Handbook of Latin American Studies. Gainesville, University of Florida Press, 1936-1961.

LEAVITT, STURGIS ELLENO, *Argentine Literature, a bibliography of literary criticism, biography, and literary controversy.* Chapel Hill, University of North Carolina Press, 1924, p. 32.

LUQUIENS, FREDERICK BLISS, *Spanish American Literature in the Yale Library.* New Haven, Yale University Press, 1939.

RONCO, AMADEO and ALFREDO O. CONDE, *Manual bibliográfico de escritores.* Buenos Aires, F. Crespillo, 1938, p. 72.